Professor Raymond's System of COMPARATIVE ÆSTHETICS

I.—Art in Theory. 8°, cloth extra $1.75

"Scores an advance upon the many art-criticisms extant. . . . Twenty brilliant chapters, pregnant with suggestion."—*Popular Science Monthly.*
"A well grounded, thoroughly supported, and entirely artistic conception of art that will lead observers to distrust the charlatanism that imposes an idle and superficial mannerism upon the public in place of true beauty and honest workmanship."—*The New York Times.*
"His style is good, and his logic sound, and . . . of the greatest possible service to the student of artistic theories."—*Art Journal* (London).

II.—The Representative Significance of Form. 8°, cloth extra. $2.00

"A valuable essay. . . . Professor Raymond goes so deep into causes as to explore the subconscious and the unconscious mind for a solution of his problems, and eloquently to range through the conceptions of religion, science and metaphysics in order to find fixed principles of taste. . . . A highly interesting discussion."—*The Scotsman* (Edinburgh).
"Evidently the ripe fruit of years of patient and exhaustive study on the part of a man singularly fitted for his task. It is profound in insight, searching in analysis, broad in spirit, and thoroughly modern in method and sympathy."—*The Universalist Leader.*
"Its title gives no intimation to the general reader of its attractiveness for him, or to curious readers of its widely discursive range of interest. . . . Its broad range may remind one of those scythe-bearing chariots with which the ancient Persians used to mow down hostile files."—*The Outlook.*

III.—Poetry as a Representative Art. 8°, cloth extra . . $1.75

"I have read it with pleasure, and a sense of instruction on many points."—*Francis Turner Palgrave, Professor of Poetry, Oxford University.*
"Dieses ganz vortreffliche Werk."—*Englische Studien, Universität Breslau.*
"An acute, interesting, and brilliant piece of work. . . . As a whole the essay deserves unqualified praise."—*N. Y. Independent.*

IV.—Painting, Sculpture, and Architecture as Representative Arts.
With 225 illustrations. 8° $2.50

"The artist will find in it a wealth of profound and varied learning; of original, suggestive, helpful thought . . . of absolutely inestimable value."—*The Looker-on.*
"Expression by means of extension or size, . . . shape, . . . regularity in outlines . . . the human body . . . posture, gesture, and movement, . . . are all considered . . . A specially interesting chapter is the one on color."—*Current Literature.*
"The whole book is the work of a man of exceptional thoughtfulness, who says what he has to say in a remarkably lucid and direct manner."—*Philadelphia Press.*

V.—The Genesis of Art Form. Fully illustrated. 8° . . $2.25

"In a spirit at once scientific and that of the true artist, he pierces through the manifestations of art to their sources, and shows the relations, intimate and essential, between painting, sculpture, poetry, music, and architecture. A book that possesses not only singular value, but singular charm."—*N. Y. Times.*
"A help and a delight. Every aspirant for culture in any of the liberal arts, including music and poetry, will find something in this book to aid him."—*Boston Times.*
"It is impossible to withhold one's admiration from a treatise which exhibits in such a large degree the qualities of philosophic criticism."—*Philadelphia Press.*

VI.—Rhythm and Harmony in Poetry and Music. Together with Music as a Representative Art. 8°, cloth extra . $1.75

"Prof. Raymond has chosen a delightful subject, and he treats it with all the charm of narrative and high thought and profound study."—*New Orleans States.*
"The reader must be, indeed, a person either of supernatural stupidity or of marvellous erudition, who does not discover much information in Prof. Raymond's exhaustive and instructive treatise. From page to page it is full of suggestion."—*The Academy* (London).

VII.—Proportion and Harmony of Line and Color in Painting, Sculpture, and Architecture. Fully illustrated. 8° . $2.50

"Marked by profound thought along lines unfamiliar to most readers and thinkers. . . . When grasped, however, it becomes a source of great enjoyment and exhilaration. . . . No critical person can afford to ignore so valuable a contribution to the art-thought of the day."—*The Art Interchange* (N. Y.).
"One does not need to be a scholar to follow this scholar as he teaches while seeming to entertain, for he does both."—*Burlington Hawkeye.*
"The artist who wishes to penetrate the mysteries of color, the sculptor who desires to cultivate his sense of proportion, or the architect whose ambition is to reach to a high standard will find the work helpful and inspiring."—*Boston Transcript.*

G. P. PUTNAM'S SONS, New York and London

POETRY

AS A

REPRESENTATIVE ART

AN ESSAY IN

COMPARATIVE ÆSTHETICS

BY

GEORGE LANSING RAYMOND, L.H.D.

PROFESSOR OF ÆSTHETICS IN PRINCETON UNIVERSITY
AUTHOR OF "THE ORATOR'S MANUAL," "ART IN THEORY," "THE REPRESENTATIVE
SIGNIFICANCE OF FORM," "PAINTING, SCULPTURE, AND ARCHITECTURE AS
REPRESENTATIVE ARTS," "THE GENESIS OF ART-FORM," "RHYTHM
AND HARMONY IN POETRY AND MUSIC," "PROPORTION AND
HARMONY OF LINE AND COLOR IN PAINTING,
SCULPTURE, AND ARCHITECTURE," ETC.

FIFTH EDITION REVISED

G. P. PUTNAM'S SONS
NEW YORK AND LONDON
The Knickerbocker Press
1909

101
R269p

COPYRIGHT, 1886
BY
G. P. PUTNAM'S SONS

Revised Edition
COPYRIGHT, 1899
BY
G. P. PUTNAM'S SONS

The Knickerbocker Press, New York

PREFACE.

THIS work is intended to be complete in itself, developing from beginning to end the whole subject of which it treats. But this subject is a part of a larger one, connected with which are many underlying principles and practical inferences not mentioned here, although some of them, apparently, are not outside even of the limited range of discussion prescribed for this book by its title. To obviate the criticism which the omission of any reference to these may naturally occasion, it seems well to state that *Poetry as a Representative Art* is only one of a series of volumes unfolding the general subject of Comparative Æsthetics in the following order:

Art in Theory, dealing with the distinctions between nature and art; between the useful and the beautiful as in æsthetic art; the different theories held concerning the latter, and their effects upon its products; the true theory, its philosophic aspects, and the classification of the arts as determined by it.

The Representative Significance of Form, discussing the kinds of truth derivable from nature and from man; the distinctions between religious, scientific, and artistic truth; between different phases of the latter developed in the epic, the realistic, and the dramatic, as expressed in all the arts; and as differently expressed in the different arts, with illustrations showing the importance of making these distinctions. The further relations of the same subject to each of the arts considered separately are unfolded in three essays, namely:

Poetry as a Representative Art;

Music as a Representative Art, printed for convenience in the volume treating of Rhythm and Harmony; and

Painting, Sculpture, and Architecture as Representative Arts.

The Genesis of Art-Form traces the derivation of the elements of form from their sources in mind or matter and the development, according to mental and physical requirements, of these elements so as to produce, when combined, the different art-forms. The volume directs attention to the characteristics of form essential to æsthetic effects in all the arts. The characteristics essential to each of the arts considered in itself, are discussed in two volumes completing the series, namely:

Rhythm and Harmony in Poetry and Music; and

Proportion and Harmony of Line and Color in Painting, Sculpture, and Architecture.

The author wishes to express his indebtedness to Messrs. D. Appleton & Co., Houghton, Mifflin & Co., and others, for their kind permission to insert in this work certain entire poems, of which they hold the copyrights.

Altered from the Preface to the First Edition,
 PRINCETON, N. J., November, 1899.

TABLE OF CONTENTS.

I.

PAGE

POETRY AND PRIMITIVE LANGUAGE . . . 1–18

Introduction, 1—All Art Representative, 3—Poetry an Artistic Development of Language, 4—Language Representative of Mental Processes through Material Sounds or Symbols, 4—This Book to show how Language, and hence, how Poetic Language, can represent Thought, by pointing out, first, how SOUNDS represent Thought in Primitive and then in Poetic Words and Intonations: and, second, how Sounds accepted as Words are used in Different SENSES, and how these represent Thought in Conventional and then in Poetic Words and Phrases, 5—Primitive Words are developed according to Principles of Association and Comparison, partly Instinctively, as in Ejaculations; partly Reflectively, as in Imitative Sounds, 5—This Theory need not be carried too far, 9—How Language is a Gift from God, 10—Agreement with Reference to Ejaculatory and Imitative Sounds would form a Primitive Language, 11—Sounds represent Thought both in Single Words and in Consecutive Intonations, 12—Elocution, the Interpreter of Sounds used consecutively, 12—Representing that Blending and Balancing of Instinctive and Reflective Tendencies which express the Emotive Nature, 12.

II.

CONVERSATION, DISCOURSE, ELOCUTION, VERSIFICATION 19–31

Representative Character of Intonations, 19—Every Man has a Rhythm and a Tune of his own, 19—Physiological Reason for this, 20—Cultivated by Public Speaking, 21—Recitative, and the Origin of Poetic and Musical Melody, 21—Poetry, Song, Dance.

all connected: but not developed from each other, 22—Poetic Pause and Accent are Developed only from Speech, 23—Pause, the Source of Verse, 25—Breathing and the Line, 25—Hebrew Parallelism; Greek, 25—The Cæsura, 26—Accent, the Source of Rhythm and Tune, 27—Feet: how produced in English, 28—In the Classic Languages, 29—Metrical Possibilities of English, 30.

III.

ELOCUTION: ITS REPRESENTATIVE ELEMENTS CLASSI-
FIED 32–36

Pause and Accent, 32—Analyzed, the Former gives us the Element of Duration, the Latter gives Duration, Force, Pitch, and Quality, 33—Must find what each Element represents in DISCOURSIVE ELOCUTION, developed from Ejaculatory or Instinctive Modes of Utterance, and in DRAMATIC ELOCUTION, developed from Imitative or Reflective Utterance; and then apply to Poetry, 33—General Statement of what is Represented by Duration, Force, Pitch, and Quality, ; Rhythm the Effect of the First Two, and Tune of the Last Two, 34.

IV.

ELOCUTIONARY AND POETIC DURATION . . 37–49

The Elements entering into Rhythm: Duration, and Force, 37—Duration: Fast Time Instinctive, representing Unimportant Ideas; Slow Time Reflective, representing Important Ideas; Movement a Combination of the Two, 37—The Pause as used in Elocution, 38—In Poetry, at the Ends of Lines, 39—In the Cæsura, 40—Run-on and End-stopped Lines, 40—Quantity, Short and Long, in Elocution and Poetry; as produced by Vowels and Consonants, 41, —Movement or Rhythm as influenced by Pause and Quantity, 44—Feet of Three Syllables should represent Rapidity, 45—Predominating Long Quantity injures English Hexameters, 46—Feet of Four Syllables represent Rapidity, 49.

V.

ELOCUTIONARY AND POETIC FORCE . . . 50–56

Force, representing Instinctive Tendency of Utterance, or Physical Energy, 50—Different Kinds of Force, 50—The Degree of Force, 51—Loud and Soft Force as Used in Elocution, 51—Their

CONTENTS. xiii

Poetic Analogues, 51—Loudness and Softness, Strength and Weakness, Great and Slight Weight as represented by Long or Short, Accented or Unaccented Syllables, 52.

VI.

FORCE AS THE SOURCE AND INTERPRETER OF POETIC MEASURES 57–81

Gradations of Force or Stress, representing Reflective Influence exerted on Instinctive Tendency, 57—What is represented by the the Different Kinds of Elocutionary Stress, 58—Why Elocutionary Stress corresponds to Poetic Measure, 59—Classification of English Poetic Measures, and their Classic Analogues, 60—What is represented by Initial Double Measure, 62—Its Classic Form, 63—By Terminal Double Measure, 65—Why used in Our Hymns, 67—Its Classic Form, 67—Triple Measures; Median, 68—Its Classic Form, 70—Initial Triple Measure, 70—Could also be termed Compound Measure, corresponding to Compound Stress, 70—Its Classic Form, 72—Its Use in Greek Pæonics, 72—In Pathos, corresponding to Tremulous Stress, 73—Terminal Triple Measure, 74—Can correspond to Thorough Stress, 74—Its Classic Form, 75—Blending of Different Triple Measures, 75—Of Triple and Double Measures to prevent Monotony, 76—Quadruple Measures, Di-initial and Di-terminal, 77—Blending of all Kinds of Measures to represent Movements, 79.

VII.

ELOCUTIONARY AND POETIC REGULARITY OF FORCE, 82–88

Regularity of Force, combining its Instinctive with Reflective Tendencies, and representing Emotive Influence, 82—Abrupt and Smooth Force, as used in Elocution, and Irregular and Regular Accentuation corresponding to them in Poetry, 82—Abruptness in short and long Lines, 85—Imitative Effects, 87.

VIII.

ELOCUTIONARY AND POETIC PITCH—TUNES OF VERSE, 89–102

Elements entering into the Tunes of Verse: Pitch and Quality, 89—Pitch representing Reflective Tendency or Intellectual Motive, 90—On its Instinctive Side by High and Low Key, 91—What each represents, 91—On its Reflective, by Rising, Falling, and Circumflex Movements, 92—What each represents, 92—When Influences from both Sides express Emotive Colorings, by Melody, 94—What Different Melodies represent, 94—Pitch as used in Poetry, 95—Which was formerly chanted, 95—And has Tunes at Present, 96—Shades of Pitch in Speech as Numerous as, and more Delicate than, in Song, 96—Scientific Proof that Short Vowels usually suggest a High Key, and Long, a Low Key, 97—Light, Gay, Lively Ideas represented by the Former, 99—Serious, Grave, Dignified by the Latter, 100.

IX.

POETIC PITCH—RISING AND FALLING TONES . 103–114

Correspondence between Elocutionary Inflections or Intonations and certain Arrangements of Verse-Harmony produced by Sounds of Vowels and Consonants combined, 103—Effects of Rising Movements produced by Lines beginning without Accents and ending with them, 104—Of falling Movements, by Lines beginning with Accents and ending without them, 105—Of Circumflex Movements, by Combinations of both Arrangements, 106—What the Marks of Accent indicated to the Greeks, and how they read them in their Poetry, 107—Illustrations of Ideas represented by Verse arranged to give Effects of Rising, Falling, and Circumflex Movements, 109—Movements of Verse in Narration and Pathos, 114.

X.

POETIC PITCH—MELODY AND RHYME . . 115–125

Variety and Monotony in Elocution and Poetry represent less or more Control over Self and the Subject, 115—True Significance of Alliteration, Assonance, etc., 116—Rhyme introduces Element of Sameness, 118—Increases effects of Versification, of Unity, of Poetic Form, of Emphasis of all Kinds, of Regularity of Movement, of Rapidity of Thought, 118—Results of Changing the Order of the Occurrence of Rhymes in Tennyson's "In Memoriam," 122—Blank Verse admitting of Great Variety Preferable for Long Productions, 124.

XI.

ELOCUTIONARY AND POETIC QUALITY . . 126–135

Quality represents the Emotive Nature of the Soul as influencing and influenced by both Instinctive and Reflective Tendencies,

126—Kinds of Quality, and what each represents in Elocution, 127—Letter-Sounds used in Verse to Produce Effects of the Aspirate Quality, 128—Guttural, 130—Pectoral, 130—Pure, 132—Orotund, 132—Illustrations of Poetic Effects of all these Kinds when combined, 133.

XII.

EFFECTS OF POETIC QUALITY CONTINUED . 136–149

Imitative Effects of Letter-Sounds corresponding to Aspirate Quality, representing Serpents, Sighing, Rapidity, Winds, Slumber, Conspiracy, Fear, Frightening, Checking, 136—Guttural Quality, representing Grating, Forcing, Flowing Water, Rattling, Effort, 139—Pectoral Quality, representing Groaning, Depth, Hollowness, 142—Pure Quality, representing Thinness, Clearness, Sharpness, Cutting, 143—Orotund Quality, representing Fulness, Roundness, Murmuring, Humming, Denying, etc., 143—These Effects as combined in Various Illustrations of Carving; Dashing, Rippling, and Lapping Water; Roaring, Clashing, Cursing, Shrieking, Fluttering, Crawling, Confusion, Horror, Spite, Scorn, etc., 145.

XIII.

THE SACRIFICE OF SENSE TO SOUND . . 150–160

Verse in which Attention to Sound prevents Representation of Thought, 150—Violating Laws of Natural Expression or Grammatical Construction, 151—Excellences exaggerated, the Sources of these Faults, 152—Insertion of Words, Pleonasm, Superfluity, 152—Transposition of Words, Inversion, Hyperbaton, tending to Obscurity, 154—Style of the Age of Dryden, 156—Alteration of Words in Accent; or by Aphæresis, Front-Cut; Syncope, Mid-Cut; or Apocope, End-Cut, 157—All these often show Slovenly Workmanship, 158.

XIV.

SACRIFICE OF SENSE TO SOUND CONTINUED . 161–172

Omission of Words, or Ellipsis, indicating Crudeness, 161—Leading to Obscurity because Meanings are conveyed by Phrases as well as by Words, 164—Misuse of Words, Enallage, 165—Poetic Sounds are Artistic in the Degree in which they really represent Thought and Feeling, 171.

XV.

MEANINGS OF WORDS AS DEVELOPED BY ASSOCIATION AND COMPARISON 173–179

Instinctive Ejaculatory Sounds, and Reflective Imitative Sounds, becoming words by Agreement, in Fulfilment of the Principle of Association or Comparison, can represent but a few Ideas, 173—Other needed Words may be due to Agreement in using Arbitrary Symbols; it is Philosophical to suppose them largely developed by Tendencies underlying the Formation of Primitive Words, 174—How these Tendencies lead to the Use of the same Word in Different Senses, 175—In the case of Words whose Meanings depend on Association, 175—How what refers to the Material comes to refer to the Immaterial, 176—Words whose Meanings depend on Comparison, 176—What refers to the Material is by Comparison used for the Immaterial, 177—Great Varieties of Meanings are developed from the same Word by Continued Processes of Association and Comparison, 178—A Knowledge of this fact, and its Results are Necessary to an Intelligent Use of Language, 179.

XVI.

MEANINGS OF PHRASES AS DETERMINED BY ASSOCIATION OR COMPARISON 180–185

Language, a Process in which Words and Ideas represented by them are used consecutively, 180—How Words in Progression can represent Mental Processes, 180—How Acts in Progression do this in Pantomime and how this is done when Words, as Symbols, are substituted for the Acts in Pantomime, 181—How Subject, Predicate, and Object are put together, 182,—Subject, Predicate, and Object of a Complete Sentence, are the Beginning, Middle, and End of a Complete Process, of which all the Parts of Speech are Logical Parts, 183—Examination of Certain Sentences, 183—How the Meanings of them, considered as Wholes, depend on the Principle of Association or of Comparison, 184

XVII.

POETIC AND UNPOETIC WORDS 186–194

Words depending for their Meanings on Association not necessarily Prosaic; nor those depending on Comparison necessarily Poetic, 186—The Latter necessitate Imagination to originate, and, at first, to interpret them, but after being used become Conventional, 187—This the Natural Tendency of all Words, 188—Poets can always cause Words to seem Poetic; First, by selecting those representing Poetic Associations, 188—This applies to Conventional Words, 189—Second, by arranging Words imaginatively so as to suggest New Comparisons or Pictures, 190—Why English of Anglo-Saxon Origin is preferred by our Poets, 190—Have Familiar Associations, 191—Sounds fit Sense, 191—Are used by us in Different Senses, 192—Figures represented in Compound Words Apparent, 192—In general more Significant, 193—Why the English Language is fitted to remain Poetic, 194.

XVIII.

Plain and Figurative Language . . 195–207

Two Kinds of Language used in Poetry, that depending for its Meaning on Association and that depending on Comparison, 195—Distinction between the Term Figurative Language, as applied to Poetry and as used in ordinary Rhetoric, 195—Figures of Rhetoric containing no Representative Pictures: Interjection, Interrogation, Apostrophe, Vision, Apophasis, Irony, Antithesis, Climax, 196—Figures of Rhetoric necessitating Representative Language: Onomatopœia, Metonymy, Synecdoche, Trope, Simile, Metaphor, Hyperbole, Allegory, 197—Laws to be observed, and Faults to be avoided, in using Similes and Metaphors, 200—When Plain Language should be used, 203—And when Figurative, 206.

XIX.

Prose and Poetry; Presentation and Representation in its Various Forms . 208–212

Tendencies of Plain Language toward Prose, and of Figurative toward Poetry, 208—Plain Language tends to present Thought, 209—Figurative to represent it, 209—All Art Representative, 210—But Plain Language may represent, and Figurative may present, 210—Poetic Representation depends upon the Character of the Thought, 211—If a Poet thinks *of* Pictures, Plain Language describing them will represent according to the Method of Direct Representation, 211—If not *of* Pictures, he may illustrate his Theme by thinking *in* Pictures, and use Figurative Language according to the Methods of Indirect Expressional or Descriptive Representation, 211—Pure Representation is solely Representative, 212—Alloyed Representation contains some Presentation, 212.

XX.

PURE DIRECT REPRESENTATION . . . 213–224

In what Sense, and how far, Thought and Feeling can be Communicated Representatively, 213—Pure Representation, as used by Tennyson, 214—Hunt, etc., 215—Pure Direct Representation, as used by Homer, Milton, Shakespear, Morris, Heine, Tennyson, Arnold, Burns, Gilbert, etc., 216—Extensive Use of this Method in all Forms of Poetry, 220.

XXI.

PURE INDIRECT OR ILLUSTRATIVE REPRESENTATION, 225–239

Illustrative in Connection with Direct Representation enables a writer to express almost any Phase of Thought representatively or poetically, 225; Examples, 226—Representation, if Direct, must communicate mainly what can he seen or heard, 228—Inward Mental Processes can be pictured outwardly and materially only by Indirect Representation, 228—Examples of this Fact from Longfellow, from Arnold, from Whittier, from Smith, from Tennyson, Aldrich, and Bryant, 229—Two Motives in using Language, corresponding respectively to those underlying Discoursive and Dramatic Elocution, namely that tending to the Expression of what is within the Mind, and that tending to the Description of what is without the Mind, 230—Examples from Longfellow of Poetry giving form to these two different Motives, 231—Careful Analysis might give us here, besides Indirect or Figurative Representation used for the purpose of Expression, the same used for the purpose of Description, but as in Rhetoric and Practice Expressional and Descriptive Illustration follow the same Laws, both will be treated here as Illustrative Representation, 231—Similes, ancient and modern, from Homer, from Morris, from Milton, from Shakespear, from Moore, from Kingsley, 232—Metaphors, ancient and modern, 235—Used in Cases of Excitation; Examples, 237.

XXII.

PURE REPRESENTATION IN THE POETRY OF HOMER, 240–261

How the Phenomena of Nature should be used in Representation—Homer as a Model, 240—His Descriptions are Mental, Fragmentary, Specific, Typical, 241—The Descriptions of Lytton, Goethe, Morris, Southey, etc,, 244.—Homer's Descriptions are also Progressive; Examples, 251—Dramatic Poems should show the same Traits, 259—Homer's Illustrative Representation, 260.

XXIII.

ALLOYED REPRESENTATION: ITS GENESIS . . 262–277

Alloy introduces Unpoetic Elements into Verse, 262—All Classic Representation Pure, 263—Tendencies in Poetic Composition leading to Alloyed Representation, 264—In Direct Representation, 264—In Illustrative Representation, 265—Lawful to enlarge by Illustrations an Idea Great and Complex, 265—Or Small and Simple, 266—Descriptions of a Meal, 269—Sunset, 270—Peasant, 271—Sailor, 272—How these Tendencies may introduce Alloy that does not represent, 273—Exaggerations in Love-Scenes, 274—In Descriptions of Natural Scenery, etc., 276—In Allegorical Poems and Sensational Plays, 276.

XXIV.

EXPLANATORY ALLOY IN DIRECT REPRESENTATION, 278–292

Alloy, if carrying to Extreme the Tendency in Plain Language, becomes Didactic; if the Tendency in Figurative Language, it becomes Ornate, 278—Didactic Alloy explains and appeals to the Elaborative Faculty, not the Imagination, 279—Rhetoric instead of Poetry, 279—Examples of Didactic Alloy where Representation purports to be Direct in Cases where the Thought is Philosophical, 280—How Thought of the Same Kind can be expressed Poetically, 281—In Cases where the Thought is Picturesque, as in Descriptions of Natural Scenery, 284—How Similar Scenes can be described Poetically, 285—Didactic Descriptions of Persons, 288—Similar Representative Descriptions, 289—How Illustrative Representation helps the Appeal to the Imagination, 289—In Descriptions of Natural Scenery and of Persons, 290—The Sensuous and the Sensual, 292.

XXV.

EXPLANATORY ALLOY IN ILLUSTRATIVE REPRESEN-
TATION 293–307
Illustrations that are not always necessarily Representative, 293—
Their Development gradually traced in Descriptions of Natural
Scenery, 295—Practical Bearing of this on the Composition of
Orations, 299—Why Common People hear Some gladly and Others
not at all, 299—Obscure Styles not Brilliant, 302—Examples of
Obscure Historical and Mythological References in Poetry, 303—
—Alloyed Representation Short-Lived, 304—How without any
such a Mixture of Main and Illustrating Thought as to destroy
Representation, References to possibly Unknown Things are made
in Poetry that lives, 305.

XXVI.

ORNAMENTAL ALLOY IN REPRESENTATION . 308–318
Poetic Development of the Far-Fetched Simile in the Illustrating
of Illustrations, 308—Examples of this from Several Modern
Writers, 309—Whose Representation or Illustration fails to repre-
sent or illustrate, 312—Poetic Development of the Mixed Meta-
phor, 312—Examples from Modern Poets, 313—In what will this
result? 314—More Examples, 315 ; How the Tendency leads the
Poet from his Main Thought to pursue Suggestions made even by
Sounds, Representing thus a Lack of Sanity or of Discipline,
neither of which is what Art should represent, 317.

XXVII.

REPRESENTATION IN POEMS CONSIDERED AS WHOLES, 319–341
Form in Words and Sentences, 319—How Visible Appearances
give an Impression of Form, 320—How Movable Appearances do
the Same, 320—Consistency and Continuity in a Sentence Neces-
sary to give it an Effect of Form, 321—A Poem a Series of Repre-
sentations and of Sentences, 321—Must have Manifest Consist-
ency and Continuity giving it Manifest Unity and Progress, as also
Definiteness and Completeness, 322—Examples of Poems with a
Manifest Form modelled on Direct Representation, 323—How
Figures can be carried out with Manifest Consistency and Conti-
nuity, 327—Complete and Broken Figures, 328—Examples of

Poems with Forms modelled on the Methods of Illustrative Representation, 328—How Excellence of Form in all Poems of whatever Length should be determined, 336—Certain Poems not representing Unity and Progress, 337—Great Poets see Pictures when conceiving their Poems ; Inferior Poets think of Arguments, 338—Same Principles applied to Smaller Poems, 338—The Moral in Poetry should be represented not presented, 339—Poetic Excellence determined not by the Thought but by the Form of the Thought, which must be a Form of Representation, 339.

XXVIII.

The Useful Ends of Poetic Representation 342-346

These are all developed from Possibilities and Methods of Expression underlying equally the Formation of Poetic and of all Language, 342—Poetry forced to recognize that Nature symbolizes Processes of Thought, 343—Influence of this Recognition upon Conceptions of Truth, Human and Divine, Scientific and Theologic, 344—And its Effects upon Feeling and Action ; Conclusion, 345.

POETRY AS A REPRESENTATIVE ART.

CHAPTER I.

POETRY AND PRIMITIVE LANGUAGE.

Introduction—All Art Representative—Poetry an Artistic Development of Language—Language Representative of Mental Processes through Material Sounds or Symbols—Primitive Words are developed according to Principles of Association and Comparison, partly Instinctive, through Ejaculations; partly Reflective, through Imitative Sounds—This Theory need not be carried too far—How Language is a Gift from God—Agreement with Reference to Ejaculatory and Imitative Sounds would form a Primitive Language—This Book to show how Language, and hence, how Poetic Language, can represent Thought, by pointing out, first, how SOUNDS represent Thought in Primitive and then in Poetic Words and Intonations; and, second, how Sounds accepted as Words are used in Different SENSES, and how these Represent Thought in Conventional and then in Poetic Words and Phrases—Sounds represent Thought both in Single Words and in Consecutive Intonations—Elocution, the Interpreter of Sounds used Consecutively—Representing that Blending and Balancing of Instinctive and Reflective Tendencies, which express the Emotive Nature.

WORDSWORTH, in one of his finest passages, says of the results of his studies in poetry:

>   I have learned
> To look on nature, not as in the hour
> Of thoughtless youth; but hearing oftentimes
> The still, sad music of humanity.
>
>   . . . And I have felt
> A presence that disturbs me with the joy

> Of elevated thoughts; a sense sublime
> Of something far more deeply interfused,
> Whose dwelling is the light of setting suns,
> And the round ocean, and the living air,
> And the blue sky, and in the mind of man:
> A motion and a spirit, that impels
> All thinking things, all objects of all thought,
> And rolls through all things.
> —*Lines Composed a few Miles above Tintern Abbey.*

How many are there who have learned for themselves this lesson — undoubtedly a valuable one — of which Wordsworth speaks? How many are there who can apprehend clearly his meaning in what he says of it? How many are there who can discover in themselves any important addition to their mental or moral development that has been due to poetry, or who can appreciate fully its best thought, if at all subtle in its nature, even though presented in the best possible form? That in our day there are very few of these, is only too apparent to any competent judge of the subject who questions the leaders in our literary circles, who reads the verses in our magazines, who examines the criticisms in our reviews, or who listens to the accounts of what students of poetry are taught in our schools. Yet in his "Defence of Poesy" Sir Philip Sidney tells us that this art "is of all other learnings the most ancient,—that from whence all other learnings have taken their beginnings,—and so universal that no learned nation doth despise it; nor no barbarous nation is without it." Bailey says that:

> Poetry is itself a thing of God.
> He made his prophets poets, and the more
> We feel of poesy do we become
> Like God in love and power.
> —*Festus.*

And Holmes assures us that—

> There breathes no being, but has some pretence
> To that fine instinct called poetic sense.
> —*A Metrical Essay.*

If statements like these, which could be multiplied indefinitely, be true, then it is both important and possible for men of all classes and conditions to have the character and methods of this art—the only one accessible to the members of every household—so explained to them that they shall be able to appreciate it, and to judge intelligently of its products, and hence to enjoy it, and to profit by it. It is with this belief that the present work has been undertaken, in which it will be maintained throughout that there are absolute standards of poetic excellence; that these can be ascertained; and that upon them can be founded a system of criticism as simple as it is scientific.

At the threshold of our undertaking, the first thing for us, of course, is to become thoroughly acquainted with the facts of the case, and the fact of primary importance for us here will be ascertained when, in some form, we have answered the question, What is poetry?

Poetry is acknowledged to be an art, ranking, like music, with the fine arts,—painting, sculpture, and architecture. It is acknowledged, also, that the peculiar characteristic of all these arts is that they have what is termed *form* (from the Latin *forma*, an external appearance). This form, moreover, is æsthetic (from the Greek αἰσθητός, perceived by the senses); and it is presented in such a way as to address the senses through the agency of an artist, who, in order to attain his end, re-presents the sounds or sights of nature. All these arts, therefore, in a broad sense of the term, are representative. What they represent is partly the phenomena of nature and partly the thoughts of man; partly that which is imitated from things perceived in the world without, and partly that which is conceived in the mind of him who, in order to express his conception, produces the imitation. Both of these factors are present in all artistic forms, and cause them to be what they are. That painting and sculpture represent, is recognized by all; that music and architecture do the same, needs to be proved to most men. As for poetry, with which we are now to deal, all perceive that it contains certain representative elements; but few are aware to what an extent these determine every thing in it that is distinctive and excellent.

The medium used in poetry is language, of which it is simply an artistic development. To understand the one, we should begin by trying to understand the other. Let us consider, then, for a little, what language is. Only a moment's thought will show, that, like the arts of which I have spoken, it, too, is representative. Through outward and perceptible sounds or symbols it makes known our inward thoughts, which, without the representation, others could not know. If, in any way, we can ascertain how it does this, we may gain a clew by which to find how poetry can do the same.

How, then, does language represent thought through the agency of sound? The best way to find an answer to this is to trace, as far as possible, the course of a few thoughts from their inception in the mind outward to the full expression of them in words. For this purpose we might imagine ourselves to be living in some early, or, at least, uncultivated age; we might ask what would be done by the members of a race with a limited number of words and desirous of expressing ideas for which they had no terms in their vocabulary. But, without taxing our imagination thus, we can accomplish our purpose by watching the children of our own time. We can note the different stages in the development of their efforts to tell us what they think; and then we can argue from analogy that there would be a similar order of development in language during the childhood of the race. Let us pursue this course. As we do so, we shall find ourselves, instinctively, making two divisions of our subject: the first dealing with the methods of originating sounds so as to represent thought; the second, with the use of them after they have been originated so as to represent different thoughts. It is best to begin by considering the former of these, and then, immediately in connection with it, its bearings on poetic forms; not because, in its relations either to language or to poetry, it occupies the more important position, but because it comes the earlier in the order of time.

The first sounds made by the babe are *instinctive*, and seem to be accepted as words in fulfilment mainly of the principle of *association*. By instinctive, as used in this book, is meant an expression allied in its nature to instinct; due, even in a rational being, to the operation less of conscious rationality than of natural forces vitalizing all sentient existence. The child cries and crows while the mother hums and chuckles, and both understand each other. They communicate through what may be termed *ejaculations* or interjections. This kind of language is little above the level of that of the brutes; in fact, it is of the same nature as theirs. The sounds seem to have a purely muscular or nervous origin; and for this reason may be supposed to have no necessary connection with particular thoughts or psychic states intended to be expressed by them. Nevertheless, we all understand the meanings of them when produced by the lower animals, as well as when made by man. Everywhere, certain ejaculations are recognized to be expressive of the general tenor of certain feelings, like those of pleasure and pain, desire and aversion, surprise and fright. This fact shows that in a true sense these ejaculations are representative; and to recognize it, is all that is necessary for our present purpose. To show why they are so, to explain how the various qualities and movements of sounds can be made to picture in one sphere the qualities and movements of thoughts which can exist only in another sphere, would require a thorough unfolding of the principles of elocution and music; and to introduce this just here would take us away from the line of thought immediately before us.

Waiving all questions with reference to any comparison or likeness that there may be between these ejaculations and the particular sensations that they express, we can all recognize how men, after they have heard the same utterance used many times with the same emotion, should come to ally or associate the two. "Expression," says Farrar, in his "Language and Languages," "is the natural and spontaneous result of impression; and, however merely animal in their nature the earliest exclamations may have been, they were probably the very first to acquire the dignity and significance of reasonable speech, because in their case, more naturally than in any other, the mere repetition of the sound would, by the association of ideas, involuntarily recall the sensation of which the sound was so energetic and instantaneous an exponent. In the discovery of this simple law, which a very few instances would reveal to the mind of man, lay the discovery of the Idea of Speech. The divine secret of language—the secret of the possibility of perfectly expressing the unseen and immaterial by an articulation of air which seemed to have no analogy with it—the secret of accepting sounds as the exponents and signs of every thing in the ' choir of heaven and furniture of earth'—lay completely revealed in the use of two or three despised interjections. To borrow a simile from the eloquent pages of Herder, they were the sparks of Promethean fire which kindled language into life."

The principle of association in connection with the use of natural exclamations, accounts probably for the origin not only of actual interjections, but of other sounds also, like the sibilants, aspirates, and gutturals, giving their peculiar qualities to the meanings of syllables like those in *hush, hist,* and *kick.* Some, too, think that it accounts for the origin of words like *is, me,* and *that,* cognate with the Sanskrit *as, ma,* and *ta ;* the first meaning to breathe, and indicating the act of breathing; the second closing the lips to shut off outside influence, and thus to refer to self; and the third opening the lips to refer to others. In the same way, too, because the organs of speech are so formed that the earliest articulated sound made by a babe is usually either *mama* or *papa,* and the earliest persons to whom each is addressed are the mother and father, people of many different races have come to associate *mama,* which, as a rule, is uttered first, with an appeal to the mother, and *papa* with an appeal to the father.

In order, however, that utterances springing from sounds like these may be used in language, it is evident that men must begin to imitate them. The principle of *imitation,* therefore, as well as that of ejaculation, must have been closely connected with the formation of the earliest words. Ejaculations, as has been said, are instinctive. As such, they come first in the order of time, furnishing men both with sounds that can be imitated, and with sounds, originated in the vocal organs, that can be modified so as to form the imitations. But the latter begin to be used as soon as the *reflective* nature begins to assert itself; and they soon extend to the reproduction of other sounds besides ejaculations—sounds that are indisputably representative in the most literal sense, and that become accepted as words as a result of actual *comparison* as well as of *association*. The sounds are first heard when the child is led to notice external objects. Then, unlike the animal which can only ejaculate, but just like his reputed father Adam, the first who had a reflective nature, he begins to give names to these objects, or to have names given to them for him by others. These names, according to the methods controlling the formation of nursery language, are always based upon the principle of imitation. Certain noises emanating from the objects designated, the *chick-chick* of the fowl, the *tick-tick* of the watch, the *cuckoo* of the bird over the clock, the *bow-wow* of the dog, and, later, the *clatter* of the *rattle*, or the *rustle* of the silk or satin, are imitated in the names applied to them; and this imitative element enables the child to recognize what the object is to which each name refers. The existence of hundreds of terms in all languages, the sounds of which are significant of their sense, like *buzz*, *hiss*, *crash*, *slam*, *bang*, *whine*, *howl*, *roar*, *bellow*, *whistle*, *prattle*, *twitter*, *gabble*, and *gurgle* (many of which are of comparatively recent origin), is a proof that the principle of imitation is an important factor in the formation of words. "Through all the stages of growth of language," says Whitney in his "Language and the Science of Language," "absolutely new words are produced by this method more than by any other."

POETRY AND PRIMITIVE LANGUAGE.

Not only so, but it is recognized universally that in our present languages certain words—and they are those which skilful writers always prefer to use, if they can—sound more like what they mean than others do. Many of these words, it is true, are in no sense traceable to an imitative origin. But they are treated as if they were; and this fact proves that there is a tendency at present, as there always has been, to derive satisfaction from imitative, mimetic, or, as they are technically termed, onomatopoetic, sounds. Of all writers, the poet, who, as an artist, is supposed to use language the most skilfully, manifests the most of this tendency. Notice the following:

>The terrible grumble and rumble and roar,
>Telling the battle was on once more.
>*—Sheridan's Ride: T. B. Read.*

>Here 's a knife; clip quick; it 's a sign of grace.
>*—Holy Cross Day: Browning.*

>So we were left galloping, Joris and I,
>* * * * * * * * *
>'Neath our feet broke the bright brittle stubble like chaff.
>*—How They Brought the Good News: Browning.*

>Roared as when the rolling breakers boom and blanch on the precipices.
>*—Boädicea: Tennyson.*

>Ancient rosaries,
>Laborious Orient ivory, sphere in sphere.
>*—The Princess: Tennyson.*

>While I nodded nearly napping, suddenly there came a tapping,
>As of some one gently rapping, rapping at my chamber-door.
>*—The Raven: Poe.*

It is only when the imitative and ejaculatory theories of the origin of words are held to the exclusion of all others, that they deserve the treatment which they have received from Max Müller, in his "Science of Language," under the names of the *bow-wow* and *pooh-pooh* theories. Müller himself, however, mentions approvingly what has been called in turn the *ding-dong* theory, originated by the German Heyse, in his "System der Sprachwissenschaft." According to this theory, as Müller states it, "a law runs through nearly the whole of nature, that each substance has its peculiar ring. . . . It was the same with man." He once possessed an instinctive faculty for giving articulate expression to the rational conceptions of his mind. But this "creative faculty, which gave to each conception, as it thrilled for the first time through his brain, a phonetic expression, became extinct when its object was fulfilled." This theory does not seem to differ materially from the ejaculatory. Of course, the fewer words a man had in his vocabulary in that early period, the more he would exclaim, and the more he used his exclamations as words, the more their character would become changed from that which they had when mere exclamations. It is true that in this sense the creative faculty, enabling him to give representative expressions, would become extinct. He would come to use conventional words instead of them. But before he possessed these words it would be, to quote from Whitney, "beyond all question as natural for the untaught and undeveloped man to utter exclamations as to make gestures."

This theory, that the very earliest words were ejaculatory and imitative, seems to accord with the commonly accepted view, that language is a gift from God, recognizing it to be so in the sense that, whereas beasts and birds are endowed with the power of representing only a few sensations through a few almost unvarying sounds, man can represent any number of thoughts and emotions through articulating organs capable of producing almost infinite combinations and variations. Place two human beings, thus constituted, in a state like that of Eden, and in a month's time, by using ejaculatory and imitative utterances, and mutually agreeing, as they necessarily would do, to associate certain ideas with certain of these, they would form a primitive language, which both could understand; and a number of their words, too, would probably not be wholly dissimilar in either sound or sense to some that we use to-day.

This fact of agreement, just mentioned, is undoubtedly the most important of the elements causing sounds to become words with definite meanings. But in the present discussion, it is important to notice that, in the beginning, there were the best of reasons for this agreement; the signs used actually represented the things signified; they were like them or allied to them; they compared with them or were associated with them, and that, too, in a natural and not, as is the case with words originated later, in an arbitrary way. Without any agreement at all, an ejaculatory or imitative word would have some meaning, and this a meaning similar to the one ultimately assigned to it by common consent.

Were we dealing with language here for its own sake, it would be in place now to pass on from these earlier sounds, originated in order to represent thought, to the consideration of the same after they have been originated and are used over again in order to represent other and different thoughts. This would introduce us into a sphere where we should find the great majority of words in every vocabulary. But we must defer any reference to these at present. Our object now is to find the connection between representation in natural and in artistic language; and, before we go further, it will be best to apply at once what has been noticed with reference to the representation of thought in sound, to its representation in those features of poetic form which depend upon sound.

So far, we have been examining how ideas can be represented in single words. But ideas, when conceived in the mind, are in constant movement. To be represented completely, they must be expressed by words, not standing alone, but following one another in the order of time. Possibly, it is because we usually hear them in this order, that most of us are inclined to give credence to the ejaculatory and imitative theories with reference to their origin. For, whatever may be true of words used separately, it is a fact that, even aside from the conventional meanings ordinarily attached to them, intonations, such as can be given only in the movements of consecutive speech, have a significance. When Bridget, according to a familiar story, was sent to the neighbors to inquire how old Mrs. Jones was, she emphasized the *old*, and paused after it, and so gave irreparable offence. Her tones represented an idea which the mere words of the message confided to her had not been intended to convey.

These intonations, as will be noticed, are representative of movement on the part of ideas. Movement is a result of the instinctive tendency, which, carried to an extreme, as in great physical passion, ends in explosion. Ideas result from the reflective tendency, which, carried to an extreme, as in the profoundest thought, ends in absolute cessation of movement, or quietness. The intonations result from the blending and balancing of both of these tendencies. But now, whenever the results of reflection are added to those of instinct, or of instinct to those of reflection; whenever neither one of these elements alone is present but both together are found in an expression, this, in distinction from either *instinctive* or *reflective*, is what we may term *emotive*. A man, for instance, may eat and sleep like an animal, instinctively, or he may think and talk reflectively, without giving any expression to what we mean by emotion. But as soon as he thinks and talks in connection with eating and sleeping, as is the case with a caterer or an upholsterer, an hotel-keeper or a housewife; or as soon as his instincts prompt and accentuate his thinking and talking, as is the case with an actor or a good story-teller, then, as a result of instinct made thoughtful, or of thought made instinctive, he begins to manifest his emotive nature, and the character of his emotion is represented by the degree in which the one or the other of the two tendencies influencing him is in excess.

We may arrive at this same conclusion through a different method. That which blends and balances the instinctive or physical and the reflective or mental tendencies, is the soul, holding body and mind together, influencing and influenced by both. But as the intonations result from the blending and balancing of these same tendencies as manifested in language, we may say that the intonations represent not only the emotive nature, as has been shown, but also the soul. Is it, then, the same thing to put *emotion* into an expression and to put *soul* into it? Ninety-nine persons out of every hundred will acknowledge that, according to their ordinary conceptions, it is. And our line of thought here will show that, in this case, ordinary conceptions are right. No one can give expression to his emotive nature without representing a blended result of nerve and thought, of instinct and reflection.

Nor can he give material embodiment to all the possibilities of expression that move his soul, without doing the same.[1]

---

[1] It may be asked here, very naturally, where, in this classification of tendencies, is the place for the expression of the will? The answer is that there is none, and that there needs to be none. What we mean by will is simply a force in the soul, emotive in its general character, which, swayed by the influence of some overbalancing tendency, ends in action. As this force, when operating in any direction, is constant or fitful, the will is said to be strong or weak. If it impel to action mainly in an instinctive direction, to the exclusion of reflective influences, the character is what is ordinarily termed wilful, and, under differing conditions, will be reckless, sensual, cruel, or, as influenced slightly by reflective tendencies, domineering, like that of a Napoleon. If the force impel to action mainly in a reflective direction to the exclusion of instinctive influences, the character, under differing conditions, will be too coldly speculative, chimerical, or, as influenced slightly by instinctive tendencies, calculating or hypocritical, like that of a Machiavelli or a Chesterfield. In case the instinctive and reflective tendencies are very evenly matched, and therefore both act, but act alternately, the character is ill-balanced and fickle, like that of many men of genius, whose susceptibility to widely separated influences is the source of their strength, but also of their weakness. In case the instinctive and reflective tendencies both act, and act simultaneously, with the reflective ruling, as is always the case when the two act together normally, the result is both natural and rational; we say that the character is "well-balanced," and the one possessing it is "level-headed,"—conditions which, at their best, produce a man like Washington. Were these facts with reference to the action of the will regarded, many faults both of opinion and training would be avoided. It would be recognized, for instance, that while there is such a thing as "converting a soul," by turning the control of its energies from its instinctive to its reflective nature, there is no such a thing as "breaking a will"; that the recklessness tending to sensuality and cruelty, or the opposite trait, tending to speculation and sometimes to hypocrisy, can neither of them be corrected, except by a careful cultivation of the tendencies that naturally balance them.

The three tendencies from which, in this work, the phenomena of expression are derived, are the same in general character as those upon which were based the principles of the "Orator's Manual," published several years ago. For the terms now used in order to refer to them, especially *instinctive* and *emotive*, as well as for certain ideas necessarily associated with these, I

It may be interesting to notice now how Herbert Spencer, in his "Essay on the Origin and Function of Music," confirms the most of what has just been said with

seem to be about equally indebted to my friends Professor J. W. Churchill, of the Andover Theological Seminary, and Moses True Brown, of the Boston School of Oratory. But this division of expressional tendencies into the instinctive, reflective, and emotive, besides being made to accord with the results of the practical experience of instructors of this rank, can be made to accord also with the classifications of many different systems of philosophy. To mention a few of these, and to go back first to the subtlest of the most ancient of them, Plato,—according to the careful analyses of his theories made by my esteemed colleague, Professor S. S. Orris, of Princeton College,—in the "Timæus," as also in the fourth and ninth books of the "Republic," divides the soul into the *sensuous*, corresponding to what is called in this work the *instinctive* tendency, under which he classes the desires for sensuous pleasures and indulgences, all the way from carnality to lust for money; the *rational*, corresponding to what is here termed the *reflective* tendency; and the *spirited*, as translators term it, under which, as appears from the "Phædrus" and the eighth and ninth books of the "Republic," he classes the *emotions* of wonder, reverence, ambition, emulation, indignation, love of honor, the beautiful, power, glory, etc. In the "Timæus," again, he locates the *rational* nature in the head, and the *spirited* in the thorax near by it, so that "it may obey the reasoning principle (the *reflective*), and in connection with it restrain the desires" (of the *instinctive* tendency),—which duty, as will be seen, is also the most important of the functions assigned in this work to the *emotive* nature.

The underlying philosophy of the writers of the New Testament, too, seems to have been very similar to that of Plato. Paul says in 1 Thes. v., 23: "I pray God your whole spirit ($\pi\nu\varepsilon\tilde{u}\mu\alpha$) and soul ($\psi\upsilon\chi\acute{\eta}$) and body ($\sigma\tilde{\omega}\mu\alpha$) be preserved blameless unto the coming of the Lord Jesus Christ." Of the three tendencies thus mentioned—for it can hardly be supposed that they are meant to indicate separate entities—the former, the $\pi\nu\varepsilon\tilde{u}\mu\alpha$, is generally taken to refer to the higher rational or reflective nature. It is represented as sometimes good and sometimes evil in character (Mark i., 23), but always as that which allies man to the divine Spirit, also described frequently as the Spirit of Truth ($\tau\grave{o}\ \pi\nu\varepsilon\tilde{u}\mu\alpha\ \tau\tilde{\eta}\varsigma\ \dot{\alpha}\lambda\eta\theta\varepsilon\acute{\iota}\alpha\varsigma$, John xiv., 17). The latter word, $\sigma\tilde{\omega}\mu\alpha$, is acknowledged to refer to the body, sometimes to the fleshly body, as in the expression "body of his flesh" ($\dot{\varepsilon}\nu\ \tau\tilde{\omega}\ \sigma\acute{\omega}\mu\alpha\tau\iota\ \tau\tilde{\eta}\varsigma\ \sigma\alpha\rho\varkappa\grave{o}\varsigma$) in Col. i., 22, and sometimes to the body supposed to take the place of the fleshly in the next world, as in the expression, "It is sown a natural

reference to the representative character of the intonations. He asserts that these furnish "the commentary of the emotions upon the propositions of the intellect"; then,

body, it is raised a spiritual body. There is a natural body and there is a spiritual body," ($\sigma\tilde{\omega}\mu\alpha\ \pi\nu\epsilon\upsilon\mu\alpha\tau\iota\varkappa\acute{o}\nu$) in 1 Cor. xiii., 43, 44. These statements would make the promptings of the $\sigma\tilde{\omega}\mu\alpha$ correspond to what is meant in this book by the instinctive tendency; for while this has been represented to be the one most nearly allied to physical vitality, it is still a tendency of *mind*, otherwise it could not be a factor in linguistic expression; and though, during the presence of the physical form it manifests itself through it, we can conceive, were this form absent, of its manifesting itself through the form taking the place of it.

The *reflective* tendency being traced to the $\pi\nu\epsilon\tilde{\upsilon}\mu\alpha$ and the *instinctive* to the $\sigma\tilde{\omega}\mu\alpha$, or, so far as concerns the present life, to this, as embodied in the flesh ($\sigma\grave{\alpha}\varrho\xi$), which we are told, in Gal. v., 17, "lusteth against the spirit," we have left the *emotive* tendency. Can this be traced to what Paul terms the soul ($\psi\upsilon\chi\grave{\eta}$)? In other words, can the $\psi\upsilon\chi\grave{\eta}$ represent the feeling connected with conscious life, either animal or rational? As for the soul's being the seat of *emotion*, it can only be said that usually, but not universally, it is the soul which in the Scriptures is represented as being pleased, Mat. xii., 18; or sorrowful, Mark xiv., 34; or troubled, John xii., 27; and this either spiritually or physically, as in Luke xii., 19, "Soul ($\psi\upsilon\chi\eta\grave{}$), eat, drink, and be merry." As for the same word's representing the principle of life in both the animal and rational natures, this seems more susceptible of proof. It is explicitly stated in I. Cor. xv., 43, 44, that when one dies his body "is sown" a soul-body ($\sigma\tilde{\omega}\mu\alpha\ \psi\upsilon\chi\iota\varkappa\grave{o}\nu$, translated in our version "a natural body") "and is raised a spiritual body. There is a spiritual body and there is a soul-body"; but it is implied just as plainly in Matt. xvi., 25, 26, that there is a soul connected with the $\pi\nu\epsilon\tilde{\upsilon}\mu\alpha$ or the rational part of man, existing after death. Otherwise what can this mean: "For what is a man profited, if he shall gain the whole world and lose his own *soul*? or what shall a man give in exchange for his *soul* ($\tau\tilde{\eta}s\ \psi\upsilon\chi\tilde{\eta}s$)?" If these passages taken together, and others like them, can be made to mean that there is a soul or an emotive tendency which, at times, can act in connection either with the *reflective* ($\pi\nu\epsilon\tilde{\upsilon}\mu\alpha$) or the *instinctive* ($\sigma\tilde{\omega}\mu\alpha$) tendency, then the philosophical theory implied in these statements corresponds exactly with what is said of the *emotive* tendency of the *soul* in this work. Possibly, too, theologians might derive a suggestion of value from the fact that the $\psi\upsilon\chi\grave{\eta}$ is the only mental element represented in the Scriptures as in danger of being *lost*. The $\pi\nu\epsilon\tilde{\upsilon}\mu\alpha$ and the σῶμα appear to be always kept, but the question seems to be asked: What would either be without the ψυχή, the seat of those emotions, from which man derives both the pleasures of existence and the power of balancing and harmonizing the tendencies of his nature toward "rationality," "thought," "the ideal," on the one hand; and toward "body," "embodiment," "form," on the other?

The classification of modes of expression given here, will be recognized also as resembling, with some differences, those of the system of Delsarte, as represented both by L' Abbé Delaumosne in his printed work, and by pupils of the French elocutionist in this country. Delaumosne traces expression to eccentric, concentric, and normal motion, corresponding respectively to the sensitive, intellectual, and moral states of the mind. For normal motion, or the effects of it, Moses True Brown, in his lectures before the Boston School of Oratory, substitutes the word *poise*, an admirable term, which I have found full of suggestions, as I have other ideas of this lecturer; and he describes the states of the mind by using the terms vital, mental, and emotional. In the present work, an attempt has been made for the first time to analyze the tendencies of expression for the purpose of showing the relation between them and the effects of poetry. But, in connection with this, will be found also the first complete classification of these tendencies, as manifested in discoursive and dramatic elocution, through the elements of duration, force, pitch, and quality. As for the theory underlying these classifications, the acceptance of which, however, is not necessary to the acceptance of the classes themselves, it differs from the others mentioned, mainly, in recognizing, as a basis for æsthetic methods of expression, only two primary forms of motion, or of mental tendencies corresponding to them; and in considering the third as the resultant of these two. In this regard, this theory is sustained by the divisions into the *subjective*, the *objective*, and the *relations between them*, which underlie the entire philosophic systems both of Schelling and Hegel. Herbert Spencer, moreover, in his "Principles of Pyschology," while maintaining that "no definite separation can be effected between the phenomena of mind and those of vitality in general," also tries to "find a true generalization of mental phenomena by comparing them with the lower vital phenomena." Of course, it would follow from this, that there are certain mental tendencies allied to the vital nature, and others allied to what is higher than it; the former of which, being first manifested in instinct, may very properly be termed, as in this work, in-

feelings; every different contraction of these muscles involving, as it does, a different adjustment of the vocal organs; every different adjustment of the vocal organs causing a change in the sound emitted;—it follows that variations of voice are the physiological results of variation of feeling; it follows that each inflection or modulation is the natural outcome of some passing emotion or sensation; and it follows that the explanation of all kinds of vocal expression must be sought in this general relation between mental and muscular excitements." Thus the philosophy of evolution confirms in a general way the conclusions, with reference to the developments of verbal sounds, that have been drawn here. The emotive element, representing the "relation between mental and muscular excitements," or, to put it in our own language, between the reflective and instinctive tendencies, using and blending the results of the former as manifested in imitative words, and of the latter as manifested in words formed from ejaculations, gives us the intonations of consecutive speech. On the representative character of these, aside from that of verbal significance, are based the principles of elocution, and on these last, as we shall find, are based the principles of poetry, so far as this is dependent on elements of sound.

---

stinctive, while the latter is a more full and complex development of that "reflex action," to use the words of Spencer, "in which we see the incipient differentiation of the psychical (or reflective) from the physical life." He also says that "the same progress which gives origin to memory and reason simultaneously gives origin to feeling," by which he must mean that the emotive nature has that in it which corresponds to the lowest as well as the highest states of conscious intelligence. He adds, too, that "so long as the actions are perfectly automatic, feeling does not exist," by which he seems to indicate that, in his opinion, will and feeling are related, as has been intimated here. Notice also in the main text the quotations from Spencer with reference to the subject immediately before us.

CHAPTER II.

CONVERSATION, DISCOURSE, ELOCUTION, AND VERSIFICATION.

Representative Character of Intonations—Every Man has a Rhythm and a Tune of his Own—Physiological Reason for this—Cultivated by Public Speaking—Recitative, and the Origin of Poetic and Musical Melody—Poetry, Song, Dance, all connected; but not developed from each Other—Poetic Pause and Accent are developed only from Speech—Pause the Source of Verse—Breathing and the Line—Hebrew Parallelism; Greek—The Cæsura—Accent, the Source of Rhythm and Tune—Feet: how produced in English; in the Classic Languages—Metrical Possibilities of English.

WE all must have noticed that a child too young to talk, a foreigner using a language unknown to us, a friend speaking at such a distance from us that his words are indistinguishable, can all reveal to us, with a certain degree of definiteness, the general tenor of their thoughts. Their tones, aside from their words, enable us to understand such facts as whether they are hurried or at leisure, elated or depressed, in earnest or indifferent, pleased or angered. This is so because these facts are directly represented by their intonations. Developed with design, these may be made to resemble those of the foremost actors and orators. Hence the art of elocution. Developed without design, they instinctively come to imitate those of the people with whom one most associates. Scotchmen, Irishmen, Englishmen, and Americans can all be distinguished by the different ways in which they utter the same phrases. No two of them will emphasize precisely alike a simple expression such as "I can't go there to-day."

Not only men of different nations can be distinguished thus, but even different individuals. Any one well known to us can be recognized in the dark by what we term his voice, by which we mean his method of using his voice ; the way, peculiar to himself, of pausing at certain intervals and hurrying at others, of sliding his sounds up and down on certain syllables and phrases, and also, perhaps, of giving in certain places an unusual stress or quality of tone. All these methods impress his individuality on every thing that he has to say. If he becomes a public speaker, his peculiarities in these regards become still more marked. Unconsciously, if not consciously, he develops them so that, in his delivery, similar intonations recur with a certain degree of regularity; in other words, he comes to have what may be termed a rhythm and a tune of his own. The reason why he comes to have these is, undoubtedly, mainly physiological, as is intimated by Herbert Spencer in his "Essay on Style," and Grant Allen in his "Physiological Æsthetics." It is owing to a natural tendency to economize labor. Just as the swinging of the hands enables one to walk more easily, so what may be termed the swinging of the tones enables one to talk more easily. So, also, as we shall find by-and-bye, do verse and measure, to which these intonations naturally lead. The two together separate the words and syllables, and make them accord with the natural actions of the lungs and throat.

But let us waive this thought, until we reach it in its proper place. Before the age of books those who prepared literature published it by repeating it in public. Every man who did this had, of course, his own peculiarities of utterance, which, as he continued to repeat his productions, he would cultivate and render more and more peculiar; just as is the case to-day with the venders who cry in our streets, the clerks who read in our courts, and the priests who intone the services in our churches. These peculiarities, moreover, would be shown not only in the elocution of the reciter, but in the arrangement of his words and sentences, so as to fit them to his elocution. At the outset, every literary man would have his own style of delivery and composition, and confine himself to it. But after a little, just as men of the same districts, and preachers and exhorters of the same religious sects— Quakers, Methodists, or Episcopalians,—imitate one another; so these public reciters would drift into imitation. Before long, too, it would be found that one style of expression, or form of words, was better suited for one set of ideas, and another for another set; so, in time, the same reciter would come to use different styles or forms for different subjects. Only a slight knowledge of history is needed in order to prove that this is what has actually taken place. Pindaric metre, and possibly Homeric, as also the Alcaic and Sapphic stanzas of the Greeks, were used first by the poets whose names they bear; but to-day they are used by many others who find them the best forms through which to express what they wish to write.

But to return to our line of thought. A further development in the direction already indicated, would cause these reciters after a time to use versification, so that their rhythms and the variations in them might be more clearly marked; and still later, that the precise length of their verses might be apparent, as well as to assist the memory in retaining them, they would use rhymes. Further developments in the direction of rhythm and tune, introducing greater variety in both, and making the tones more and more sustained, would lead to the singing of songs—that is, to poetry set to musical melody.

Such, crudely outlined, seems to be the most rational explanation of the rise of poetic forms. It is true that some, like Dr. J. H. Heinrich Schmidt, in his "Introduction to the Rhythmic and Metric of the Classic Languages," hold that "poetry and music had their origin in the dance and song," and that " it must be carefully borne in mind that recited poetry was developed from song." But while he maintains this theory, Dr. Schmidt is obliged to admit that it cannot be substantiated by the known facts of history. He says that the march-melodies, dance-melodies, and purely lyric melodies, which, he believes, to have preceded recitative poetry, were so inferior in quality that none of them have come down to us. Of the products which have come down to us, "recitative poetry, powerfully developed in the great national epics (Homer, Hesiod, Arctinus, Stasinus, etc.), comes first. Then purely lyrical poetry appears with Callinus, Archilochus, etc. The first march-melodies were written by Tyrtæus for the Spartans. And about the same time we hear of the first choric compositions (*i. e.*, dance-melodies), those, namely, of Alcman and Stesichorus."

This order of development, it will be seen, corresponds to that of the theory just presented here. But, while we hold this theory, perhaps we should be going too far, did we carry it to the extreme that Herbert Spencer does in his "Essay on the Origin and Function of Music," in which he seems to argue that every thing that we have in music is merely a development of the forms of speech. It seems more likely that both music and speech, the one instinctive in its nature, and the other reflective, are equally differentiated from a primitive ejaculatory form of utterance. Speech, as we have it, originated with man; but long before the existence of man, there must have been lower orders of creation in which the tendencies subsequently developed into speech and music, both existed in distinct and different forms. In fact, all the modes of expression mentioned by Schmidt—talking, singing, and dance-gesturing—have correspondences, respectively, in the chirping, singing, and fluttering of the bird. Spencer is undoubtedly right in saying that poetry is "a form of speech used for the better expression of emotional ideas." It, and all the higher forms of eloquence, are developed from talking with a musical or— what is the same thing—an emotional motive. And Schmidt is undoubtedly right in recognizing that the three forms of expression which he mentions have a tendency to run into one another. Whether one start out to talk, or sing, or gesture, he may end by doing all three. This fact has been true, probably, as long as man has existed; and in this sense, dance and song—*i. e.*, music in connection with rhythmical language, undoubtedly preceded the earliest known recitative poems. But it is a different thing to say that poetry, which is distinctively an artistic development of language, is nothing but a development of dance and song. In no true sense can this be affirmed, although of course poetry, music, and dancing have all influenced one another, and in important particulars the principles underlying all are the same.

It has been shown from analogy that language, as used by the early reciters, had a natural tendency to become rhythmical; also from history, that the various forms of existing poetry were developed from the recitative. The strongest argument in favor of the view just advanced, however, has yet to be presented. It is found in the fact that the elements of all poetic, as well as of elocutionary forms, can be traced to the physical requirements of the organs of speech, and to these not as they are used in singing, but, distinctively, in talking, One can sing without suggesting any thing that can be developed into verse or rhythm; but it is impossible for him to talk, without suggesting what can be developed into both. In order to recognize the truth of this statement, we have merely to listen to a man talking. As we do so, two characteristics of speech will at once attract our attention. One is the pause or cessation of sound, following groups of syllables, which form phrases or sentences, containing anywhere from two to a dozen words; the other is the accent, given to every second, third, or fourth syllable. This word *accent* is used here, by the way, not in its restricted classic etymological sense (from *ad* and *cano, to sing to*), which will be explained hereafter, but in its modern English sense, meaning merely the emphasis or *ictus* given to certain syllables. Results that are universal—and the pause and accent are so, notwithstanding the alleged lack of the latter in the French language—are usually founded on requirements of nature.

The *pause* results, primarily, from the construction of the human lungs; the *accent*, from that of the human throat. The speaker checks his utterance in order to breathe; he accents it because the current of sound—in talking, but not in singing—flows through the vocal passages in a manner similar to that in which the blood pulses through the veins, or fluid is emptied from the neck of a bottle—*i. e.*, with what may be termed alternate active and passive movements. The active movements, which cause the accents, open the throat more freely than the passive ones, and in doing so may change, as will be shown hereafter, either the duration, force, pitch, or quality of the tone, or all of these together. Observe the difference between the accented and unaccented syllables of *tartarize, Singsing, murmuring, barbarous, sassafras, Lulu, papa.*

It is only necessary to observe these facts in order to recognize that the line in verse, at the end of which, when regularly constructed, the reader necessarily pauses, is an artistic development of the phrase, which we find in all natural conversation. In fact, Aristotle, in his Rhetoric, seems to hint at some such a development in prose, for he says the period must be divided into clauses, easily pronounced at a breath, εὖ ἀνάπνευστος. It is generally acknowledged that the principal mental process involved in art-construction is comparison. This causes all men, both consciously and unconsciously, both for convenience and pleasure, to take satisfaction in putting like with like. The moment this tendency is applied to groups of syllables separated by pauses, it leads men to place, if possible, a like number of syllables in each group, and thus have between the pauses like intervals of time. But an arrangement of this kind is the primary characteristic of verse. Take one of the earliest verse-forms—Hebrew parallelism —so called because made up of two phrases, each of which contains a parallel or equivalent statement :

> I will bless the Lord at all times ;
> His praise shall continually be in my mouth.
>
> My soul shall make her boast in the Lord ;
> The humble shall hear thereof, and be glad.
>
> O magnify the Lord with me ;
> And let us exalt his name together.

> I sought the Lord, and he heard me ;
> And delivered me from all my fears.
> —Psalms xxxiv., 1–4.

Even the English translation shows that this was constructed according to the principle just mentioned. The Hebrew, feeling that the end of the sentence was the appropriate place in which to pause, and wishing to pause at regular intervals, tried to make his sentences of equal length. This was his way of producing the same effect that we have in our verse. The method of the early Greek, too, seems to have been the same. "In recitative poetry," says Schmidt, to whom I have already referred, "which appropriated to itself the simplest forms, occurs the most primitive sort of rhythmical period, the recitative verse; this consists of two sentences," similar in arrangement to that of the Hebrew, "which either have equal length, or the second of which is catalectic or 'falling,' or is even shortened by an entire measure."

In the later Greek poetry, however, as in our own, the length of the line does not determine the length of the sentence. But it does, or at least should, determine the length of the phrases; because, as we have found, the reader naturally pauses at the end of the line. If this be long, he also pauses at some other place, usually in the middle of the line. This latter pause is called the cæsura, from a Latin word meaning a division. Here are lines with the cæsura indicated by a bar:

> Brought from the woods | the honeysuckle twines
> Around the porch, | and seems in that trim place
> A plant no longer wild ; | the cultured rose
> There blossoms, strong in health, | and will be soon
> Roof high ; | the wild pink crowns the garden wall,
> And with the flowers | are intermingled stones
> Sparry and bright, | rough scatterings of the hills.
> —*Excursion*, 6 : *Wordsworth.*

The cæsura pause need not necessarily come in the middle of the line, *e. g.* :

>—Death his dart
>Shook, | but delayed to strike, though oft invoked.
>>—*Par. Lost*, II : *Milton.*

>Have found him guilty of high treason. | Much
>He spoke and learnedly.
>>—*Henry VIII.*, 2 ; 1 : *Shakespear.*

For reasons to be given hereafter, the pause at the end of the line is much more apparent where rhymes are used, *e. g.* :

>In arguing, too, the pastor owned his skill,
>For e'en though vanquished he could argue still,
>While words of learnéd length and thundering sound
>Amazed the gazing rustics ranged around,
>And still they gazed and still the wonder grew,
>That one small head could carry all he knew.
>>—*Deserted Village : Goldsmith.*

In the same way as the pause is developed into verse, accent is developed into rhythm and the tunes of verse, —two characteristics of poetic form which necessarily go together, just as do their analogues in the arts appealing to the eye, proportion and color. Some may doubt that accent is the basis of rhythm and tune, but it is really about all that the majority of men know of either. With exceptions, the fewness of which confirms the rule, all of our English words of more than one syllable must necessarily be accented in one way ; and all of our articles, prepositions, and conjunctions of one syllable are unaccented, unless the sense very plainly demands a different treatment. These two facts enable us to arrange any number of our words so that the accents shall fall on syllables separated by like intervals. The tendency to compare things, and to put like with like, which is in constant operation where there are artistic possibilities, leads men to take satisfaction in this kind of an arrangement; and when they have made it, they have produced rhythm.

A larger rhythm makes prominent as in prose, every second or third accent; but metrical rhythm, *i. e.*, *metre*, regards every accent. When reading verse, the accents seem to mark it off; if marching, our feet would keep time to them. Hence, as many syllables as can be grouped about one syllable clearly accented, are termed a *measure* or *foot*,—words synonymous as applied to English verse; though the classic measure sometimes contained two feet. Here are feet separated by bars:

Tell me | not in | mournful | numbers
The train | from out | the cas | tle drew
Over the | roadways and | on through the | villages
There came to | the beach a | poor exile | of Erin
O'er the land | of the free | and the home | of the brave
Roses are in | blossom and the | rills are filled with | water-cresses
The king has come | to marshal us | in all his ar | mor dressed.

The number of measures in a line determines its metre; Hence the use of the Greek terms, monometer, meaning a line of one measure, and dimeter, trimeter, tetrameter, pentameter, hexameter, etc., meaning respectively a line of two, three, four, five, and six measures.

All this, however, need scarcely be known as a preparation either for writing or reading English verse. The poet has only to arrange his words so that the accents will recur at like intervals, and very few for whom he writes will fail to recognize the character of his rhythm, and to measure it off correctly in their reading. It is true that, if unusual measures are used, it may be necessary to put long words, or those in which the accent is unmistakable, at the beginning of the first line or two, but, the clew once given, the rhythm will take care of itself. The smallest children, able to talk, catch with ease the movements of Mother Goose's melodies, some of which contain metres as complicated as are ever constructed.

In the classic languages metre was determined by the quantities or relative lengths of the vowel-sounds or consonant-sounds composing the syllables. Our own language is not spelled phonetically, and therefore we fail to notice the effect of similar elements in it. Yet they are present to a greater extent than we ordinarily suppose, as will be brought out clearly when we come to consider quantity, especially that which is used in the English hexameter. Any one acquainted with the subject, knows that it is a mistake to hold that quantity has nothing whatever to do with the movements of our metres, and an analogous mistake, probably, would be made in supposing that the emphasis of ordinary pronunciation had nothing to do with the movements of the classic metres. Notice what Schmidt has to say on this subject in the quotation from his "Introduction to the Rhythmic and Metric of the Classic Languages," given in the ninth chapter of this work. It is true that, in constructing verse, the Greeks and Romans subordinated every thing else to quantity; but they did so in order to produce a rhythmic effect when chanting their lines, analogous to that which we produce when reading ours according to accent. Unlike ourselves, however, if, in composing, they came to a word in which long quantity and the ordinary accent did not go together, they seem always to have been at liberty to disregard the accent, and occasionally, too, to change the quantity. At the same time, that which controlled their action in the matter appears to have been largely a consideration of convenience. In serious poetry, it was lawful for them to produce results not wholly unlike that in the third rhyme of the following, the classic quality of which some of us hitherto may not have recognized:

> For he might have been a Roosian,
> A French, or Turk, or Proosian,
>   Or perhaps I-tal-i-an.
> But in spite of all temptations
> To belong to other nations,
>   He remains an Englishman.
> —*Pinafore : Gilbert.*

Our poets, on the contrary, base the rhythms of their verse on the accents of the standard pronunciation, and to these subordinate all considerations of quantity. The result, as compared with the language of our prose, is more natural than that reached by the other method; and in its way is fully as artistic. Nor, in other regards, is English inferior to the classic tongues in its capabilities of artistic treatment. Owing to an extensive use of terminations in nouns, articles, pronouns, adjectives, and verbs, in order to indicate different grammatical relationships, the Greeks and Romans could change the order of words in a sentence without changing its meaning. In their language, "The dog ate the wolf," with slightly varied terminations, could read, " The wolf ate the dog." For this reason, they could alter their phraseology, in order to accommodate it to the requirements of metre, as is not possible for us; and so far they had an advantage over us. Nevertheless, for some reason, when they came to put their words into verse, every school-boy who tries to scan, knows that they produced a language which, like the present French poetic diction, sounded unlike that of conversation. Even supposing, with some scholars, that in reading they did not scan their verses as we do now, nor even chant them invariably, as some infer was the case, their poetical language was not the same as their spoken language. Aristotle tells us, when mentioning things which it is legitimate for the poet to do, that he can invent new words, that he can expand old ones, either by lengthening vowels or by adding syllables, that he can contract them by shortening vowels or omitting syllables, and that he can alter them in various other ways. Spenser and others since him have applied similar methods to English poetic diction ; but, at present, such changes are not considered admissible, except in rare instances, and this because they are recognized to be unnecessary. The fact that they are not admissible in our language, and were admissible in the classic languages, proves that, in one regard at least, our language is superior to them as a medium of metre. The following is a typical English stanza. In it there are no changes from ordinary prose in the arrangement, spelling, or pronunciation of any of the words:

" Tell me not in mournful numbers
Life is but an empty dream,
For the soul is dead that slumbers,
And things are not what they seem."
—*Psalm of Life* : *Longfellow.*

CHAPTER III.

ELOCUTION: ITS REPRESENTATIVE ELEMENTS CLASSIFIED.

Pause and Accent—Analyzed, the Former gives us the Element of Duration; the Latter gives Duration, Force, Pitch, and Quality—Must find What each Element represents in DISCOURSIVE ELOCUTION, developed from Ejaculatory or Instinctive Modes of Utterance, and in DRAMATIC ELOCUTION, developed from Imitative or Reflective Utterance; and then apply to Poetry—General Statement of What is represented by Duration, Force, Pitch, and Quality; Rhythm the Effect of the First Two, and Tune of the Last Two.

HAVING sufficiently established now the general fact that certain poetic forms are traceable to the pause and accent of ordinary conversation, we are prepared to pass on and ask what these forms represent? To answer this we must decide first what the pause and accent represent; and, after that, try to determine whether, in any sense, they represent corresponding ideas when developed into the forms of poetry. Let us pursue our inquiry in the order thus suggested.

What the pause and accent represent can be ascertained only by a reference to the principles of elocution. This art, as we know, has the power of producing an almost endless variety of effects, and all these, as a moment's thought will show us, simply by making more or less emphatic the very pauses and accents now engaging our attention. In these, therefore, must be enfolded many possibilities of expression capable of development. Let us try to ascertain what they are. Looking first, then, at the pause, it is easy to see that its only element is that of duration. We can extend it over longer or shorter time. In accent, however, on comparing the accented and unaccented syllables of words like *barbarous, murmuring, tartarize, Singsing,* and *papa,* we can clearly detect four elements. The accented syllable differs slightly from the unaccented—first, in *duration:* it is sounded in longer time; second, in *force:* it is sounded with more energy; third, in *pitch:* it is sounded on a key that, if used in music, would be relatively higher or lower in the musical scale; and fourth, in *quality:* it is sounded with more fulness or sharpness of tone. Simply by increasing the degree in which any of these elements enter into ordinary accentuation, we can increase the degree of emphasis represented by them. We have noticed, already, how the pause influences the division of consecutive words into verses. As applied to individual words, *i. e.,* when used after or before them, it has evidently the same general effect as the prolongation of a sound; it gives the ideas expressed in the words more duration.

Let us examine now what phases of thought different kinds of duration, force, pitch, and quality are fitted to represent, and see how far they can aid us in determining what can be represented by analogous poetic forms. To attain our end, it will be necessary for us to go to elocution.

All the principles of this art can be classed under two heads, those of *discoursive* and of *dramatic* elocution. The first, generally termed the elocution of emphasis, is developed from instinctive methods of expression, and corresponds, in this regard, to words formed from ejaculations. It is used mainly in oratory. The second, generally termed the elocution of personation, is developed by the reflective powers as a result of impressions received from without. Mimicry, in some form, underlies all its effects; for which reason, it will be seen at once to correspond to words formed as a result of imitation, and to be the phase of delivery used mainly in dramatic acting. Of course, the best elocution combines all the possibilities of the art; but, as a rule, the orator's chief aim is to give expression to his own thoughts; the actor's, to seem properly impressed by thoughts suggested by his surroundings.

In treating of duration, force, pitch, and quality, it will be best to consider, first, the discoursive, and then the dramatic, uses of each; and, in immediate connection with them, to direct attention to the corresponding developments in poetic form. More extended explanations and illustrations of the elocutionary part of this subject may be found in the author's "Orator's Manual." For our present purpose, it will be sufficient to state, briefly, as introductory to what will be unfolded more fully as we go on, that, of the four elements of emphasis to be examined, *duration* is merely an external effect of sound, while *force, pitch*, and *quality* are all essential to the very formation of it; different degrees of *force*, as we learn from science, being determined by the relative size of the vibrations causing the tone; of *pitch*, by their relative rapidity; and of *quality*, by the relative size and rapidity of those compounded together, in order to produce any apparently single tone—almost every tone, as science has ascertained, being a compound.

With reference to the significance of these elements, while it is true that all, in a general way, represent, as has been said, emotive effects, all of them represent also certain peculiar phases of such effects. These, as manifested in dramatic elocution, of course interpret themselves. In discoursive elocution, duration *measures* the utterance—that is, it represents the mind's measurement of its ideas,—one indication, by the way, of the appropriateness of the poetic term, meters, or measures, which result from giving different kinds of duration to syllables; force *energizes* utterance; pitch *aims* it; and quality *tempers* it. Of the last three, again, force imparts *physique* to delivery; pitch, *intellectuality*, and quality, *emotion* or *soul*, by which, as has been explained, is meant that balancing and blending of physical and intellectual tendencies which manifest the degree in which the man is master or slave of body or mind. Or, finally, to make a classification as comprehensive as possible of all the factors in our problem, it may be said that duration, in a general way, represents the promptings of the *instinctive* feelings, and the other three elements those of the *reflective* feelings. Pure instinct leads to fast time, reflective instinct to slow time, and the general movement or measure is the resultant of both. The degrees of instinctive influence connected with reflective feeling are represented in force; of purely reflective influence, in pitch; and of the equilibrium maintained between the instinctive and reflective influences, in quality. Besides this, it is well to notice that duration and force together are essential to the effects of *rhythm*, and pitch and quality together to those of *tune;* rhythm resulting from the measure of time or movement by regularly recurring impulses perceptible in the physical world; and tune from a similar cause, detected only by scientific analysis, operating through vibrations upon our inner nervous and mental organism.

These statements are preliminary. They will be explained and illustrated when the proper time comes—that is, in places where they will fall into line, so as to further the object of our present undertaking, which, as we must remember, is to show not what these forms are, but what, in elocution and poetry, they are fitted to represent.

CHAPTER IV.

ELOCUTIONARY AND POETIC DURATION.

The Elements entering into Rhythm, Duration, and Force—Duration: Fast Time Instinctive, representing Unimportant Ideas; Slow Time Reflective, representing Important Ideas; Movement a Combination of the Two—The Pause as used in Elocution; in Poetry, at the ends of Lines; in the Cæsura—Run-on and End-stopped Lines—Quantity, Short and Long, in Elocution and Poetry; as produced by Vowels and Consonants—Movement or Rhythm as influenced by Pause and Quantity—Feet of Three Syllables should represent Rapidity—Predominating Long Quantity injures English Hexameters—Feet of Four Syllables represent Rapidity.

WE have now to consider representation in rhythm, resulting, as has been said, from a combination of the effects of duration and force. Taking up the first of these, it is evident that in elocution duration may be short or long, or both; in the latter case making possible all the artistic developments of metre. Both experience and reflection show us that in the degree in which utterances are instinctive, as they are when under the influence of mere spontaneity, they find expression in short duration, or—what is the same thing—in fast time. But when one becomes conscious of surrounding influences to which he must conform his phraseology, these put him into a reflective mood, and under the sway of his impressions, he stops to think—sometimes to think twice—of what he is to say, and so uses slow time; or, to look at the subject from a different view-point, a speaker, when not desirous of conveying to others the impression that what he is saying demands their serious consideration, may talk rapidly. But when he wishes to convey the opposite impression—that they should weigh his statements with the utmost care,—he talks slowly. From noticing facts like these, we learn that duration assigns, as has been said, a *mental weight* or *measure* to ideas. If these appeared for us in space, we could mete them out in measurements of space. But as they are heard in words, which occupy successive intervals of time, we must indicate their weight or bulk, by shortening or lengthening their duration. *Less or more time* given to an utterance, gives a hearer less or more time in which to think of the thoughts expressed in it, suggesting, therefore, that, in the opinion of the speaker, they are of *less or more relative importance.*

This principle we will apply, first, to the elocutionary *pause*, which leads us in reading to check our utterance not only at the ends of phrases, as already noticed, but also before or after important words, like those preceding the bars in these quotations.

> The people | will carry us | gloriously | through | this struggle.
> He is pleasing ; | but ‖ is he honest ?

The same principle applied to consecutive words causes us to read the *unimportant* parenthesis in the following, rapidly :

> He girt his fisher's coat unto him (for he was naked), and did cast himself into the sea.—John xxi., 7.

And the *important* one in the following, slowly :

> Let us hold fast the profession of our faith without wavering (for he is faithful that promised), and let us consider one another, to provoke unto love and to good works.—Heb. x., 23, 24.

According to dramatic elocution, fast time indicates that which moves *rapidly*, and slow time that which moves *slowly ; e. g.:*

Fast. { He stayed not for brake, and he stopped not for stone,
{ He swam the Eske River where ford there was none ;

Slower. { But ere he alighted at Netherby gate,
{ The bride had consented, the gallant came late ;

Slow. { For a laggard in love, and a dastard in war,
{ Was to wed the fair Ellen of brave Lochinvar.
—*Lochinvar: Scott.*

Turning now to poetic form, we find that the same principles apply to it. Notice in these stanzas how almost all the important words are placed before the pause at the end of the line, or before the cæsura-pause in the middle of it.

    Go not, happy day,
    Till the maiden yields.
    Rosy is the west,
    Rosy is the south,
    Rosy are her cheeks,
    And a rose her mouth.
    When the happy Yes
    Falters from her lips,
    Pass and blush the news
    O'er the glowing ships.
    Over blowing seas,
    Over seas at rest,
    Pass the happy news,
    Blush it through the West,
    Till the red-man dance, etc.
      —*Maud: Tennyson.*

Earth has not any thing | to show more fair ;
Dull would he be of soul | who could pass by
A sight so touching | in its majesty.
 * * * * * *
Never did sun | more beautifully steep
 In his first splendor | valley, rock, or hill ;

Ne'er saw I, never felt, | a calm so deep.
　The river glideth | at his own sweet will.
Dear God, the very houses | seem asleep ;
　And all that mighty heart | is lying still.
　　　　　　　　—*Westminster Bridge : Wordsworth.*

Of man's first disobedience | and the fruit
Of that forbidden tree, | whose mortal taste
Brought death into the world | and all our woe,
With loss of Eden, | till one greater man
Restore us, | and regain the blissful seat,
Sing, heavenly Muse.
　　　　　　　　—*Paradise Lost*, I : *Milton.*

Comrades, leave me here a little, | while as yet 't is early morn ;
Leave me here ; and, when you want me, | sound upon the bugle-horn.
　　　　　　　　—*Locksley Hall : Tennyson.*

Notice, too, the inartistic effects produced, when the voice does not naturally pause where the lines are ended ; *e. g. :*

　　　Cross down her quiet hands, and *smooth*
　　　　Down her patient locks of silk,
　　　Cold and passive as in truth
　　　　You your fingers in spilt milk
　　　Drew along a marble floor.
　　　　　　　　—*Little Mattie : Mrs. Browning.*

　　　The speech in the commons, which *hits you*
　　　　A sketch off, how dungeons must feel,—
　　　The official despatch, which commits you
　　　　From stamping out groans with your heel,—
　　　Suggestions in journal or *book for*
　　　　Good efforts are praised as is meet.
　　　　　　　　—*Summing up in Italy : Idem.*

　　　With that he fiercely at him flew, and *laid*
　　　On hideous strokes, with most importune might.
　　　　　　　　—*Faerie Queen : Spenser.*

　　　　—And some in file
　　　Stand spelling false, while one might walk to *Mile-*
　　　End green.
　　　　　　　　—*Sonnet, On the Detraction, etc. : Milton.*

In blank verse, these *run-on* lines, as they are termed, in contrast to *end-stopped*, are less objectionable. Yet, considered in themselves, they are inartistic. In another place, I intend to speak of Shakespear's use of them. The following are examples of this.

> —and then to breakfast *with*
> What appetite you have.
> —*Henry VIII.*, 3, 2.
>
> Yet, if that quarrel, Fortune do *divorce*
> It from the bearer, etc.
> —*Idem*, 2, 3.

The effects of duration, however, are produced not only by the absence or presence of the pause before and after words, but also by shortening or prolonging what is termed the *quantity* of a syllable. In elocution, quantity may sometimes be prolonged at will; in poetry, it is usually determined by the letter-sounds forming the syllable. The rule is, that syllables composed of short vowel-sounds, and of consonant-sounds easy to pronounce, are short in an absolute sense, as distinguished from a relative sense, of which I shall speak by-and-bye. A predominance of these short sounds in the style fits it to represent comparatively *unimportant* ideas; *e. g.*:

> At a pleasant evening party, I had taken down to supper
> One whom I will call Elvira, and we talked of love and Tupper.
> * * * * * * * * *
> Then we let off paper crackers, each of which contained a motto,
> And she listened while I read them, till her mother told her not to.
> —*Ferdinando and Elvira : Gilbert.*

And, also, *things that move rapidly*, as in the quotation from Scott above, as well as in these:

> And he chirped and sang and skipped about, and laughed with laughter hearty.
> He was wonderfully active for so very stout a party.
> —*Idem.*

> Singing through the forests;
> Rattling over ridges;
> Shooting under arches,
> Rumbling over bridges;
> Whizzing through the mountains;
> Buzzing o'er the vale,—
> Bless me, this is pleasant,
> Riding on the rail.
> —*Railroad Rhyme: Saxe.*

A predominance, on the contrary, of decidedly long vowel-sounds, or of consonant-sounds difficult to pronounce, makes the rhythm move slowly, and fits it, therefore, according to the principles already unfolded, to represent *important* ideas; *e. g.*:

> Nor you, ye proud, impute to these the fault,
> If memory o'er their tomb no trophies raise,
> Where through the long-drawn aisle and fretted vault
> The pealing anthem swells the note of praise.
> —*Elegy in a Country Church-Yard: Gray.*

And also *things that move slowly; e. g.*:

> The curfew tolls the knell of parting day;
> The lowing herd winds slowly o'er the lea;
> The plowman homeward plods his weary way,
> And leaves the world to darkness and to me.
> —*Idem.*

> First march the heavy mules securely slow;
> O'er hills, o'er dales, o'er crags, o'er rocks they go.
> —*Pope's Tr. of the Iliad.*

Notice in the following how the short syllables in connection with the irregular accentuation of the rhythm in the earlier lines contrast with the long quantities and strongly marked accents of the last line. Here we have an exact poetic analogue for fast and slow time, as also for weak and strong force, as used in elocution:

ELOCUTIONARY AND POETIC DURATION. 43

> The cherubim descended ; on the ground
> Gliding meteorious, as evening mist
> Ris'n from a river o'er the marsh glides,
> And gathers round fast at the laborer's heel
> Homeward returning. High in front advanced
> The brandished sword of God before them blazed.
> —*Par. Lost*, 12 : *Milton.*

Here, again, notice the *unimportance* and *rapidity* expressed in the italicized words :

> Each creek and bay
> With fry *innumerable* swarm, and shoals
> Of fish that with their fins and shining scales
> Glide *under the* green wave.
> —*Idem*, 7.

Notice in the following, too, how, in the lines beginning with *A league of grass*, Tennyson, by lengthening the unaccented syllables in *washed*, *broad*, *Waves*, and *creeps*, retards the movement of his verse to make it represent the slow flowing of the water:

> Not wholly in the busy world, nor quite
> Beyond it, looms the garden that I love.
> News from the humming city comes to it
> In sound of funeral or of marriage bells ;
> And sitting, muffled in dark leaves, you hear
> The windy clanging of the minster clock ;
> Although between it and the garden lies
> A league of grass, *washed* by a slow, *broad* stream,
> That, stirred with languid pulses of the oar,
> *Waves* all its lazy lilies, and *creeps* on,
> Barge-laden, to three arches of a bridge
> Crowned with the minster-towers.
> —*The Gardener's Daughter.*

Slowness, in the instances already mentioned, has been produced mainly by long vowel-sounds. In the fourth, fifth, and sixth lines of the following quotation, all of which is to the point here, it is produced by consonant-sounds combined so as to be difficult to pronounce:

> Soft is the strain when zephyr gently blows,
> And the smooth strain in smoother numbers flows.
> But when loud surges lash the sounding shore,
> The hoarse rough verse should like the torrent roar.
> When Ajax strives some rock's vast weight to throw,
> The line too labors and the words move slow ;
> Not so when swift Camilla scours the plain,
> Flies o'er the bending corn, and skims along the plain.
> —*Essay on Criticism : Pope.*

It has been intimated that in poetry there is, besides an absolute, a relative quantity of syllables. This latter depends upon the places in the verse where the accent falls—*i. e.*, upon the measure, which itself, as has been said, results from the combined effects of the tendencies, already considered, to movement and to rest, or to fast and slow time. Just as intelligence measures off phrases and words to represent their relative importance, so psychic emotion, or the artistic feeling within us which regulates our constructive method, seems to take satisfaction in making their accents conform to what in a subtle way, perhaps, it recognizes to be representative of the regularities of life, —regularities, which—to say nothing about those which are external to him—every living man experiences in the recurring tread of his feet when walking, in the heaving of his chest when breathing, in the beating of his heart, and even in the vibrating of his nerves when receiving or imparting impressions. But whatever may be the cause or character of these regular arrangements, which will be unfolded more fully under the head of force, they exist, and have an important bearing on those measurements of ideas which we have been considering.

When we are reading verse, the accented syllables seem

to be used at regular intervals; that is to say, about the same amount of time is expected to intervene between these syllables, no matter by how many unaccented ones they may be separated. Hence, as a rule, *the more unaccented syllables* there are in a line, or—what is the same thing—in a measure, *the more rapidly* is it uttered. Each of the four following lines, for instance, is read in nearly the same time. Yet the first contains only seven syllables, and the last eleven. Of course, these latter, in order to be uttered in the same time as the preceding seven, must be read more rapidly.

>She had dreams all yester night
>Of her own betrothéd knight,
>And she in the midnight wood will pray
>For the weal of her lover that 's far away.
>   —*Christabel: Coleridge.*

Rapid movement represents, as has been indicated, what is comparatively *unimportant, light*, or *trivial* in its character. Notice, therefore, the inappropriateness of the metre used to express the thought in the following:

>My soul is beset
>   With grief and dismay;
>I owe a vast debt,
>   And nothing can pay.
>
>I must go to prison,
>   Unless the dear Lord,
>Who died and is risen,
>   His mercy afford.
>   —*Guest's History of English Rhythms.*

Especially, as contrasted with the following expression of the same thought:

>My former hopes are fled,
>My terror now begins;

> I feel alas ! that I am dead
> In trespasses and sins.
> —*Idem.*

For the reasons given, metres in which the accented syllables are fewer than the unaccented ones, are favorites with those who wish to describe events or scenes characterized by rapidity of movement,—in such poems, for instance, as Scott's *Lochinvar :*

> Oh, young Lochinvar is come out of the west,
> Through all the wide border his steed was the best.

or Read's *Sheridan's Ride, e. g. :*

> Up from the South at break of day,
> Bringing to Winchester fresh dismay,

or Browning's *How They Brought the Good News from Ghent,* a poem, which, with its galloping measures, is probably the best phonetic representation of a horseback ride in the language, equally true to the requirements of discoursive and of dramatic elocution :

> I sprang to the stirrup, and Joris, and he ;
> I galloped, Dirck galloped, we galloped all three ;
> "Good speed !" cried the watch, as the gate-bolts undrew ;
> "Speed !" echoed the wall to us galloping through.
> Behind shut the postern, the lights sank to rest,
> And into the midnight we galloped abreast.

A metre similar in effect to those just mentioned is the classic hexameter, used by Homer and Virgil. In most of the English imitations of this metre, however, the easy flow of the movement, which, as readers of Greek and Latin know, is its chief characteristic, fails to be produced. One reason for this is that our language, largely because it lacks the grammatical terminations of the classic tongues, contains fewer short syllables then they ; and, in the place of the only foot of three syllables allowed in their hexameter—I mean the dactyl, containing one long and two short syllables,—our poets often use long syllables only, influenced to do this, probably, by the false theory that quantity has nothing to do with English metres. Another reason is, that notwithstanding the poverty of our language in short syllables, many seem to think that the hexameter necessarily requires a large number of them. But Greek and Latin lines are frequent in which measures containing short syllables are few, *e. g.*:

ἀρνύμενος ἥν τε ψυχὴν καὶ νόστον ἑταίρων.—*Homer.*
Illi inter sese magna vi brachia tollunt.—*Virgil.*

Both of these causes serve to make our English hexameters slow and heavy. Besides this, most of those who write them, misled by the notion that they must crowd as many syllables as possible into their lines, are tempted to use too many words, and thus to violate another principle not of poetry only, but of rhetoric. Take the following, for instance, from Longfellow's *Children of the Lord's Supper*:

Weeping he spake in these words : and now at the beck of the old man,
Knee against knee, they knitted a wreath round the altar's enclosure.
Kneeling he read then the prayers of the consecration, and softly,
With him the children read ; at the close, with tremulous accents,
Asked he the peace of heaven, a benediction upon them.

An English verse representing accurately—what is all that is worth representing—the movement of the classic hexameter, would read more like this, which, itself, too, would read better, did it contain fewer dactyls; but to show the possibilities of our verse these have been intentionally crowded into it :

> Weeping he told them this, and they, at the villager's bidding,
> Knitting with knee to knee a wreath at the altar's railing,
> Knelt as he softly led in the prayer of the consecration.
> In it the children joined, until in a tremulous accent
> Closing the prayer he had asked for the Lord's benediction upon them.

This passage from Longfellow is a typical specimen of what is called English hexameter. Here is another (not so good), from Frothingham's translation—in many respects an admirable one—of Goethe's *Hermann and Dorothea*:

> Thitherward up the new street as I hasted, a stout-timbered wagon
> Drawn by two oxen I saw, of that region the largest and strongest,
> While with vigorous step a maiden was walking beside them ;
> And, a long staff in her hand, the two powerful creatures was guiding,
> Urging them now, now holding them back, with skill did she drive them.

Not until such lines have been reduced to a form more like the following, can we be prepared to debate whether or not the effects of the classic hexameter can be reproduced in English. Those, too, who choose to compare these lines with the original, will find this translation more literal than the last.

> Now my eyes, as I made my way along the new street there,
> Happened to light on a cart with a frame of the heaviest timber,
> Drawn by a pair of steers of the largest breed and stoutest.
> By their side was a maid, and with vigorous gait was walking,
> Waving a staff in her hand, and guiding the strong pair onward.
> Urging or holding them in, right skilfully did she drive them.

In these last lines, there are more spondaic verses,—verses, that is, in which the fifth foot contains two syllables—than were often used in the classic hexameters. But this fact does not change the general effect of the movement. Matthew Arnold says of the following, that, "it is the one version of any part of the Iliad which in some degree reproduces for me the original effect of

Homer." It is a translation from the third book made by Dr. Hawtrey of Eton College:

Clearly the rest I beheld of the dark-eyed sons of Achaia,
Known to me well are the faces of all ; their names I remember.
Two, two only remain, whom I see not among the commanders,—
Castor fleet in the car,—Polydeukes brave with the cestus,—
Own dear brethren of mine,—one parent loved us as infants.
Are they not here in the host, from the shores of loved Lacedæmon?
Or though they came with the rest in ships that bound through the waters,
Dare they not enter the fight, or stand in the council of heroes,
All for fear of the shame, and the taunts my crime has awakened?

Instead of two we sometimes find three consecutive unaccented syllables, combined with which there is occasionally a slight but secondary accent on the second of these. As the general effect of this kind of rhythm is to cause four syllables to be uttered in the time usually given to two, it increases the rapidity of the movement ; *e. g.:*

The king has come to marshal us in all his armor dressed,
And he has bound a snow-white plume upon his gallant crest,
He looked upon his people, and a tear was in his eye ;
He looked upon the traitors, and his glance was stern and high ;
Right graciously he smiled on us, as rolled from wing to wing,
Down all the line in deafening shout, God save our lord the king !

* * * * * * * *

" And if my standard-bearer fall,—as fall full well he may,
For never saw I promise yet of such a bloody fray,—
Press where ye see my white plume shine amid the ranks of war,
And be your oriflame to-day, the helmet of Navarre."
— *The Battle of Ivry : Macaulay.*

CHAPTER V.

ELOCUTIONARY AND POETIC FORCE.

Force, representing Instinctive Tendency of Utterance, or Physical Energy—Different Kinds of Force—the Degree of Force—Loud and Soft Force as used in Elocution—Their Poetic Analogues—Loudness and Softness, Strength and Weakness, Great and Slight Weight as represented by Long or Short Accented or Unaccented Syllables.

THE next rhythmical element of expression to be considered, is force. This is to sounds what different degrees of light and shade are to objects of sight; and is essential to the effects of rhythm in the same way that shading is to those of proportion. In elocution, no one in feeble physical health can manifest an excess of force, while, at times, without it, his delivery may be characterized by the greatest amount of intelligence and soul, of thought and the emotion that is connected with thought. For these reasons, it seems right to infer that force represents physique rather than intellect or spiritual feeling; in other words, energy that is instinctive and connected with the physical nature rather than any thing that is reflective and connected with the psychical. As used for emphasis, force differs mainly in three regards, which, according to the principle of classification pursued hitherto, may be stated thus: first, on its purely instinctive or physical side, it differs in *degree*—it may be loud or soft; second, on its reflective or intellectual side, it differs in *gradation*—it may be strongest at the beginning,

ELOCUTIONARY AND POETIC FORCE. 51

middle, or end of the utterance of a syllable or word; and third, in emotive relations, affected more or less by both instinctive and reflective influences, it differs in *regularity* —it may be abrupt or smooth.

Let us consider, first, the *degrees* of force. It is probably not necessary to illustrate the statement that, in elocution *loud* force indicates a great degree of energy, and *soft* force a slight degree of it. As loud and soft are relative terms, it is evident that in poetry their analogues are found in forms in which the relative force is decidedly greater on certain syllables than on others; therefore, in metres in which the accents are strongly marked. This condition is realized, as a rule, where the accented syllables are long, in quantity, and the unaccented short. Here are metres of this character:

>Louder, louder chant the lay;
>Waken lords and ladies gay!
>Tell them youth and mirth and glee
>Run a course, as well as we;
>Time, stern huntsman! who can balk?
>Stanch as hound and fleet as hawk?
>Think of this and rise with day,
>Gentle lords and ladies gay!
>—*Hunting Song: Scott.*

>When, wide in soul and bold of tongue,
>Among the tents I paused and sung,
>The distant battle flashed and rung.
>—*Two Voices: Tennyson.*

>Strike, and when the fight is over,
>If ye look in vain for me,
>Where the dead are lying thickest
>Look for him who was Dundee.
>—*Burial March of Dundee: Aytoun.*

>How firm a foundation, ye saints of the Lord,
>Is laid for your faith in his excellent word!
>—*Hymn: Kirkham.*

If both the accented and unaccented syllables are short in quantity, the movement is rapid, indicating, as has been said before, thought that is *unimportant ;* and we have a *rattling* effect, analogous to loudness that does not convey an impression of strength—*e. g. :*

> Then we let off paper crackers, each of which contained a motto,
> And she listened while I read them, till her mother told her not to.
> —*Ferdinando and Elvira : Gilbert.*

> Now elderly men of the bachelor crew,
>   With wrinkled hose
>   And spectacled nose,
> Don't marry at all ;—you may take it as true,
>   If ever you do,
>   The step you will rue,
> For your babes will be elderly, elderly too.
> —*The Precocious Baby : Idem.*

> " O maidens," said Pattison, touching his hat,
> " Don't blubber, my dears, for a fellow like that ;
> Observe I 'm a very superior man,
> A much better fellow than Angus McClan."
> —*Ellen McJones Aberdeen : Idem.*

If both the accented and unaccented syllables are long in quantity, the movement is *slow*, indicating thought that is *important*, and the accent is less decidedly marked. This gives us the poetical equivalent for force characterized by *weight* and *strength*, though not necessarily by loudness— *e. g. :*

> O good gray head which all men knew ;
> O voice from which their omens all men drew ;
> O iron nerve to true occasion true ;
> O fall'n at length that tower of strength
> Which stood four square to all the winds that blew !
> —*Ode on the Duke of Wellington : Tennyson.*

> The woods shall wear their robes of praise,
>   The south winds softly sigh,

> And sweet, calm days in golden haze
> Melt down the amber sky.
> —*My Psalm: Whittier.*

> Though hearts brood o'er the past, our eyes
> With smiling futures glisten;
> For, lo, our day bursts up the skies,—
> Lean out your souls and listen.
> —*To-day and To-morrow: Gerald Massey.*

When the accented and unaccented syllables are indiscriminately long and short, the accent is least decidedly marked, and we have the poetic equivalent for soft force. This may convey an impression of *strength*, if it contain several long syllables—*e. g.*:

> Never any more
> While I live,
> Need I hope to see his face
> As before.
> Once his love grown chill
> Mine may strive,—
> Bitterly we re-embrace,
> Single still.
> —*In a Year: R. Browning.*

> And so my silent moan begins and ends,
> No world's laugh or world's taunt, no pity of friends
> Or sneer of foes, with this my torment blends.
> —*Only a Woman: Mulock.*

But it must convey an impression of *weakness*, if made up mainly of short syllables—*e. g.*:

> Though not disordinate, yet causeless suffering
> The punishment of dissolute days; in fine,
> Just or unjust, alike seem miserable,
> For oft alike both come to evil end.
> —*Samson Agonistes: Milton.*

> —Let him slip down,
> Not one accompanying his declining feet.
> —*Timon I., 1: Shakespear.*

—Nothing routs us but
The villany of our fears.
—*Cymbeline V.*, 2 : *Idem.*

Here are distinctively imitative effects, first, of *loudness :*

And my pulses closed their gates with a shock on my heart, as I heard
The shrill-edged shriek of a mother divide the shuddering night.
* * * * * * * *
And the vitriol madness flushes up in the ruffian's head,
Till the filthy by-lane rings to the yell of the trampled wife.
* * * * * * * *
Is it peace or war ? better war ! loud war by land and by sea !
War with a hundred battles and shaking a hundred thrones.
—*Maud : Tennyson.*

And here of *loudness* with more or less *strength :*

On came the whirlwind,—steel-gleams broke
Like lightning through the rolling smoke ;
   The war was waked anew.
Three hundred cannon mouths roared loud,
And from their throats, with flash and cloud,
   Their showers of iron threw.
Beneath their fire in full career,
Rushed on the ponderous cuirassier ;
The lancer couched his ruthless spear,
And, hurrying as to havoc near,
   The cohorts' eagles flew.
In one dark torrent, broad and strong,
The advancing onset rolled along,
Forth harbingered by fierce acclaim,
That from the shroud of smoke and flame
Peal'd wildly the imperial name.
—*The Charge at Waterloo : Scott.*

Loud sounds the axe, redoubling strokes on strokes—
On all sides round the forest hurls her oaks
Headlong. Deep echoing groan the thickets brown,
Then rustling, crackling, crashing thunder down.
—*Iliad*, 23 : *Pope.*

Here of *weight* or *strength:*

> When Ajax strives some rock's vast weight to throw,
> The line too labors, and the words move slow.
> —*Essay on Criticism : Pope.*

> Then those eight mighty daughters of the plow
> Bent their broad faces toward us, and addressed
> Their motion.
> —*The Princess : Tennyson.*

Here of *softness:*

> And let some strange mysterious dream
> Wave at his wings in aëry stream,
> Of lively portraiture display'd,
> Softly on my eyelids laid.
> And, as I wake, sweet music breathe
> Above, about, or underneath,
> Sent by some spirit to mortal's good,
> Or the unseen genius of the wood.
> —*Il Penseroso : Milton.*

> While I nodded, nearly napping, suddenly there came a tapping
> As of some one gently rapping, rapping at my chamber door.
> —*The Raven : Poe.*

> Within, the waves in softer murmurs glide,
> And ships secure without their haulsers ride.
> —*Odyssey*, 3 : *Pope.*

> There is sweet music here that softer falls
> Than petals from blown roses on the grass,
> Or night dews on still waters between walls
> Of shadowy granite in a gleaming pass.
> —*The Lotus Eaters : Tennyson.*

And here of *weakness:*

> So he with difficulty and labor hard
> Moved on with difficulty and labor he.
> —*Par. Lost*, 2 : *Milton.*

> So she low-toned, while with shut eyes I lay
> Listening, then looked. Pale was the perfect face ;
> The bosom with long sighs labored ; and meek
> Seemed the full lips, and mild the luminous eyes,
> And the voice trembled and the hand.
> —*The Princess : Tennyson.*

Look once more now at the passage from weak force to strong, as well as from fast time to slow, in the following:

> The cherubim descended ; on the ground
> Gliding meteorous, as evening mist
> Ris'n from a river o'er the marsh glides,
> And gathers round fast at the laborer's heel
> Homeward returning. High in front advanced,
> The brandish'd sword of God before them blazed,
> Fierce as a comet.
> —*Par. Lost,* 12 : *Milton.*

CHAPTER VI.

FORCE AS THE SOURCE AND INTERPRETER OF POETIC MEASURES.

Gradations of Force or Stress, representing Reflective Influence exerted on Instinctive Tendency—What is represented by the Different Kinds of Elocutionary Stress—Why Elocutionary Stress corresponds to Poetic Measure—Classification of English Poetic Measures, and their Classic Analogues—What is represented by Initial Double Measure—Its Classic Form—By Terminal Double Measure—Why used in Our Hymns—Its Classic Form—Triple Measures; Median—Its Classic Form—Initial Triple Measure—Could also be termed Compound Measure, corresponding to Compound Stress—Its Classic Forms—Its Use in Greek Pæonics—In Pathos, corresponding to Tremulous Stress—Terminal Triple Measure—Can correspond to Thorough Stress—Its Classic Forms—Blending of Different Triple Measures—Of Triple and Double Measures to prevent Monotony—Quadruple Measures, Initial and Terminal—Blending of all Kinds of Measures to represent Movements.

WE pass on now to the next way, in which the force employed in emphasis has been said to differ—namely, in *gradation*, or what is technically termed *stress*. In discoursive elocution, the force or exertion necessary for the pronunciation of any given syllable or word may be used because of an internal or an external motive, or of a combination of the two; in other words, either because a man desires to *express an idea for his own sake;* or because he wishes to *impress it upon others;* or because he wishes to do *both*. In the first case, the sound bursts forth explosively, as if the speaker were conscious of nothing but his own vocal organs to prevent the accomplishment of his object; and the loudest part of the sound is on the first part of the utterance. This is the most instinctive, and, in this sense, physical, form of stress. In the second case, the sound is pushed forth expulsively, as if the man were conscious of an outside possibility of opposition, and of the necessity of pressing his point; and the loudest sound is at the end of the utterance. This is a deliberative stress, force given with a design; and, in this sense, is reflective and intellectual. In the third case, the sound is uttered so that it blends the effects of both the other methods, either as in the effusive median stress, or in the ways indicated in the descriptions given below of compound, thorough, and tremulous stress. In dramatic elocution, of course, these same methods would represent things having a bursting or pushing sound or tendency, or both of these together.

These two methods of applying energy to articulation, and different combinations of them, give us the different kinds of stress: termed, if the chief force is used at the beginning of the accented utterance, *Initial*, indicated thus >, and used in this:

> Up, comrades, up !—in Rokeby's halls
> Ne'er be it said our courage falls !

If at its end, *Terminal*, <, and used in this:

> Let the consequences be what they may, I am determined to proceed.

If in its middle, *Median*, <>, and used in this:

> O joy to the people and joy to the throne.

If at both its beginning and end, *Compound*, ×, and used in this:

> Ye blocks, ye stones, ye worse than senseless things.

If at its beginning, middle, and end, with strong force, *Thorough* ⋉⋊, and used in this:

> Lend, lend your wings, I mount, I fly.
> O grave, where is thy victory?

If at all three, with weak force, *Tremulous* ∿, and used in this:

> Pity the sorrows of a poor old man.

It may be difficult for those not acquainted with elocution to detect at once what is meant by *stress;* but it will become clearer as we proceed. The first important thing for us to notice in connection with it, is that, though given mainly on the accented syllable, it is often, especially in flexible voices, communicated to more than one syllable. In the following, for instance, the same kind of compound stress is used on the one syllable in *hard* and on the two syllables in *cruel*, and might be used on the three syllables in a word like *villanous*, were it substituted for *cruel*.

> ⋊   > <
> O ye *hard* hearts, ye *cru-el* men of Rome.

So it is with other kinds of stress. The three syllables in *misery* might receive the same gradations in force as the one in *woe*. It is owing to this fact with reference to force that analogies, important though subtle, may be detected between different kinds of stress and different kinds of poetic measure. An accent, as has been noticed, falls on every second, third, or fourth syllable of a verse, and the number of accents in a line determines the number of feet or measures in it, a foot being composed of one accented syllable and, as the case may be, of one, two, or three unaccented syllables. Below, separated by bars, will be found all the principal kinds of feet. A moment's glance at them will detect that the character of each measure is determined by the place in it, whether its beginning, its middle, or its end, on which the accent falls. In the same way, the character of any given kind of stress is determined by the place in the utterance, whether composed of one or of more syllables, on which the chief force falls. In other words, poetic accent influences syllables grouped in feet or measures, precisely as elocutionary stress influences syllables grouped in words. For this reason, the measures in the paragraph below are named according to the analogy between the places in them on which the accents fall, and the places in words made most prominent by the different kinds of stress. The Greek names for corresponding measures are also given.

Initial measure, or *initial double measure*, is determined by what may be called initial accent, and corresponds, if composed of one long syllable followed by one short, to the Greek trochee or choree; if of two long, to the Greek spondee; *e. g.* :

Tèll me | nòt in | mòurnful | nùmbers.

Terminal measure, or *terminal double measure*, is determined by what may be called terminal accent, and corresponds to the Greek iambus, composed of one short followed by one long syllable; *e. g.* :

The tràin | from oùt | the càs | tle drèw.

Initial triple measure is usually the same as the Greek dactyl.

Òver the | ròadways and | òn through the | vìllages.

Median, or *median triple measure*, is usually the same as the Greek amphibrach; *e. g.* :

There càme to | the bèach a | poor èxile | of Èrin.

Terminal triple measure is usually the same as the Greek anapæst; *e. g.*:

O'er the lànd | of the frèe | and the hòme | of the bràve.

Compound triple measure is the same as the Greek amphimacrus, or as feet used in certain of the pæonic stanzas.

Nèarer mý | Gòd to thèe | È'en though ìt | bè a cròss.

Diinitial quadruple measure is usually the same as the Greek ditrochee, with a primary accent on every first, and a secondary on every third syllable; *e. g.*:

Ròses are in | blòssom and the | rìlls are filled with | wàter-cresses.

Diterminal quadruple measure is usually the same as the Greek diiambus, with a primary accent on every second; and a secondary on every fourth syllable; *e. g.*:

The kìng has come | to màrshal us,

Quadruple measures might have their primary accent on their third or fourth syllable, *i. e.*, on their final double foot, and be termed, therefore, *Final diinitial* or *Final diterminal;* or they might be *Compound*, having an initial and terminal foot, and be termed, to indicate the foot coming first, *Initial-terminal* or *Terminal-initial*. I can recall, however, no English measures of these kinds.

Now let us see what ideas each of these measures, according to elocutionary analogy, is fitted to represent. We will begin with *Initial* stress, called radical also. As has been said, this characterizes utterances that burst forth abruptly with their loudest sound at their beginning, as in the sentence, "Go on, I say; get along; I tell you I 'll not wait for you; move on." In fulfilment of the principles stated above, this stress is used when one seems to be conscious of nothing but his own organs to prevent the expression of his ideas, and when therefore his main wish is to *express himself* so as to be distinctly understood. In its milder form, it serves to render articulation *clear* and utterance *precise;* in its stronger form, it indicates great physical momentum, and therefore *bold*, and sometimes vehement *assurance, positiveness,* and *dictation.*

Bearing in mind now what has been shown before, that the important places in a line of verse are its beginning, before which, and its end, after which, the voice of the reader naturally pauses, it may be said, that whenever lines containing feet of two syllables begin or end with a foot, the first syllable of which is accented, the emphasis characterizing the verse is the same in general tendency as when single words receive initial stress. It is possible, for instance, to read the following with any kind of elocutionary stress; but the arrangement of accented and unaccented syllables is such, that, when read without design, one naturally gives to each foot the kind of emphasis characterizing initial stress. We may call this, therefore, the measure of initial accent or *Initial measure.* Here is an example of its milder form, representing, like initial stress, *clearness* and *precision* of statement :

>Take the open air, the more you take the better ;
>Follow nature's laws to the very letter.
>Let the doctors go to the Bay of Biscay,
>Let alone the gin, the brandy, and the whiskey.
>—*Advice : Anon.*

>Go where glory waits thee,
>But when fame elates thee, etc.—
>—*Go Where, etc. : Moore.*

>Should you ask me, whence these stories,
>Whence these legends and traditions,

> With the odors of the forest,
> With the dew and damp of meadows,
> With the curling smoke of wigwams,
> With the rushing of great rivers,
> With their frequent repetitions,
> And their wild reverberations
> As of thunder in the mountains?
> I should answer, I should tell you,
> " From the forests and the prairies."
> —*Hiawatha : Longfellow.*

> Then with deep sonorous clangor,
> Calmly answering their sweet anger,
> When the wrangling bells had ended,
> Slowly struck the clock eleven,
> And from out the silent heaven,
> Silence on the town descended.
> —*Carillon : Longfellow.*

And this is the stronger form, representing *bold assurance, positiveness,* and *dictation :*

> Honor, riches, marriage, blessing,
> Long continuance and increasing,
> Hourly joys be still upon you!
> Juno sings her blessings on you.
> —*Tempest, iv.,* 1 : *Shakespear.*

> Shake the casements,
> Break the painted
> Panes that flame with gold and crimson ;
> Scatter them like leaves of autumn.
> —*Golden Legend : Longfellow.*

As has been said, this metre existed among the Greeks in two principal forms. The first was composed of one long syllable followed by a short, and called Trochee from τρέχω, *to run,* or τροχός, *a wheel,* and also Choree from χορεῖος, *belonging to a chorus or dance.* These terms in themselves signify little. They might be applied to many other movements. But Schmidt, emerging for a moment from the too frequent lack of endeavor to interpret the meanings of metres, which characterizes the voluminous literature on this subject, tells us, in his "Rhythmic and Metric of the Classic Languages," that it is "a somewhat *vivacious* measure, serving for the expression of *individual* feeling," and this is all he says; but the correspondence between this, and saying, as has just been done here, that the metre has an *internal* motive and represents *assurance, positiveness*, and *dictation*, will be recognized by all. The other Greek form of this metre was the Spondee, so called from σπονδαί, *the drink-offerings*, and was used in religious hymns, like this, for instance, to Helios by Dionysius:

εὐφαμείτω πᾶς αἰθήρ
γῆ καὶ πόντος καὶ πνοιαί.

This is simply initial measure to which has been added the effect of predominating long quantity on unaccented syllables. The spondaic hymn would sound something like the following, which is an attempt to reproduce the effect of the Latin original:

DIES IRÆ, DIES ILLA.

Day of wrath, that day of burning,
All shall melt to ashes turning,
All foretold by seers discerning.

*　　*　　*　　*

All aghast then, Death shall shiver,
And great Nature's frame shall quiver,
When the graves their dead deliver.
—*Translated by A. Coles.*

The limited number of final syllables in our language which can end effectively lines of this kind, as well as the positive assurance expressed by them, sometimes passing, as in the *Dies Iræ* above, into almost fatalistic acquiescence, gives initial measure little popularity with our own hymn writers. A few instances, indeed, can be cited of the use of a similar measure, but almost always in connection with occasional terminal measures, as in this; *e. g.*:

> Glorious things of thee are spoken,
> Zion, city of our God.
> He whose word can not be broken,
> Formed thee for his own abode.
> —*Newton.*

All of our Long, Common, and Short Metre hymns, however, are written entirely in terminal measures. And this is what we should expect, for these measures themselves, as well as their tunes, to which I shall refer by-and-bye, express the effort of the soul as it reaches forth with a pushing *persistence* and *determination* toward that which is beyond itself, which means in the case of religious thought, *aspiration*,—a feeling especially in harmony with the spirit of the modern church.

The second kind of stress, called *Terminal*, and also Final and Vanishing, is applied when an utterance begins softly, and gradually increases in force, till it ends with its loudest sound. It seems to be used, as has been said, when one is conscious of outside opposition, obliging him to press his point, and so when his main wish is to *impress his thoughts upon others*. Its milder form may indicate merely *complaint* or *peevishness*, demanding consideration, as when the child whines out, "I sha'n't"; its stronger form indicates energy used with an intelligent design, and so a pushing *pertinacity, persistence*, or *determination*, in view of what is either liked or disliked, as in the exclamation, used either in banter or contempt, "Aha!" or in the sentences, "I am determined to remain true to my cause," "I despise the man."

The arrangement of accented and unaccented syllables

analogous to this is found evidently, for reasons similar to those already given, in a line containing feet of two syllables, that begins or ends with a foot, the first syllable of which is unaccented. We may call the following, therefore, *Terminal measure.* Here is its milder form, representing *complaint* demanding consideration :

  O let the solid ground
   Not fail beneath my feet,
  Before my life has found
   What some have found so sweet.
       —*Maud : Tennyson.*

  Alas ! I have nor hope nor health,
  Nor peace within nor calm around,
  Nor that content surpassing wealth
  The sage in meditation found,
  And walked with inward glory crowned.
      —*The Sun is Warm : Shelley.*

Here is its stronger form, representing *earnest persistence, determination :*

  If that the world and love were young,
  And truth in every shepherd's tongue,
  These pretty pleasures might me move
  To live with thee and be thy love.
      —*Nymph's Reply : Raleigh.*

  I cannot hide that some have striven,
  Achieving calm to whom was given
  The joy that mixes man with heaven ;

  Who rowing hard against the stream,
  Saw distant gates of Eden gleam,
  And did not dream it was a dream.
      —*Two Voices : Tennyson.*

  Think not, thou eagle Lord of Rome,
   And master of the world,
  Though victory's banner o'er thy dome
   In triumph now is furled,

> I would address thee as thy slave,
> But as the bold should greet the brave.
> —*Caractacus: Bernard Barton.*

As applied to spiritual relations, this pushing earnestness of terminal measure properly represents, as was said a moment ago, *aspiration*. Hence the use of the metre in most of our popular hymns; *e. g.*:

> Praise God from whom all blessings flow.
>
> My soul, be on thy guard.

The Greek measure corresponding to this, was the Iambic, a term supposed to have been derived from ἰάπτο *to drive forth, shoot, assail.* Prof. Jebb, in his "Greek Literature," says it "was first used" (as in the case of the *aha!* cited above), "in raillery, which entered into the worship of Demeter as into a modern carnival." "It was the form in which the more intense and original spirits loved to utter their scorn, or their deeper thought and emotion." It "was fitted to express any pointed thought." This explanation of its uses evidently corresponds with that which has just been said of it here, viz.: that it represents an external aim, and is indicative of *petulancy, push, persistence, determination*, and in certain cases of *aspiration*. Schmidt endeavors to identify this metre with the Trochaic, because in this, as in that, every other syllable is accented. Of course, the rhythmical movements of both metres are the same, except at the beginnings and ends of lines. But, unfortunately for Schmidt's theory, these two places in the line give it its whole character, and a difference in them necessitates a difference in the ideas which the lines represent, and this not only in their metres, but also, as we shall find, by-and-bye, in their tunes. The two metres, therefore, should not be identified.

Let us pass on now to triple measures. When considering duration, it was noticed that, as contrasted with double measures, the triple give to the movement the effect of greater rapidity, inasmuch as the time usually allotted to two syllables is in them allotted to three. It is important to notice here, in addition to this, that in the degree in which the accented syllable in triple measures is rendered emphatic, there is a tendency to give it the same time as that given to the two unaccented syllables in the same foot, and thus, by way of contrast, to thrust it into greater prominence. Accordingly, initial and terminal accents in triple measure are stronger forms of the same in double measure. They convey, too, an added effect of *rapidity*, representing, therefore, more drift and momentum in the general thought expressed in the passage. But in triple measure there is also a middle syllable in the foot, which syllable, as well as the one before it or after it, can be emphasized. This fact gives rise to a measure of a new kind, which, as it influences somewhat both of the other kinds of triple measure, needs to be considered before them.

The accent given on the middle of the foot corresponds to what elocutionists term *Median* stress, in which the voice swells out on the middle of an utterance, as in reading the line: "O joy to the people and joy to the throne." Median stress begins like terminal, indicating, like it a *reflective* motive,—a desire to *impress* one's thought on others; and ends like initial, indicating an *instinctive* motive,—a desire to *express* one's thought for its own sake. The two forms together seem to indicate, therefore, any thing that is felt to be worth the attention both of others and of one's self. It is accordingly the natural expression for emotion or for *eloquence* of

MEANINGS OF THE METRES.   69

thought, for any thing deemed to be intrinsically attractive and interesting whether because *beautiful* or *pathetic*. Notice how graceful is the general effect of this kind of verse :

> There is a green island in lone Gougaune Barra,
> Where Allua of songs rushes forth as an arrow ;
> In deep valleyed Desmond—a thousand wild fountains
> Come down to that lake from their home in the mountains.
> High sons of the lyre, O how proud was the feeling,
> To think while alone through that solitude stealing,
> Though loftier minstrels green Erin could number,
> I only awoke your wild harp from its slumber,
> And mingled once more with the voice of those fountains
> The songs even Echo forgot on her mountains.
> —*Gougaune Barra : J. J. Callanan.*

> " What makes you be shoving and moving your stool on,
> And singing all wrong the old song of ' The Coolun' ? "
> There 's a form at the casement,—the form of her true love,—
> And he whispers with face bent : " I 'm waiting for you, love ;
> Get up on the stool, through the lattice step lightly,
> We 'll rove in the grove while the moon 's shining brightly."
> —*The Spinning-Wheel Song : J. F. Waller.*

Median measures are frequently changed to terminal measures at the ends of the lines ; *e. g.* :

> How dear to my heart are the scenes of my childhood,
>   When fond recollection presents them to view.
> The orchard, the meadow, the deep-tangled wildwood,
>   And every loved spot which my infancy knew.
> *Old Oaken Bucket : S. Woodworth.*

> In slumbers of midnight the sailor boy lay,
>   His hammock swung loose to the sport of the wind :
> But watch-worn and weary his cares flew away,
>   And visions of happiness danced o'er his mind.
> —*The Sailor Boy's Dream : Dimond.*

> Society, friendship, and love,
>   Divinely bestowed upon man.

> O had I the wings of a dove,
> How soon would I taste you again !
> —*Selkirk : Cowper.*

The following are terminal triple measures, but owing to the fact that there is no break in the regularity of the metre after the pause at the end of each line, their effect is about the same as that of median triple measures :

> For the moon never beams without bringing me dreams
> Of the beautiful Annabel Lee,
> And the stars never rise but I feel the bright eyes
> Of the beautiful Annabel Lee.
> And so all the night-tide I lie down by the side
> Of my darling, my darling, my life and my bride,
> In the sepulchre there by the sea,
> In her tomb by the sounding sea.
> —*Annabel Lee : Poe.*

The Greek metre corresponding to median is the Amphibrach, from ἀμφί, *on both sides,* and βραχύς, *short.* Scholars usually treat it as a form of the anapæst or terminal triple measure, and as significant of the same mental tendency. As the last two quotations have shown, these two measures are often used interchangeably, and, when we come to treat of terminal triple measure, we shall find that there is a reason why this should be so. Any further consideration, therefore, of what the measure represents may better be deferred until then.

In uttering measures termed *Initial Triple*, of which examples are given below, it will be noticed that there is a natural tendency to use more emphasis with the second than with the first of the unaccented syllables, producing therefore a stronger tone at the end as well as at the beginning of the measure. In this respect a foot thus accented corresponds in effect to what elocutionists term *Compound* stress ; and for this reason might be termed

Compound measure. Compound stress characterizes an utterance the first and last parts of which receive more force than its middle. It may be used for a strong form of initial stress, especially where there are long slides, the beginnings and ends of which need to be brought out with distinctness, as in the word *now* in the question: "*What will you do now?*" or it may be used, as its form (×) suggests, especially with abrupt irregular rhythm, for a combination of the ideas expressed by initial and terminal stress—*i. e.*, for *assured, positive,* and *dictating earnestness, persistence,* and *determination,* as in these words that are italicised.

"You *blocks*, you *stones*, you *worse* than *senseless* things."

Here are examples of the poetic equivalent for this kind of stress, indicating persistence or determination. They introduce occasionally an initial double measure ; *e. g.:*

> Come away, come away, hark to the summons ;
> Come in your war array, gentles and commons,
>   *   *   *   *   *   *
> Come as the winds come when forests are rended,
> Come as the waves come when navies are stranded ;
> Faster, come faster, come faster and faster,
> Chief, vassal, page and groom, tenant and master.
>   —*Gathering Song of Donald the Black: Scott.*

> Flashed all their sabres bare,
> Flashed as they turned in air,
> Sabring the gunners there,
> Charging an army while
> All the world wondered :
> Plunged in the battery-smoke
> Right through the line they broke ;
> Cossack and Russian
> Reeled from the sabre-stroke.
>   —*Charge of the Light Brigade: Tennyson.*

Several Greek measures correspond to this, chiefly perhaps the Dactyl from δάκτυλος, *a finger*, which, like the measure, consists of three members, divided at the joints into one long and two short parts. Schmidt tells us that this "was used (especially in choric poetry) to denote an exalted *God-trusting state* of mind, or to express warnings with *solemn earnestness*"—both of which uses could evidently be made of a metre representing the ideas just attributed to this. The measure corresponds also to Schmidt's representation of the pæonic, which with some quadruple feet derived its main effect from feet containing a long syllable followed by a short and a long. This, as will be noticed, is more nearly analogous to *Compound* stress than is the dactyl. But in English both measures would be read in nearly the same way, and would always be used interchangeably. The pæonic measure, according to Schmidt, indicated "*overwhelming enthusiasm*," as well as another state to be spoken of in a moment. Of course, the "enthusiasm" here mentioned can very properly be classed as a manifestation of the *highest degree of assurance* and *positiveness*, which have been said to characterize this metre. The other state of feeling which Schmidt says that this metre sometimes represents, is apparently just the opposite of enthusiasm—*i. e.*, "*uncertainty, wavering*, and *helplessness*." We find an exact parallel to this conflicting use of the Greek pæonics in the employment of initial triple measure in such a poem as Hood's *Bridge of Sighs ; e. g.:*

    Touch her not scornfully,
    Think of her mournfully,
     Gently, and humanly.
    Not of the stains of her,
    All that remains of her
     Now is pure womanly.

> Make no deep scrutiny
> Into her mutiny,
>   Rash and undutiful;
> Past all dishonor,
> Death has left on her
>   Only the beautiful.

And in Browning's *Evelyn Hope*; *e. g.*:

> Beautiful Evelyn Hope is dead.
>   Sit and watch by her side an hour.
> That is her book-shelf,—this her bed;
>   She plucked that piece of geranium-flower
> Beginning to die too in the glass.

The pathetic effect here may be owing to the blending of the spirit of assurance,—as if a man would say: "I know all about it; I am making no mistake,"—with the sad nature of the facts represented; or, possibly, the pathos may be owing to the uncertain effect of the metre, when read, as it would be in such a poem, without strongly marked accents. In this case, the immediate proximity of two syllables like *not* and *scorn* and *her* and *mourn*, both of them apparently accented, yet not both able to receive a strong accent, would of themselves suggest uncertainty, and make this kind of metre analogous to the trembling tone produced by the elocutionist's *Tremulous stress*. This is a form of stress, too, which, like the Greek pæonics, may be used both for *great grief* and for *great joy*—for any thing, in fact, showing that a man has not complete mastery over himself. Hence the appropriateness of the metre in the following—

> Though like a wanderer,
>   Daylight all gone,
> Darkness be over me,
>   My rest a stone,
> Yet in my dreams I 'd be

> Nearer, my God, to thee,
> Nearer to thee.
>
> —*Hymn: S. F. Adams.*

and also in this verse of the same hymn, where the assured earnestness and persistence or, what is the same thing, the aspiration, is represented in effects that blend those of tremulous and thorough stress:

> Or if on joyful wing
> Cleaving the sky,
> Sun, moon, and stars forgot,
> Upward I fly,
> Still all my song shall be,
> Nearer, my God, to thee,
> Nearer to thee.
>
> —*Idem.*

Not a little of the success of a hymn like this, or of any poem, depends on the happy choice—usually made, of course, unconsciously—of a metre for it.

As was shown in the examples quoted under median measure, *Terminal Triple Measure*, is often used interchangeably with median, which is thus more closely allied to it than to initial measure; in fact, the terminal accent, in this measure, can be regarded as a strong form of median. In this regard, these terminal effects resemble those of what elocutionists term *Thorough* stress, which, though sometimes described as a combination of initial, median, and terminal stress, has in it much more of the latter two than of the former—*i. e.*, it indicates both the subjective feeling of the median in view of that which is *intrinsically eloquent*, *beautiful*, and *sublime*, and also the objective *persistence* and *push* of the terminal, therefore *rapture*, *triumph*, *vehemence*, etc. Here are examples of terminal accent in triple measures:

Now it catches the gleam of the morning's first beam;
In full glory reflected now shines on the stream;
'T is the star-spangled banner. Oh, long may it wave
O'er the land of the free and the home of the brave.
—*Star-Spangled Banner: Key.*

Now there 's peace on the shore, now there 's calm on the sea,
Fill a glass to the heroes whose swords kept us free,
Right descendants of Wallace, Montrose, and Dundee.
—*The Broad-Swords of Scotland: Lockhart.*

Over hill, over dale,
  Thorough bush, thorough brier,
Over park, over pale,
  Thorough flood, thorough fire.
—*Midsummer Night's Dream*, ii., 1 : *Shakespear.*

The Greek measure corresponding to this is the Anapæst, from ἀναπαίω, *to strike back*. This, as Schmidt says, is "the proper march measure," used "in the march songs (in particular those of the Spartans), of which fragments have been preserved. The chorus in tragedy also generally entered the orchestra (in the parodus) and left it (in the exodus) while reciting anapæsts, the recitation in both cases being in a chanting tone." This use of the anapæst would correspond exactly with that appropriate for our terminal triple measure, as just interpreted.

In order to prevent monotony, as well as too great rapidity of movement, all kinds of triple measure are usually combined with double measure, initial triple, for instance, with initial double, as in the following:

Under my window, under my window,
All in the midsummer weather.
—*Under my Window: T. Westwood.*

Work and pure slumbers shall wait on thy pillow;
Work thou shalt ride o'er Care's coming billow;
Lie not down 'neath Woe's weeping willow.
—*To Labor is to Pray: F. S. Osgood.*

This combination is that which is found in the classic hexameter; *e. g.*:

Hearty and hale was he, an oak that is covered with snow-flakes;
White as the snow were his locks, and his cheeks as brown as the oak-
    leaves.   —*Evangeline: Longfellow.*

Terminal triple measure is usually joined with terminal double; *e. g.*:

    With fingers weary and worn,
    With eyelids heavy and red.
                —*Song of the Shirt: Hood.*

Let them sing who may of the battle fray,
And the deeds that have long since passed.
                The Good Old Plough: Anon.

And median triple measure is used sometimes with initial double; *e. g.*:

Glen Orchy's proud mountains, Coalchurn and her towers,
Glenstrae and Glenlyon no longer are ours:
We're landless, landless, landless, Grigalach.
Landless, landless, landless.
              —*Macgregor's Gathering: Scott.*

But it is used more frequently with terminal double measure; *e. g.*:

I wield the flail of the lashing hail,
    And whiten the green plains under;
And then again I dissolve it in rain;
    And laugh as I pass in thunder.
              —*The Cloud: Shelley.*

In some compositions all forms, both of double and triple measure, are combined, the only essential consideration in the mind of the poet being to arrange the accents so that, when read, they can be separated by like intervals; *e. g.*:

> Day after day, day after day,
> We stuck, not land nor motion,
> As idle as a painted ship
> Upon a painted ocean.
>
> Water, water everywhere,
> And all the boards did shrink ;
> Water, water everywhere,
> Nor any a drop to drink.
>
> *   *   *   *   *   *
>
> I closed my lids and kept them close,
> And the balls like pulses beat ;
> For the sky and the sea, and the sea and the sky
> Lay like a load on my weary eye,
> And the dead were at my feet.
> —*The Ancient Mariner : Coleridge.*

Quadruple measure is made up of two feet of double measure, one of the accented syllables of which receives more stress than the other. Here, for instance, is the Ditrochaic measure of the Greeks, or what may be termed *Diinitial Quadruple* measure. In it there are two trochaic feet.

> Róses are in | blóssom, and the | rílls are filled with | wàter-cresses.
> —*Anon.*

And here is the Greek Diiambic measure, in which there are two iambic feet. It may be called *Diterminal Quadruple* measure.

> The kìng has come | to màrshal us | in àll his ar | mor drèssed,
> –*Battle of Ivry : Macaulay.*

The first of these is evidently an example of initial accent, and the second of terminal accent, and each must indicate the same as in double measure, with the exception that in quadruple measure the movement is more rapid, and represents, therefore, more buoyancy and momentum in the thought.

If necessary, a distinction might be drawn between these two forms of Quadruple measure and those forms of it in which the primary accent belongs to the second of its two Double measures. The following, for instance, is usually considered to be an example of Initial Double measure. But it might be divided into feet like these, and termed *Final Diinitial Quadruple* measure, because the primary accent belongs to the final double foot constituting the Quadruple measure:

> We the faìries | blithe and àntic,
> Of dimensions not gigantic;
> Though the moonshine mostly keep us,
> Oft in orchards frisk and peep us.
> —*Fairies' Song : Thomas Randolph.*
> *Trans. by Leigh Hunt.*

And this, for similar reasons, might be termed *Final Diterminal Quadruple* measure:

> Domestic blìss | has proved my bàne
> A harder case you never heard,
> My wife (in other matters sane)
> Pretends that I'm a Dicky-bird !
> —*Bains Carew : Gilbert.*

In such cases, however, it is better to attribute the greater prominence given to certain of the accented syllables, not to the supposed fact that the lines containing them are composed in Quadruple measure, instead of—as seems to be the case—in Double measure; but to the effects, considered in Chapter Fourth, of short quantity which increases the rapidity of the movement, and of the pauses in the middle and at the end of each line which increase the emphasis of the accented syllables immediately preceding them. If we call the measures that we have just examined Quadruple, what is to prevent our supposing that verses, written in triple measure like the following, contain *feet* composed of four, or even six, syllables?

> Guvener B. | is a sensible man ;
> He stays to his home | an' looks arter his folks.
> —*The Biglow Papers : Lowell.*

We have seen now that all the different kinds of elocutionary stress have correspondences in poetic measures. It remains to be said that, just as different kinds of stress may be used in reading different parts of the same sentence, so different kinds of measures may be used in the same verse, either for the sake of variety, or to give peculiar emphasis to some word or syllable thus thrust into unusual and unexpected importance.

Here terminal accent is used for initial, at the beginning of a line :

> Hears amid the chime and singing
> *The bells* of his own village ringing.
> —*Carillon : Longfellow.*

And here at the end of a line :

> Silence on the town descended,
> Silence, silence *everywhere.*
> —*Idem.*

Here initial accent is used for terminal, at the beginning of a line, and also at its end :

> *Blaze* with your serried *columns,*
> I will not bend the knee.
> —*The Seminole's Defiance : G. W. Patten.*

And here at its end :

> O sacred head now *wounded,*
> With grief and shame weighed down.
> —*Hymn : Bernard through Gerhardt tr. by J. W. Alexander.*

In the following, with the variety that is common in triple measure, we have initial accent in *Sunbeam;* terminal, in *From cape;* median, in *The mountains;* initial triple, in *Over a;* and terminal tripple, in *with a bridge,* etc.

> From cape to cape with a bridge-like shape,
>   Over a torrent sea,
> Sunbeam-proof, I hang like a roof,
>   The mountains its columns be.
>   —*The Cloud: Shelley.*

Corresponding to the methods of dramatic elocution, changes in measure are often made in order to represent the movements of certain objects described. Notice, in the following terminal double measures, how the placing of the accent on the first syllable of many of the feet, serves, by changing them into initial triple measures, to convey the impression of rapidity:

> Each creek and bay
> With fry *innumerable* swarm, and shoals
> Of fish that with their fins and shining scales
> Glide *under the* green wave, in sculls that oft
> *Bank the mid* sea ; part single or with mate,
> *Graze the sea-weed, their* pasture, and through groves
> Of coral stray, or *sporting with* quick glance
> *Show to the* sun their wav'd coats dropt with gold.
>   —*Paradise Lost,* 7: *Milton.*

Notice here, too, the words italicized:

> Far along
> From peak to peak, the rattling crags among,
> *Leaps the live thunder.* Not from one lone cloud,
> But every mountain now hath found a tongue.
>   —*Childe Harold: Byron.*

And the representation of the movement of the leaf, when the poet comes to speak of it, in the following:

Is it the wind that moaneth bleak?
There is not wind enough in the air
To move away the ringlet curl
From the lovely lady's cheek,—
There is not wind enough to twirl
The one red leaf, the last of its clan,
That dances as often as dance it can,
Hanging so light, and hanging so high,
On the topmost twig that looks up at the sky.
—*Christabel: Coleridge.*

CHAPTER VII.

ELOCUTIONARY AND POETIC REGULARITY OF FORCE.

Regularity of Force, combining its Instinctive with Reflective Tendencies, and representing Emotive Influence—Abrupt and Smooth Force, as used in Elocution—Irregular and Regular Accentuation corresponding to them in Poetry—Abruptness in Short and Long Lines—Imitative Effects, etc.

THIS subject of changes in metre introduces us, naturally, to the third way in which force on different words may differ—namely, in regularity. It may be abrupt or smooth, each respectively representing the amount of mere instinct or of reflection in the emotion accompanying the momentum. Abrupt force indicates *interruption, excitement, vehemence, anger;* smooth force *continuity, satisfaction, gentleness, delight.* The poetic equivalent for the first seems to be found in lines in which there is a break in the regularity of the rhythm, either because two accented syllables are brought together, or a larger number of unaccented ones than the rhythm warrants. For instance, we must all perceive the abrupt effects produced by the first syllables of *Battering*, and *belching*, and by the word *Far* in the following, coming, respectively, as they do, immediately after the accented words, *sob, wide,* and *flame*:

> I will not cease to grasp the hope I hold
> Of saintdom, and to clamor, mourn, and sob,
> *Battering* the gates of heaven with storms of prayer.
> —*St. Simeon Stylites: Tennyson.*

> The gates that now
> Stood open wide, *belching* outrageous flame
> *Far* into chaos. —*Paradise Lost*, 10 : *Milton.*

Notice, too, the abrupt effects occasioned by the three unaccented syllables *Are the in-*, and the two *With im-*, in the following:

> I 'll cavil on the ninth part of a hair.
> *Are the in*dentures drawn ? shall we be gone ?
> —1 *Henry IV.*, iii., 1 : *Shakespear.*

> On a sudden open fly,
> *With im*petuous recoil and jarring sound
> Th' infernal doors. —*Paradise Lost*, 2 : *Milton.*

Abruptness is sometimes characteristic of the entire metre of a poem. In these cases, it is usually produced in connection with the pauses between the lines. At times it results from ending one line with an accented syllable, and beginning the next with another, as in these:

> Every day brings a ship,
> Every ship brings a word ;
> Well for those who have no fear,
> Looking seaward well assured
> That the word the vessel brings
> Is the word they wish to hear.
> —*Letters : Emerson.*

> Here let us sport,
> Boys, as we sit.
> Laughter and wit
> Flashing so free.
> Life is but short ;
> When we are gone,
> Let them sing on
> Round the old tree.
> —*The Mahogany Tree : Thackeray.*

> Forward the light brigade!
> Was there a man dismayed?
> Not though the soldiers knew
>   Some one had blundered;
> Theirs not to make reply,
> Theirs not to reason why,
> Theirs but to do and die.
> Into the valley of death
>   Rode the six hundred.
> —*Charge of the Light Brigade : Tennyson.*

> Lo, the leader in these glorious wars
> Now to glorious burial slowly borne,
> Followed by the brave of other lands.
> He on whom from both her open hands
> Lavish honor showered all her stars.
> —*Ode on the Duke of Wellington : Tennyson.*

> Up the street came the rebel tread,
> Stonewall Jackson riding ahead.
>
> Under his slouched hat, left and right
> He glanced : the old flag met his sight.
>
> "Halt!"—the dust-brown ranks stood fast.
> "Fire!"—out blazed the rifle blast.
> —*Barbara Frietchie : Whittier.*

At times, this abrupt effect is produced by ending a line with an unaccented syllable and beginning the next with another one, *e. g.*:

> As she lay on her death-bed,
>   The bones of her thin face, boys,
> As she lay on her death-bed,
>   I don't know how it be, boys,
> When all 's done and said ;
>   But I see her looking at me, boys,
> Wherever I turn my head.
> —*Tommy's Dead : Dobell.*

> The fountains mingle with the river,
> And the rivers with the ocean ;

> The winds of heaven mix forever
> With a sweet emotion.
> >   —*Love's Philosophy: Shelley.*

> With deep affection
> And recollection
> I often think of
>   Those Shandon bells;
> Whose sound so wild would,
> In the days of childhood,
> Fling round my cradle
>   Their magic spells.
> >   —*The Bells of Shandon: F. Mahony.*

> They lock them up and veil and guard them daily;
>   They scarcely can behold their male relations;
> So that their moments do not pass so gaily
>   As is supposed the case with northern nations.
> >   —*Beppo: Byron.*

As characteristic abruptness in verse is produced in connection with the pauses at the ends of the lines, the shorter the lines are, the more frequent are the instances of abrupt force, and the more do the verses seem to manifest the sort of nervous energy which this represents. Compare the quotations above in which the lines are long with those in which they are short; or compare the two following stanzas:

> Where corpse-light
> Dances bright,
> Be it by day or night,
> Be it by light or dark,
> There shall corpse lie stiff and stark.
> >   —*Halcro's Verses in The Pirate: Scott.*

> Not in vain the distance beacons, Forward, forward let us range,
> Let the old world spin forever down the ringing grooves of change.
> >   -*Locksley Hall: Tennyson.*

This latter couplet has almost the effect of perfect regularity of rhythm, which, as has been said, characterizes metre corresponding to smooth force, representing therefore *continuity*, *satisfaction*, *gentleness*, *delight*, such, for instance, as one would naturally have in the *tender*, *lovely*, *beautiful*, *grand*, or *sublime*. In all the following quotations it will be noticed that the final syllable of each line joins without a break the rhythm of the following line. They all furnish illustrations of the poetic equivalent for smooth force.

> From gold to gray
> Our mild sweet day
> Of Indian summer fades too soon ;
> But tenderly
> Above the sea
> Hangs white and clear the hunter's moon.
> —*Eve of Election : Whittier.*

> When gathering clouds around I view,
> And days are dark and friends are few,
> On Him I lean who not in vain
> Experienced every human pain.
> —*Hymn : Grant.*

> Till their chimes in sweet collision
> Mingled with each wandering vision,
> Mingled with the fortune-telling
> Gypsy bands of dreams and fancies,
> Which, amid the waste expanses
> Of the silent land of trances,
> Have their solitary dwelling.
> —*Carillon : Longfellow.*

> My eyes, how I love you,
> You sweet little dove you,
> There 's no one above you,
> Most beautiful Kitty.
> —*Kitty : Anon.*

> At Paris it was, at the opera there,
> And she looked like a queen in a book that night,
> With a wreath of pearl in her raven hair,
> And the brooch on her breast so bright.
> —*Aux Italiens : Lytton.*

> Our bugles sang truce, for the night cloud had lowered,
>   And the sentinal stars set their watch in the sky,
> And thousands had sunk on the ground overpowered,
>   The weary to sleep and the wounded to die.
> —*The Soldier's Dream : Campbell.*

Here is the same in our regular English blank verse:

> So all day long the noise of battle rolled
> Among the mountains by the winter sea,
> Until King Arthur's table, man by man,
> Had fallen in Lyonesse about their lord.
> —*The Idyls of the King : Tennyson.*

Abrupt and smooth poetic effects, corresponding to those of imitative elocution, have been noticed often, and scarcely need mention here. The following are abrupt:

> The pilgrim oft
> At dead of night 'mid his oraison hears
> Aghast the voice of time-disparted towers,
> Tumbeling all precipitate down—dash'd
> Rattling around, loud thundering to the moon.
> —*The Ruins of Rome : Dyer.*

> Then broke the whole night in one blow,
> Thundering ; then all hell with one throe
> Heaved, and brought forth beneath the stroke
> Death, and all dead things moved and woke.
> —*Epilogue : Swinburne.*

> On a sudden open fly,
> With impetuous recoil and jarring sound,
> The infernal doors, and on their hinges grate
> Harsh thunder.
> —*Paradise Lost*, 2 : *Milton.*

And these are smooth:

> Heaven open'd wide
> Her ever-during gates, harmonious sound,
> On golden hinges moving.
> —*Idem*, 7.

Follow'd with acclamation, and the sound
Symphonious of ten thousand harps that tuned
Angelic harmonies ; the earth, the air
Resounded.
—*Idem*, 7.

Collecting, projecting,
Receding and speeding,
And shocking and rocking,
And darting and parting.
* * * * * *
Dividing and gliding and sliding,
And falling and brawling and sprawling,
And diving and riving and striving,
And sprinkling and twinkling and wrinkling.
* * * * * *
Retreating and beating and meeting and sheeting,
Delaying and straying and playing and spraying.
* * * * * *
And so never ending, but always descending,
Sounds and motions for ever and ever are blending,
All at once, and all o'er with a mighty uproar,
And this way the water comes down at Lodore.
The Cataract of Lodore : *Southey.*

CHAPTER VIII.

ELOCUTIONARY AND POETIC PITCH—TUNES OF VERSE.

Elements entering into the Tunes of Verse : Pitch and Quality—Pitch representing Reflective Tendency or Intellectual Motive—On its Instinctive Side by High and Low Key—What each represents—On its Reflective, by Rising, Falling, and Circumflex Movements—What each represents—When Influences from both Sides express Emotive Tendencies, by Melody—What Different Melodies represent—Pitch as used in Poetry—Which was formerly chanted—And has Tunes at Present—Shades of Pitch in Speech as Numerous as, and more Delicate than, in Song—Scientific Proof that Short Vowels are sounded on a High Key, and Long on a Low Key—Light, Gay, Lively Ideas represented by the Former; Serious, Grave, Dignified by the Latter.

WE are to take up, now, the elements of elocutionary expression which enter into the effects of what are termed the *tunes of verse*. The first of these elements is pitch.

This word means the same in elocution as in music, and indicates that the consecutive sounds of speech are related to one another in a way analogous to that in which, in singing, they move up and down the musical scale. A whole passage may be delivered on what is termed a *high* pitch or key, as when one is shouting to a person at a distance ; or it may be delivered on a *low* one, as when one is groaning. Besides this, in uttering a whole passage, or a single syllable with what is termed an inflection, it is possible for the voice to *rise*, as is said, from a low to a high pitch, or to *fall* from a high to a low one.

It is important to notice, also, that, in giving different degrees of pitch, it is not essential to manifest much either of physical energy or of those instinctive modes of psychical emotive expression most allied to it. A hand-organ, in which every note is sounded with the same force and quality, can nevertheless illustrate degrees of pitch so far as concerns this alone. But though neither physical energy nor psychical emotion is represented by pitch, we find that every man, in talking, directs his voice first to one key and then to another; and that, by so doing, he represents to us the general tenor of his reflections. Intelligence of these, therefore, is communicated by pitch; and, usually, too, very definite intelligence of them. What a man wishes to have his tones commumunicate, we can often infer by overhearing them, even amid circumstances rendering it impossible for us to distinguish clearly his words. Often, indeed, his words may mean one thing, and his intonations another, as when a teacher tells the parents of a boy in his school that their son is "doing very well," at the same time using a very decided rising inflection on the word "well."

It seems proper to say, therefore, that, in the main, pitch is that part of the generally emotive language of the intonations which is most reflective, representing what may be termed, distinctively, the mental movements, or—what underlie these—the mental *motives* or *aims*. Thus the rising pitch on the word "well," as just quoted, indicates the speaker's *motive* in what he says. As affected by instinctive or physical tendencies, in the degree in which the predominance of reflective influences is least, the tones are kept on a high level of pitch, or on a "high key"; but as reflective influences become stronger, the tones are kept on a lower level of pitch, or on a "low key." In their strictly reflective or intellectual phases, the motives cause the pitch to "rise" or "fall" in accordance with the tendency or direction of the ideas,—and this mainly in the inflections. The balance maintained between the instinctive and the reflective tendencies—that is, between the different kinds of keys and of the "rising" and "falling" movements, determines the melody, and represents, of course, the tendency in one or the other direction of the psychic nature.

Considering pitch, first, as influenced by the instinctive nature, it has been noticed that when a man is light-hearted, carrying the least amount of thought, either in quantity or quality,—in other words, when there is nothing to *weigh* him *down*, and that which is moving him is *light*, *gay*, and *lively* in its character, he uses *high* pitch, as in uttering this:

> O, then I see Queen Mab has been with you.
> —*Romeo and Juliet*, i., 4: *Shakespear.*

But if, on the contrary, his reflective nature is in operation to such an extent and with such subjects that he does feel *weighed down*, as is the case when that which is moving him is *serious*, *grave*, and *dignified* in its character, calling for more or less expression of soul from him, he uses low pitch, and keeps his voice on it, as in this:

> Roll on, thou deep and dark blue ocean, roll.
> —*Childe Harold: Byron.*

It is hardly necessary to add that, as related to these two extremes, words conveying intelligence of merely ordinary matters, would be uttered at a medium pitch, somewhere between the two. It is equally evident that in dramatic elocution a high key imitates sounds that are high, as in the cry, "Yell! yell! why don't you!"; and a low key imitates sounds that are low, as in saying, "Who's there? he growled."

In *discoursive* elocution, again, the *rising* and *falling* movements of the voice, whether used in continuous passages or in the inflections given to single words, represent, as has been said, the direction or tendency of the current of ideas in the mind of the speaker. To extend and explain this, they represent the *flowing* or *checking* of his motives as influenced by the instinctive or reflective operations of his mind. The *rising* movement opens, and, if an inflection, emphatically *opens, the channel of thought*, as if to speed its current forward. Those listening to it feel, therefore, that the speaker has not yet arrived at a word, or completed an idea, upon which he wishes them very particularly to reflect. This movement produces, therefore, an *anticipative* or *indecisive* effect, and indicates what, as compared with the falling movement, is *subordinate, negative*, or *questionable*. The *downward* movement *closes*, and, if an inflection, emphatically *checks*, the current of thought, points out to the audience that which has been said, leads them to reflect upon it, and so produces a *conclusive, decisive* effect, and indicates what is comparatively *important, positive*, or *affirmative*. Besides this, there is often, on the same passage or syllable, a movement both upward and downward, or what, if on a single word, is termed a *circumflex* inflection. This, of course, imparts something of the effects of both the rising and falling movements, though often, especially in the inflections, in accordance with the principle of contrast, it is chiefly employed to give increased effect to the rising or falling movement of the voice with which the circumflex ends, the end of this inflection being that which indicates its main significance.

To recognize the accuracy of these explanations of the meanings of the inflections, we have only to notice how the significance of the following sentences is changed upon our uttering them with a rising (´) or falling (`) or with a circumflex inflection, ending with a rising (ᵕ) or a falling (ᴀ) movement.

If só I will gó.	If sò I will gò.
It múst be so.	It mùst be so.
It depénds.	It depènds.
John declaims wéll.	John declaims wèll.
Of coúrse it ís.	Of coùrse it ìs.
You are nót to do thát.	You are nòt to do thàt.
Is n't she beáutiful?	Is n't she beàutiful?
Yŏu—you meant no hărm.	Yôu—you meant no hârm.

Sidney Lanier, in his "Science of English Verse," has directed attention, as had been done before, to the way in which this truth, with reference to the different meanings that may be conveyed by the simple movements of the voice, wholly aside from the words used, is brought out by Shakespear in his *All's Well that Ends Well*, where he makes the clown declare:

I have an answer will serve all men.

Countess.—Marry; that's a bountiful answer, that fits all questions.

*   *   *   *   *   *   *   *   *

Clown.—From below your duke to beneath your constable; it will fit any question.

Countess.—It must be an answer of most monstrous size, that must fit all demands.

Clown.—But a trifle, neither, in good faith, if the learned should speak truth of it. Here it is, and all that belongs to 't . . . Ask me if I am a courtier. . . .

Count.—I pray you, sir, are you a courtier?

Clown.—O Lord, sir,—there's a simple putting off,—more, more, a hundred of them.

Count.—Sir, I am a poor friend of yours, that loves you.

Clown.—O Lord, sir,—thick, thick, spare not me.

Count.—I think, sir, you can eat none of this homely meat.
Clown.—O Lord, sir,—nay, put me to 't, I warrant you.
Count.—You were lately whipped, sir, as I think.
Clown.—O Lord, sir,—spare not me.

*   *   *   *   *   *   *

Count.—I play the noble housewife with the time
　　To entertain it so merrily with a Fool.
Clown.—O Lord, sir,—why there 't serves well again.
　　　　　　　　　—*All's Well that Ends Well*, ii., 2.

In dramatic elocution, rising, falling, or circumflex movements of the voice, simply imitate things with which movements or sounds of these kinds are in some way associated. The following, for instance, require movements of the voice in both directions:

> He saw a crowd assembled round
> A person dancing on the ground,
> Who straight began to leap and bound
> 　With all his might and main.
> To see that dancing man he stopped,
> Who twirled and wriggled, skipped and hopped,
> Then down incontinently dropped.
> 　And then sprang up again.
> 　　　　—*The Bishop of Rum-ti-Foo : Gilbert.*

> But the babe with a dig that would startle an ox,
> 　With his " C'ck ! Oh, my !—
> 　Go along wiz 'oo, fie ! "
> Would exclain : " I 'm affaid 'oo a shocking ole fox."
> 　Now a father it shocks,
> 　And it whitens his locks,
> When his little babe calls him a shocking old fox.
> 　　　　—*Precocious Baby : Gilbert.*

As has been said, the blending of the effects of high and low key with those of the rising and falling of phrases and syllables, leads to what is termed *melody*, the general character of which represents the mental motive as influenced by the soul, or the higher emotive nature. If the key be *greatly varied*, therefore, it represents a *minimum of self-control* or poise ; if *slightly varied* or *monotonous*, a *maximum of this*,—statements which will be sufficiently illustrated while we go on to apply, as we shall now do, all these elocutionary principles of pitch to the subject immediately before us.

Probably few have noticed to what an extent pitch enters as a factor into the effects of poetry. They know in a general way, of course, that in early modes of communicating thought, intonations, like gestures, were almost as significant as words ; but they do not realize that the same is true in our own day, least of all that changes in pitch are and always must be elements entering into the significance of the effects produced by poetic rhythm. They know, again, if at all acquainted with the history of the art, that there was a time when poetry was associated with both dancing and music. It was so, as we are told, in the time of King David, who, on one occasion, at least, danced as well as sang his psalms before the ark. In Greece, not only lyric but dramatic poetry was chanted, and often accompanied by the lyre. As late as the sixteenth century, declamation accompanied by music, flourished in England and in Italy. In the latter country it then passed into the opera, which did not follow, as some suppose, but preceded all that is noteworthy in the development of the pure music, unaccompanied by words, of modern times. In our own day, however, when poetry is merely read, the movements of the waltz, the polka, the sonata, the symphony, seem to belong to an art so different, that it is difficult to conceive that it was once appropriate to speak of ballad poetry, because the Italian *ballare* meant to dance, or of a sonnet, because the lute was *sounded* while poetry was being chanted. The truth is, however, that even to-day, also, poetry and music are allied. As has been said already, the chanting of verse was not originally the cause of its tunes, but the result of them, springing from an endeavor to develop artistically the tunes natural to speech. These tunes our poetry, notwithstanding its present separation from music, still retains. They differ from those of music, yet are analogous to them. Let us consider the more important of the resemblances and differences between the two.

As most of us know, science has ascertained that all musical sounds result from regularly recurring vibrations caused by cords, pipes, reeds, or other agencies. About thirty-three of these vibrations per second produce the lowest tone used in music, and about three thousand nine hundred and sixty, the highest. That the number of vibrations in any note may be increased and its pitch made higher, it is necessary to lessen the length or size of the cord, or of whatever causes the vibrations. When the vibrating cord is lessened by just one half, the tone produced is separated from its former tone by an interval of sound which in music is termed an octave. Between the two extremes of pitch forming the octave, eleven half tones, as they are called, caused by sounds resulting from different lengths of the cord, between its whole length and its half length, have been selected, for reasons to be given in another place, and arranged in what is termed a musical scale. These half-tones, seven of them constituting the *do, re, me, fa, sol, la,* and *si* of the gamut, are all that can be used in music between the two notes forming the octave. There are about seven octaves, or, what is the same thing, seven scales, each containing twelve sounds of different pitch,—in all, about eighty-four degrees of pitch that are used in music. In the speaking voice only about two octaves are used, so that in this regard its range is more narrow than that of music. Between any two octave notes, however, the speaking voice can use whatever sounds it chooses; it is not confined to the twelve that constitute the musical scale. For instance, the note of the bass voice called by musicians *C*, is sounded by producing one hundred and thirty-two vibrations a second, and *C* of the octave above by producing two hundred and sixty-four vibrations. Between the two, therefore, it is possible to conceive of forming one hundred and thirty-one distinct tones, each vibrating once a second oftener than the sound below it. It is possible, too, to conceive that the speaking voice can use any of these tones. Music, however, between the same octave notes, can use but eleven tones. Therefore, the different degrees of pitch used in speech, though not extending over as many octaves, are much more numerous than those used in music. For this reason, the melodies of speech cannot be represented by any system through which we now write music. There are not enough notes used in music to render it possible to make the representation accurate. Nor probably would much practical benefit be derived from an attempt to construct a system of speech-notation; though it, like other things, may be among the possibilities of acoustic development in the future.

In applying to poetic form the principles determining pitch in elocution, let us take up first those in accordance with which certain syllables are uttered on a high or low key. The former key seems suggested by vowels formed at the mouth's *front*, as in *beet, bate, bet, bit, bat*, etc.; the latter by *back* vowels, as in *fool, full, foal, fall*, etc. The best of reasons underlies this suggestion. It is the fact that the pronunciation of every front or back vowel-sound naturally tends to the production of a high or low musical note. Donders first made the discovery that the cavity of the mouth, when whispering each of the different vowels, is tuned to a different pitch. This fact gives the vowel its peculiar quality. Instruments, moreover, have been constructed, by means of which most sounds can be analyzed, and their component tones distinctly and definitely noted; and now the theory is accepted that the voice, when pronouncing vowel-sounds, at whatever key in the musical scale it may start them, has a tendency to suggest—if not through its main, or what is termed its *prime* tone, at least through associated, or what are termed its *partial* tones—that pitch which is peculiar to the vowel uttered.

Exactly what this pitch is, in the case of each vowel, it is not important for us to know here. In fact, it has not yet been definitely determined. Helmholtz, in his "Sensations of Tone," says, for instance, that the series, which may be represented in English by *a* in *father*, *a* in *man*, *e* in *there*, and *i* in *machine*, forms an ascending minor chord of *G″*—thus: *d‴*—*g‴*—*b‴ flat*—*d″″;* and the following represents the results of Merkel's experiments with the German vowels given in his "Physiologie der Menschlichen Sprache":

U O Oa A   Ö Ü Ä E I

But what concerns us, at present, is merely the fact that there is a pitch peculiar to the sound of each letter, and that the pitch of the sounds approximating long *u* is actually, and not ideally, lower in tone than that of the sounds approximating the long English *e*.

With this understanding of the actual connection existing between the sounds represented by certain letters and pitch, it follows, as a matter of natural law, that elocutionary high pitch—to begin with this—should find its poetic analogue in a predominating use of the latter class of vowel-sounds, especially when connected with consonant-sounds that cannot be prolonged, and therefore cannot introduce into the tone other strong elements of pitch. Poetic passages, therefore, composed of vowels and consonants of this character are suited, like elocutionary high pitch, to represent light, gay, and lively effects,—a fact which, as will be noticed, sustains and puts upon a scientific basis all that has been said with reference to the unimportant, or— what is the same thing—the light, gay, and lively character of the ideas represented by what are usually the same sounds in short quantity. With these explanations, the reader will understand in what sense the following illustrate high pitch as used in poetry:

> He took a life preserver, and he hit him on the head,
> And Mrs. Brown dissected him before she went to bed.
> —*Gentle Alice Brown : Gilbert.*

> Haste thee, Nymph, and bring with thee
> Jest and youthful Jollity,
> Quips, and Cranks, and wanton Wiles,
> Nods, and Becks, and wreathèd Smiles,
> Such as hang on Hebe's cheek,
> And love to live in dimple sleek ;
> Sport that wrinkled Care derides
> And Laughter holding both his sides.
> —*L'Allegro : Milton.*

Vowels of the same kind together with unprolonged

consonant-sounds are used also to imitate sounds that are high; *e. g.*:

> Then rose the cry of females shrill
> As goss-hawk's whistle on the hill,
> Denouncing misery and ill,
> Mingled with childhood's babbling trill
> Of curses stammered slow.
>
> * * * * *
>
> A sharp and shrieking echo gave,
> Coir-Uriskin, thy goblin cave,
> And the gray pass where birches wave
> On Beala-nam-bo.
> —*Lady of the Lake : Scott.*

> What news? what news? come tell to me
> What news? what news? thou little Foot-page?
> I 've been whacking the foe till it seems an age
> Since I was in Ingoldsby Hall so free.
> —*Ingoldsby Penance : Ingoldsby Legends.*

> Bird of the wilderness,
> Blithesome and cumberless,
> Sweet is thy matin o'er moorland and lea!
> Emblem of happiness
> Blest be thy dwelling-place!
> O to abide in the desert with thee!
> —*The Skylark : Hogg.*

> O hark! what mean those yells and cries?
> His chain some furious madman breaks.
> He comes!—I see his glaring eyes!
> Now, now, my dungeon grate he shakes.
> Help! help!—He 's gone—O fearful woe,
> Such screams to hear, such sights to see!
> My brain, my brain—I know, I know
> I am not mad—but soon shall be.
> —*The Maniac : M. G. Lewis.*

Sounds of the nature of ū, ō, â, on the contrary, especially when combined with consonant-sounds that can easily be prolonged, produce the serious, grave and dignified effects of low pitch, as in the following:

> Insulted, chained, and all the world our foe,
> Our God alone is all we boast below.
> —*The Captivity: Goldsmith.*

> Then dying of a mortal stroke,
> What time the foeman's line is broke,
> And all the war is rolled in smoke.
> —*Two Voices: Tennyson.*

Or as in these imitative effects:

> Thus long ago,
> Ere heaving bellows learned to blow,
> While organs yet were mute,
> Timotheous to his breathing flute
> And sounding lyre
> Could swell the soul to rage or kindle soft desire.
> —*Alexander's Feast: Dryden.*

> And waft across the waves' tumultuous roar
> The wolf's long howl from Oonalaska's shore.
> —*Pleasures of Hope: Campbell.*

Notice how Swinburne, with his exquisite sense of the meanings of sounds, passes from low pitch to high pitch, or the reverse, in order to bring out the changes in sentiment in the following:

> Old glory of warrior ghosts
> Shed fresh on filial hosts,
> With dewfall redder than the dews of day.
> —*Birthday Ode.*

> Being bird and God in one.
> —*On the Cliffs.*

> Whose heart was ever set to song, or stirred
> With wind of mounting music blown more high
> Than wildest wing may fly.
> —*On the Cliffs.*

With songs and cries
That sang and shrieked their soul out at the skies,
A shapeless earthly storm of shapes began
From all ways round to move in on the man,
Clamorous against him silent; and their feet
Were as the winds' are fleet,
And their shrill songs were as wild birds' are sweet.
—*Thalassius.*

CHAPTER IX.

POETIC PITCH—RISING AND FALLING TONES.

Correspondence between Elocutionary Inflections or Intonations and certain Arrangements of Verse-Harmony produced by Sounds of Vowels and Consonants combined—Effects of Rising Movements produced by Lines beginning without Accents and ending with them—Of falling Movements, by Lines beginning with Accents and ending without them—Of Circumflex Movements, by Combinations of both Arrangements—What the Marks of Accent indicated to the Greeks, and how they read them in their Poetry—Illustrations of Ideas represented by Verse arranged to give Effects of Rising, Falling, and Circumflex Movements—Movements of Verse in Narration and Pathos.

THE poetic effects, corresponding to the rising and falling of the voice, especially as used in the inflections, will now be examined. There is a sense in which these movements of the voice enter into the pronunciation of every syllable containing more than one letter-sound. In uttering, for example, the word *an*, the sound of the *a* is at a different pitch from that of the *n*. In talking rapidly, however, the two sounds seem usually uttered, not in succession but simultaneously. Their effects, therefore, when combined, are analogous, not to those of musical melody, but of harmony, and of these much more closely than at first might be supposed. In flexible, well-trained voices, belonging to those familiar with the relations of musical tones, there is a tendency to sound the two at such intervals of pitch from each other as to form a true musical chord. One reason why vocal culture increases the sweetness and resonance of the speaking voice is because it enables one to sound distinctly all the elements of tone needed, in order to produce this speech-harmony.

The rising and falling of the voice with which we have to deal now, however, are not those subtile ones allying speech to harmony, but those more obvious ones which give it a very apparent melody. The effects in poetry corresponding to elocutionary inflections, are produced by the same arrangements of the syllables in the line that we have already noticed when considering metre. In our language, as a rule,—a rule which the elocutionist, of course, can violate in order to produce what for him are the more important effects of delivery,—an accented syllable is sounded on a key higher than an unaccented one. To illustrate this, in the ordinary pronunciation of *còniure*, meaning to practise magical arts, the *con* is sounded higher than the *jure;* but in *conjùre* meaning to summon solemnly, the *con* is sounded lower. Therefore, if a line of poetry end with an accented syllable, or have what is termed a *masculine* ending, the voice in pausing on this, as it generally does at the end of a line, will pause, as a rule, on a key higher than that on which it has uttered the preceding syllable. Notice this *snow* and *below:*

>   I sift the snow
> On the mountains below,
> And their great pines groan aghast.
> —*The Cloud: Shelley.*

Or again, if a line begin with an unaccented syllable, the voice will pass upward from this to the accented syllable; and this movement, begun with the line, will continue to its end, especially if there be an accented syllable there. The effect produced, therefore, in both cases, is that of a constant repetition of the rising inflection; *e. g.:*

> The triumphal arch
> Through which I march
> With hurricane, fire, and snow,
> When the powers of the air
> Are chained to my chair,
> Is the million colored bow. —*Idem*.

For similar reasons, if a line close with an unaccented syllable, having what is termed a *feminine* ending; or begin with an accented syllable, the effect is that of a constant repetition of the falling inflection. In fact, the Greeks, though arriving at their result through a different process, actually termed lines ending thus *catalectic* or *falling*; *e. g.*:

> Love he comes, and love he tarries,
> Just as fate or fancy carries,
> Longest stays when sorest chidden,
> Laughs and flies when pressed and bidden.
> —*The First Kiss: Campbell*.

Perhaps the contrast between this movement and the former one can be made more apparent by quoting two exceptional lines of the same poem used for illustration there:

> I am the daughter
> Of earth and water.
> —*The Cloud: Shelley*.

Very few, without making a special effort to do so, could read these lines, giving rising inflections on the syllable *ter* at the ends of them. Nor is it without significance that there is a natural tendency for musical composers, when preparing tunes for words, to arrange their melodies so that there is an emphatic rising of the voice where the final syllables either of the feet or of the lines, but especially of the latter, are accented, and a falling of it, where they are unaccented. Notice the following, and also the musical illustrations, especially the hymn termed *Bayley*, in the next chapter,—all of which were selected in a very few moments from an ordinary hymn-book.

It was said, a little time ago, that the circumflex inflections, in accordance with the principle of contrast, make stronger the rising or falling movements with which they end. In like manner, certain arrangements of syllables augment the rising or falling poetic movements which we are now considering. If, for instance, series of lines both end and begin with accented syllables, the impression conveyed by the rising movement at the end of a line is increased, because it is immediately repeated at the beginning of the next line; and the voice, before repeating it, must necessarily pause for a little, thus directing additional attention to it; *e. g.*:

<pre>
          On a hill there grows a flower,
             Fair befall the dainty sweet,
          By that flower there is a bower,
             Where the heavenly muses meet.
                     —*Phillis the Fair: N. Breton.*
</pre>

ELOCUTIONARY AND POETIC INFLECTIONS. 107

For a similar reason, if lines both end and begin with unaccented syllables, the effect of the falling movement is increased ; *e. g.*:

> O mistress mine, where are you roaming?
> O stay, and hear; your true love 's coming.
> —*Twelfth Night*, ii., 3 : *Shakespear.*

It is interesting to notice that this incidental use of the spoken accent in our language in order to represent pitch, is just that which the best authorities, both ancient and modern, agree in acknowledging to have been the main use of the written accent in the classic languages. The word accent comes from the Latin *accentus*, from *ad* and *canere* meaning *to sing to*, and the Greek word for the same προσῳδία comes from πρός and ᾠδή, and means a mark *for singing*, or for tones of voice, and not merely for stress or the ictus. All the Greek terms used for specific accents, too, were borrowed from those used in music. The acute accent was called ὀξεῖα, meaning *sharp* or *high*, the grave βαρεῖα, meaning *heavy* or *low*, and the circumflex περισπωμένη, from περισπάω meaning *to draw around*. This circumflex, by-the-way, was almost always used upon syllables that had been contracted, and this for the simple purpose, as will become evident upon reflection, of representing in a single syllable movements of the voice that before had been represented in two : τι-μά-ω, for instance, when contracted, would become τι-μῶ.

It will be seen from this that the accents, as used by the Greeks, indicated not stress of voice, but tones not wholly dissimilar from those indicated by precisely the same marks when used to-day in our works on elocution. Dr. Schmidt, in the "Rythmic and Metric of the Classic Languages," says: "It is easy to see that a Greek verse can and must be pronounced throughout with the prose accents, and that this can be done without any conflict arising between the prose accents and the quantity of syllables and their ictus in poetry. The following verse, therefore, may be read:

Ἄν - δρα μοι ἔν - νε - πε, Μοῦ-σα, πο - λύ-τρο-πον, ὅς   μά- λα   πολ - λά.

"Here, as it happens, the high tone and the ictus coincide in the first measures, but not in the fifth and sixth. But in English, as before remarked, the high tone is almost always joined to the ictus. . . . The following verse is accented in reading as follows:

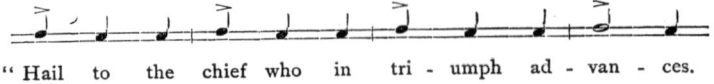

"Hail   to   the   chief who   in   tri - umph   ad - van - ces.

In this way there arises a regularity in the succession of the high and low tones which very closely resembles singing." As Schmidt says truly, in modern verse, because it is read, not chanted, the ictus and the high tone are connected more invariably than in the ancient verse. For this reason the ictus or stress, when given at the beginning or end of the line, must indicate very nearly the same thing as the high tone when used at these places. What the former indicates was shown when treating of stress and the measures. What the latter indicates is to be shown now. Those who choose to compare the two results will find that, practically, they agree, and so, while considering accent as related to pitch, will derive a confirmation of the truth of the principles unfolded when considering it as related to force.

Let us take up, then, the different kinds of accent already mentioned as necessitating the rising and falling movements of the voice. The accent accompanying terminal measure, in which the high tone ends but does not begin the line, and corresponding to the rising inflection, according to elocutionary principles, must emphatically *open* the channel of thought, as if to speed it forward, producing thus an *anticipative* effect. Accents accompanying initial measure, in which the high tone begins but does not end the line, and corresponding to the downward inflection, must emphatically *close* the channel of thought, producing thus a *conclusive* effect. Now contrast the following. Is it not a fact that the rising movements have a constant tendency to sweep the thought along with their current, and the falling to check it? This is rising:

>   Though my back I should rub
>   On Diogenes' tub,
>   How my fancy could prance
>   In a dance of romance.
>   —*Life of Napoleon:* Scott.

>   Over hill, over dale,
>   Thorough bush, thorough brier,
>   Over park, over pale,
>   Thorough flood, thorough fire.
>   —*Midsummer Night's Dream*, ii., 1: *Shakespear.*

>   Past cannon they dashed,
>   Past cannon that flashed,
>   Past cannon that crashed
>   Through their columns in vain.
>   —*A Charge:* Anon.

And these are falling:

> Down they tear, man and horse,
> Down in their awful course;
> Trampling with bloody heel
> Over the crashing steel,—
> All their eyes forward bent,
> Rushed the Black Regiment.
> —*The Black Regiment: Boker.*

> Cannon to right of them,
> Cannon to left of them,
> Cannon in front of them
> Volley'd and thundered.
> —*Charge of the Light Brigade: Tennyson.*

These, again, are rising:

> Oh, young Lochinvar is come out of the west,
> Through all the wide border his steed was the best.
> —*Lochinvar: Scott.*

> I sprang to the stirrup, and Joris, and he,
> I galloped, Dirk galloped, we galloped all three.
> —*How They Brought the Good News: Browning.*

> When dark December glooms the day
> And takes my autumn joys away;
> When short and scant the sunbeam throws
> Upon the weary waste of snows
> A cold and profitless regard,
> *   *   *   *   *   *
> When such the country cheer, I come,
> Well pleased, to seek my city home;
> For converse and for books to change
> The forest's melancholy range,
> And welcome with renewed delight
> The busy day and social night.
> —*Marmion: Scott.*

And these are falling:

> Buried and cold when my heart stills her motion,
> Green be thy fields, sweetest isle of the ocean.
> —*Exile of Erin: Campbell.*

But amid my broken slumbers
Still I heard those magic numbers,
 * * * * *
Till their chimes in sweet collision
Mingled with each wandering vision,
Mingled with the fortune-telling
Gypsy bands of dreams and fancies,
Which amid the waste expanses
Of the silent land of trances
Have their solitary dwelling.
    —Carillon : Longfellow.

These are rising :

Among the fancies tell me this,
What is the thing we call a kiss?
I shall resolve ye what it is.
    —The Kiss : R. Herrick.

A higher hand must make her mild
 If all be not in vain ; and guide
 Her footsteps moving side by side
With wisdom like the younger child.
    —In Memoriam : Tennyson.

And these are falling :

How delicious is the winning
Of a kiss at love's beginning,
When two mutual hearts are sighing
For the knot there's no untying.
    —The First Kiss : Campbell.

And all fancies yearn to cover
 The hard earth whereon she passes,
 With the thymy-scented grasses.
And all hearts do pray, "God love her."
    —A Portrait : Mrs. Browning.

The two effects under consideration may not be apparent to the reader in all of these quotations; but if we turn to the stronger methods of securing the same end—those corresponding to the rising and falling circumflex,—none probably will fail to recognize them. Notice, in the following, how the effect of the rising movement is increased when an accented syllable at the end of one line is followed immediately by an accent at the beginning of the next line:

> Comrades, leave me here a little, while as yet 't is early morn;
> Leave me here; and when you want me, sound upon the bugle-horn.
> —*Locksley Hall: Tennyson.*

In the same way, the *checking* effect of the falling movement is stronger when an unaccented syllable at the end of one line is followed by another unaccented syllable at the beginning of the next; *e. g.*:

> With deep affection
> And recollection,
> I often think of
>   Those Shandon bells;
> Whose sounds so wild would,
> In the days of childhood,
> Fling round my cradle
>   Their magic spells.
> —*The Bells of Shandon: F. Mahony.*

But the rhythm corresponding to the rising inflection, besides emphatically opening the channel of thought, as if to speed its current onward, should also, according to the principles of elocution, have the effect of representing *anticipation, hope.* Look at this:

> When ends life's transient dream,
> When death's cold sullen stream
>   Shall o'er me roll,
> Blest Saviour, then in love,
> Fear and distrust remove,
> O bear me safe above,
>   A ransomed soul.
> —*Hymn: Palmer.*

And that corresponding to the falling inflection should

represent *conclusiveness*, therefore *confidence, assurance;* e. g.:

> There no sigh of memory swelleth;
> There no tear of misery welleth;
> * * * * *
> Past is all the cold world's scorning,
> Gone the night and broke the morning.
> —*Hymn : Anon.*

Here again, too, is *anticipation, expectancy, hope:*

> Come, rest in this bosom, my own stricken deer,
> Though the herd have fled from thee, thy home is still here;
> Here still is the smile that no cloud can o'ercast,
> And a heart and a hand all thine own to the last.
> —*Come, Rest, etc.: Moore.*

And here, *conclusiveness, confidence, assurance:*

> Come in the evening, or come in the morning;
> Come when you're looked for, or come without warning;
> Kisses and welcome you'll find here before you,
> And the oftener you come here, the more I'll adore you.
> —*The Welcome: T. Davis.*

This again, like the rising inflection, represents *indecision, doubt:*

> That men with knowledge merely played,
> I told thee—hardly nigher made,
> Though scaling slow from grade to grade;
>
> Much less this dreamer, deaf and blind,
> Named man, may hope some truth to find,
> That bears relation to the mind.
> —*Two Voices: Tennyson.*

And this, corresponding to the falling inflection, represents so much *decision* and *disregard of doubtful considerations* as to seem *flippant:*

> Ah, but traditions, inventions,
>   (Say we and make up a visage,)
> So many men with such various intentions,

> Down the past ages must know more than this age!
> Leave the web all its dimensions!
> > —*Master Hugues of Saxe-Gotha: Browning.*

The old fashioned *narrative* that dealt with facts, concerning which one could be decided and sure, could find a satisfactory expression in the hexameter; *e. g.*:

> This is the forest primeval; but where are the hearts that beneath it
> Leaped like the roe when he hears in the woodland the voice of the huntsman?
> > —*Evangeline: Longfellow.*

But the present age is *analytic*. Its narratives deal with motives, concerning which no one can be sure. Is this one reason why we prefer a more *indecisive, hesitating* movement? as in our heroic metre:

> Of man's first disobedience, and the fruit
> Of that forbidden tree, whose mortal taste
> Brought death into the world and all our woe, etc.
> > —*Paradise Lost: Milton.*

Or that we feel, instinctively, that the more *decisive* metre is fitter for the mock heroic?—

> Tell me whither I may hie me—tell me, dear one, that I may know,
> Is it up the highest Andes? down a horrible volcano?
> > —*Ferdinando and Elvira: Gilbert.*

Or for the pathetic,—in a case like this, in which the very *decisiveness* of the mood, the *remorseless assurance of being right*, that is conveyed by the style, enhances the effect? Notice it:

> One more unfortunate,
> Weary of breath,
> Rashly importunate,
> Gone to her death.
> > —*Bridge of Sighs: Hood.*

CHAPTER X.

POETIC PITCH—MELODY AND RHYME.

Variety and Monotony in Elocution and Poetry representing less or more Control over Self and the Subject—True Significance of Alliteration, Assonance, etc.—Rhyme introducing Element of Sameness—Increases effects of Versification, of Unity of Poetic Form, of Emphasis of all Kinds, of Regularity of Movement, of Rapidity of Thought—Results of Changing the Order of the Occurrence of Rhymes in Tennyson's In Memoriam—Blank Verse admitting of Great Variety Preferable for Long Productions.

PASSING on now, to consider the poetic analogues for *variety* and *monotony* in elocutionary melody, it will be recognized at once that the first is found in verse in which the sounds *differ greatly*, and the second in that in which they are *very similar*. The following, therefore, corresponding to varied melody, represent, and very appropriately, too, a *buoyant, unrestrained* mood, in which the soul is exercising very *little control* over either itself or its modes of expression (see page 95):

>   Her feet beneath her petticoat
>   Like little mice stole in and out,
>   As if they feared the light :
>   But oh, she dances such a way
>   No sun upon an Easter-day
>   Is half so fine a sight !
>   —*Ballad upon a Wedding: Suckling.*
>
>   Hast thou seen the down in the air,
>   When wanton blasts have tossed it ?

> Or the ship on the sea.
> When ruder winds have crossed it?
> —*Lute Song: Suckling.*

> When Israel marched along the desert land,
> Blazed through the night on lonely wilds afar,
> And told the path—a never setting star:
> So, heavenly Genius in thy course divine,
> Hope is thy star, her light is ever thine.
> —*Pleasures of Hope: Campbell.*

And the following, in which there is much alliteration (*i. e.*, repetition of the same consonant-sounds), and assonance (*i. e.*, repetition of the same vowel-sounds), represent a very high degree of restraint on the part of the soul, and *control* exercised over itself and its modes of expression.

> Lo, the leader in these glorious wars,
> Now to glorious burial slowly borne,
> Followed by the brave of other lands,
> He on whom from both her open hands;
> Lavish honor showered all her stars,
> And affluent fortune emptied all her horn.
> —*Ode on Duke of Wellington: Tennyson.*

> More strong than strong disaster,
>   For fate and fear too strong;
> Earth's friend, whose eyes look past her,
>   Whose hands would purge of wrong;
> Our lord, our light, our master,
>   Whose word sums up all song.
> —*Garden of Cymodoce: Swinburne.*

These quotations, and the principle they illustrate, show us the true significance of passages in which we find grouped the same sounds, as in *assonance* and *alliteration* just mentioned; or similar sounds, as in *poetic gradation* (*i. e.*, a series of vowels all different, in which each is at the smallest remove of all from the one following it), and *syzygy* (*i. e.*, a combination of consonants easy to pronounce). All these sprang, originally, from that tendency at the basis of all art-construction, to bring together, as a result of comparison, things that are alike or allied. But their significance, which alone concerns us at present, is this: if no attention whatever be paid to the succession of vowels and consonants; if those combined be arranged so that they cannot be pronounced easily and smoothly, the verses appear devoid of art, the chief effect of which is to reduce that with which it has to deal to order and form. In the following, for instance, the writer manifests no control over his own powers of expression or his ideas. He presumably meant to give them an artistic form, but as arranged they produce no artistic effect.

>Numerous were the friends that gathered,
>When in the good ship " Hibernia "
>They weighed anchor in the harbor
>Of the Metropolitan City.
>It would take too long to narrate
>All the many things that happened
>In their voyage across the ocean.
>—*Sketches of Palestine : Hammond.*

If, on the contrary, the writer has made too much of qualities like *assonance* and *alliteration*, the impression conveyed is that of *too much suppression* and *control*. There seems to be no spontaneity in his work. The following produces, as is its intention, an artificial effect.

>*Holofernes*, I will somewhat affect the letter, for it argues facility:
>The preyful Princess pierced and prick'd a pretty pleasing pricket;
>Some say a sore; but not a sore, till now made sore with shooting.
>—*Love's Labor's Lost*, iv., 2 : *Shakespear.*

Swinburne is sometimes almost equally artificial.

>His eyes gat grace of sleep, to see
>The deep divine dark day-shine of the sea,
>Dense water-walls and clear dusk water-ways,

> Broad-based or branching as a sea-flower sprays
> That side or this dividing.
> —*Thalassius.*

The following are better, because in the sense there is some reason for the alliteration.

> O wind, O wingless wind that walk'st the sea,
> Weak wind, wing-broken, wearier wind than we.
> —*On the Cliffs: Swinburne.*

> And dulled to death with deep dense funeral chime
> Of their reiterate rhyme.
> —*Idem.*

Between the two extremes that have been mentioned, however, the poet can find every degree of sameness and change, unity and variety, with which to represent every kind of thought truthfully.

It is evident, from what has been said, that the chief effect of *rhyme*, or the recurrence of similar sounds at the ends of lines, is to introduce into the verse the element of *sameness*. This sameness of itself, as has been intimated in another place, increases the effects of *versification* by directing attention to the ends of the lines and thus separating them. Besides this, especially if the rhymes be used at like intervals, as is generally the case, they tend to give *unity* to the form. Their influence in this regard is precisely analogous to that of the cadences and half cadences, which, coming at the ends of musical phrases, give the effect of unity to musical composition. Notice in the following how often the alternate lines, both in the music and words, end at the same pitch. Notice, too, at the close of each line, as in the illustration in the last chapter, how the music of the melody rises with accented or masculine verse-endings, the analogues of rising inflections; and falls with unaccented or feminine verse-endings, the analogues of falling inflections. Of course there are

MELODY AND RHYME. 119

tunes set to words in which correspondences of this kind are less apparent; but the following represent arrangements sufficiently common to justify what is here said of them.

Lines Ended with Like Effects of Pitch in the Melody of both Music and Verse.
Falling or Feminine Endings.   Rising or Masculine Endings.

WILMOT.

Still we wait for thine ap-pear-ing;   Life and joy thy beams im-part,

Chas-ing all our fears, and cheer-ing   Ev-ery poor, be-night-ed heart.

BAYLEY.

Love di-vine, all loves ex-cell-ing,   Joy of heaven, to earth come down!

Fix in us thine hum-ble dwell-ing;
D. S. Vis-it us with thy sal-va-tion;   All thy faith-ful mer-cies crown;
                                          En-ter ev-ery trem-bling heart.

Je-sus! thou art all com-pass-ion,   Pure un-bound-ed love thou art;

Like these similarly ending cadences and half cadences in music, rhymes furnish a framework about which, or rather within which, all the other form-elements of the verse are brought together. This is the reason why it is easier for beginners to write poetry in rhymes than in blank verse. All successful verse must have form, and rhymes of themselves tend to give it this.

Not only so, but—what is of main importance in our present treatment of the subject—they serve equally to furnish a framework for the poetic thought. The *rhyming words*, especially the last of two or three that rhyme, always appear to be especially *emphatic*. In fact, they seem to add to the emphasis in almost every possible way. They augment the effects of duration or quantity, because at the end of the line, where the rhyme usually is, the voice, as a rule, pauses; of force, because rhyming syllables, at least the last ones in which a sound is repeated, appear to be pronounced more strongly than others; of pitch, because, as we have found, where the vowel-sounds are the same, the pitch seems the same; and of quality, as we shall find, because the likeness of the rhyming syllables necessarily attracts attention. For all these reasons, rhymes necessarily tend to thrust into prominence the ideas expressed in them. Notice this fact as exemplified in the following:

> Know, then, thyself; presume not God to scan;
> The proper study of mankind is man.
> —*Essay on Man: Pope.*

> All are but parts of one stupendous whole
> Whose body nature is, and God the soul.
> —*Idem.*

> All nature is but art unknown to thee;
> All chance, direction which thou canst not see;

All discord, harmony not understood;
All partial evil, universal good;
And spite of pride in erring reason's spite,
One truth is clear, Whatever is, is right.
       —*Idem.*

She dwelt among the untrodden ways
 Beside the springs of Dove,
A maid whom there were none to praise,
 And very few to love :

A violet by a mossy stone
 Half hidden from the eye—
Fair as a star when only one
 Is shining in the sky.

She lived unknown, and few could know
 When Lucy ceased to be ;
But she is in her grave, and oh,
 The difference to me !
    —*The Lost Love : Wordsworth.*

In connection with the effect of unity, and as one factor of it, *regularly recurring rhymes* also impart an effect of *regularity* to the movement, as in these :

Vital spark of heavenly flame,
Quit, oh, quit this mortal frame.
Trembling, hoping, lingering, flying,
Oh, the pain, the bliss of dying !
    —*Dying Christian to his Soul : Pope.*

A kind and gentle heart he had,
 To comfort friends and foes ;
The naked every day he clad,—
 When he put on his clothes.
   —*Elegy on the Death of a Mad Dog : Goldsmith.*

Singing through the forests ;
 Rattling over ridges ;
Shooting under arches ;
 Rumbling over bridges ;

> Whizzing through the mountains;
>   Buzzing o'er the vale,—
> Bless me, this is pleasant,
>   Riding on the rail.
>   —*Railroad Rhyme: Saxe.*

In the degree in which the rhymes are near together, they give an effect of rapidity to the movement—not so much of the form, as in short quantity, as of the thought. It has been said that the rhyming words emphasize strongly the ideas expressed through them. They convey the impression, therefore, that something important has been said; and if they occur frequently, they suggest that many important things have been said, and said in a short time, or—what is equivalent to this—that the thought in the poem is moving on rapidly, an effect that could not be produced by the same words arranged differently. Of course, it follows that the nearer together the rhymes are, the more rapid seems to be the movement. Compare these two stanzas, both from Sir Walter Scott's *Eve of St. John:*

> The baron returned in three days' space,
>   And his looks were sad and sour,
> And weary was his courser's pace,
>   As he reached his rocky tower.

> My lady each night sought the lonely light
>   That burns on the wild Watchfold,
> For from height to height the beacons bright
>   Of the English foemen told.

Perhaps no more interesting study of the different effects of rhyme that have just been mentioned is anywhere afforded than in Tennyson's *In Memoriam.* In several of the stanzas of this poem the third and fourth lines may change places without detriment to the sense. But if this change be made, the rhymes at the ends of the first and fourth lines are brought nearer together, thus increasing the effect of rapidity as well as the emphasis at the end of the latter line. Moreover, all four lines are then heard at regular intervals, thus increasing also the effect of regularity. The consequence is, that the slow and therefore judicial, the unemphatic and therefore doubtful, the irregular and therefore hesitating impression conveyed by the thought of the poem, as arranged in its present form, almost disappears, giving place to the easy and even flow of unwavering assurance. Those who doubt whether poetic sound has much to do with poetic representation, may learn a lesson by examining the following stanzas in these two forms. Read these first:

> Thou wilt not leave us in the dust :
>   Thou madest man he knows not why ;
>   He thinks he was not made to die ;
> And thou hast made him : thou art just.
>
> Thou seemest human and divine,
>   The highest, holiest manhood, thou :
>   Our wills are ours, we know not how ;
> Our wills are ours to make them thine.
>
> Our little systems have their day ;
>   They have their day and cease to be :
>   They are but broken lights of thee,
> And thou, O Lord, art more than they.
>
> We have but faith : we cannot know :
>   For knowledge is of things we see ;
>   And yet we trust it comes from thee,
> A beam in darkness : let it grow.

And now read these:

> Thou wilt not leave us in the dust :
>   Thou madest man he knows not why ;
>   And thou hast made him : thou art just :
> He thinks he was not made to die.

> Thou seemest human and divine,
>   The highest, holiest manhood, thou :
> Our wills are ours to make them thine ;
>   Our wills are ours, we know not how.
>
> Our little systems have their day ;
>   They have their day and cease to be :
> And thou, O Lord, art more than they :
>   They are but broken lights of thee.
>
> We have but faith ; we cannot know,
>   For knowledge is of things we see ;
> A beam in darkness : let it grow ;
>   And yet we trust it comes from thee.

Where rhymes are used, these effects of unity, regularity, and rapidity are always present to some extent, and all, if continued too long, become monotonous and tiresome, besides being unfitted for the representation of varying moods and scenes. Therefore, for long productions, poets usually prefer blank-verse,—either regular, as in Shakespear's plays and the " Paradise Lost "; *e. g.*:

> My tongue shall hush again this storm of war,
> And make fair weather in your blust'ring land.
>   —*King John*, v., 1 : *Shakespear.*

or irregular or broken, as in Goethe's *Faust* and Southey's *Thalaba* ; *e. g.* :

> How beautiful is night !
> A dewy freshness fills the silent air ;
> No mist obscures, nor cloud nor speck nor stain
>   Breaks the serene of heaven :
>   In full-orbed glory yonder moon divine
>   Rolls through the dark blue depths.
>   —*Thalaba*, 1 : *Southey.*

Blank-verse, in a sense not true of verse that rhymes, admits of irregular accents; as, for instance, in the following, in which only the last line is absolutely regular :

> Upon our sides it never shall be broken.
> And noble Dolphin, albeit we swear
> A voluntary zeal and an unurged faith
> To your proceedings, yet believe me, prince,
> I am not glad that such a sore of time
> Should seek a plaster by contemned revolt.
> —*King John*, v., 2 : *Shakespear.*

It is not necessary to argue that verse admitting of changes like these can be continued almost indefinitely without becoming monotonous, and can be used in describing almost all possible varieties of moods and scenes, without ceasing to be representative.

CHAPTER XI.

ELOCUTIONARY AND POETIC QUALITY.

Quality represents the Emotive Nature of the Soul as influencing and influenced by both Instinctive and Reflective Tendencies—Kinds of Quality, and what each represents in Elocution—Letter-Sounds used in Verse to produce Effects of the Aspirate Quality—Guttural—Pectoral—Pure—Orotund—Illustrations of Poetic Effects of all these Kinds when combined.

THE last elocutionary element, the influence of which upon poetic form we have to consider, and the second that has to do with the tunes of verse, is quality; or, as it is sometimes called, on account of that to which it corresponds in painting, tone-color. Its different varieties are determined by the relative proportions in which noise and music are combined in them; or, in other words, by the different actions of the organs of utterance in causing more or less of the breath, while leaving the lungs, to be vocalized and rendered resonant.

What different kinds of quality are fitted to represent, it needs but little observation to discover. It certainly is not physical energy. When Patti passes from a loud to a soft, or from an abrupt to a smooth tone, she changes greatly the kinds of energy, but her voice still retains the same Patti-quality. Nor does quality represent mere intellectuality. A man, without changing in the least an habitual nasal or wheezing quality, may give every inflection needed in order to represent the merely mental phases of that which actuates him. But if we *frighten* him severely, we may make it impossible for him to use any other sound than a *whisper ;* if in connection with this, we *anger* him, he will *hiss ;* or, if at length he recovers his voice, he will use the harsh, jarring, interrupted hard-*g* quality of tone, termed the *guttural ;* or, if that which he would repel is too great to make anger appropriate, it may widen and stiffen his throat so as to produce the hollow, almost inarticulate indication of *awe* and *horror* given by what is termed the *pectoral* quality. Release him now from the influence of affright, anger, or horror, and put him into a *gently satisfied* mood, and he will use his nearest approach to *pure* quality. Stir him then to *profound emotion*, inspired by what is *deeply satisfying*, and all his vocal passages will expand again, and he will produce his nearest approach to the full, round, resonant quality termed *orotund.*

For these reasons, it seems indisputable that quality represents the feelings, the temper, the spiritual condition of the higher emotive nature,—what I have termed the soul, by which is meant, as needs scarcely be said again, the principle of life holding body and mind together, influencing and influenced by both. The soul communicates with the external world never wholly through the instinctive nature, nor wholly through the reflective, but always through one of the two modified by its connection with the other. The quality of sound, therefore, represents the quality of the feeling that vivifies the soul. This feeling, on its physical side, and with its most physical coloring, gives us, first, the serpent-like *hissing aspirate ;* next, with an intellectual coloring the *guttural* quality ; and last, with an emotional coloring, the *pectoral.* On its intellectual side, it gives us first, with a physical coloring, the soft *whispering aspirate ;* next, with an intellectual coloring, the *pure* quality ; and last, with an emotional coloring, the *orotund*. Of these six forms of quality, the first four are classed in a general way as *impure*, because there is in them more breath or noise than vocal tone or music ; and the last two are classed as *pure*.

The first three again refer to what one wishes to repel ; the *hissing aspirate* indicating feelings like *affright, amazement, indignation,* and *contempt ;* the *guttural,* as has been said, *hostility ;* and the *pectoral, awe* or *horror*. The last three refer to what, if not wholly satisfactory, at least, excites in one no movement aimed against it. The *soft whisper* indicates feelings like *surprise, interest,* or *solicitude ;* the tone termed distinctively the *pure* represents *gentle contemplation of* what may be either *joyous* or *sad ;* and the *orotund, deep delight, admiration, courage,* or *determination,* as inspired by contemplation of the *noble* or *grand*.

All these different qualities can be given by good elocutionists when vocalizing almost any of the consonants or vowels ; but the poet for his effects must depend upon the sounds necessarily given to words in ordinary pronunciation. For instance, certain consonants, called variously aspirates, sibilants, or atonics, viz. : *h, s, z, w, sh, wh, th, p, t, f,* are aspirate in themselves ; that is, we are obliged to whisper when we articulate them. Therefore in poetic effects, considered aside from those that are elocutionary, the aspirate must be produced by using words containing some of these consonants ; and, if it be the repellant aspirate or the hiss, by using also consonants giving guttural effects, like *g, j, ch,* and *r*. Here, for instance, is the poetic *aspirate* of *amazement, affright, indignation, contempt*.

Out of my sight, thou serpent; that name best
Befits thee with him leagued, thyself as false
And hateful; nothing wants but that thy shape
Like his and color serpentine may show
Thy inward fraud.
—*Paradise Lost*, 10: *Milton.*

What's the business
That such a hideous trumpet calls to parley
The sleepers of the house? speak! speak!
—*Macbeth*, ii., 1: *Shakespear.*

You souls of geese
That bear the shapes of men, how have you run
From slaves that apes would beat.
—*Coriolanus*, i., 4: *Shakespear.*

Ay, in the catalogue ye go for men;
As hounds and greyhounds, mongrels, spaniels, curs,
Shoughs, water-rugs, and demi-wolves are clep'd
All by the name of dogs.
—*Macbeth*, iii., 1: *Shakespear.*

And here the poetic *aspirate* of *surprise, interest,* and *solicitude.*

What? keep a week away? seven days and nights?
Eightscore eight hours,—and lover's absent hours,—
More tedious than the dial eightscore times?
—*Othello*, iii., 4: *Shakespear.*

The red rose cries, "She is near, she is near";
And the white rose weeps, "She is late";
The larkspur listens, "I hear, I hear";
And the lily whispers, "I wait."

—*Maud: Tennyson.*

Jul.—Sweet, so would I;
Yet I should kill thee with much cherishing.
Good-night   good-night; parting is such sweet sorrow,
That I shall say good-night till it be morrow.
Rom.—Sleep dwell upon thine eyes, peace in thy breast—
Would I were sleep and peace so sweet to rest.
—*Romeo and Juliet*, ii., 2: *Shakespear.*

The aspirated sounds do not depend upon the use of the vowels. But this is not true of the other qualities. In the poetic *guttural* and *pure* tones, front * or else short vowel-sounds like those in the words *pin, met, hat, fur*, and *far*, among which we must include also the long and front * ones in *me* and *ale* usually predominate. In the poetic *pectoral* and *orotund*, long and back * vowel-sounds like those in *moor, more, cow, boil, all*, among which we must include the short but back * sound of *u* in *but*, usually predominate. Besides this, for the *guttural*, certain palatic and lingual consonant-sounds, like those of *g, j, k, ch, r*, and, at times, especially when used in combination with other consonants, dental and labial sounds, like those in *b, d*, and *v*, are essential. Here are examples of the guttural indicating, as has been said, *hostility*.

> Thou cream-faced loon,
> Where gottest thou that goose look?
> —*Macbeth*, v., 3 : *Shakespear.*

> Despised by cowards for greater cowardice,
> And scorned even by the vicious for such vices
> As in the monstrous grasp of their conception
> Defy all codes.
> —*Marino Faliero*, v., 3 : *Byron.*

> But the churchmen fain would kill their church,
> As the churches have killed their Christ.
> —*Maud : Tennyson.*

> Till I, with as fierce an anger, spoke,
> And he struck me, madman, over the face,
> Struck me before the languid fool,
> Who was gaping and grinning by.
> —*Idem.*

The elocutionary *pectoral*, with its hollow tones, always suggests more or less of a breathing quality. Therefore the poetic pectoral requires, in addition to the use of the

* See page 97.

ELOCUTIONARY AND POETIC QUALITY. 131

long and back* vowel-sounds like those of long, *o, oo, ou, oi*, broad *a*, and short *u*, that of the aspirate consonants like *h, s, z, w, sh, wh, th, r, p, t, f*, and sometimes *b, d*, and *v*. Notice the preponderance of these letters in all of the following expressions of *awe* or *horror:*

> For a charm of powerful trouble,
> Like a hell-broth boil and bubble.
>
> *All.*—Double, double toil and trouble;
> Fire burn and cauldron bubble.
>
> *   *   *   *   *   *   *   *   *
>
> *All.*—Seek to know no more.
> *Macb.*—I will be satisfied: deny me this,
> And an eternal curse fall on you! Let me know—
>
> *   *   *   *   *   *   *   *   *
>
> 1*st Witch.*—Shew!
> 2*d Witch.*—Shew!
> 3*d Witch.*—Shew!
> *All.*—Shew his eyes and grieve his heart!
> Come like shadows, so depart.
> *Macb.*—Thou art too like the spirit of Banquo; down!
> Thy crown does sear mine eyeballs:—and thy hair
> Thou other gold-bound brow, is like the first.
> —*Macbeth*, iv., 1 : *Shakespear.*

> And with blood for dew, the bosom boils;
> And a gust of sulphur is all its smell;
> And lo, he is horribly in the toils
> Of a coal-black giant flower of hell.
> —*The Heretic's Tragedy: R. Browning.*

> So wills the fierce avenging sprite,
> Till blood for blood atones.
> Ay, though he 's buried in a cave,
> And trodden down with stones,
> And years have rotted off his flesh,—
> The world shall see his bones.
> —*The Dream of Eugene Aram : Hood.*

> A dungeon horrible, on all sides round,
> As one great furnace, flamed; yet from those flames
> No light but rather darkness visible,

* See page 97.

> Served only to discover sights of woe,
> Regions of sorrow, doleful shades, where peace
> And rest can never dwell, hope never comes.
> —*Paradise Lost*, 1 : *Milton.*

> Ghastly dethronement, cursed by those the most
> On whose repugnant brow the crown next falls.
> —*Epilogue* : *R. Browning.*

Notice the rhymes, too, in the following :

> "Dust and ashes." So you creak it, and I want the heart to scold.
> Dear dead women, with such hair, too—what's become of all the gold
> Used to hang and brush their bosoms ? I feel chilly and grown old.
> —*A Toccata of Galuppi's* : *R. Browning.*

The poetic *pure* tone necessitates, as has been said, the use of the short or the front vowel-sounds. In connection with these almost any of the consonants, except the guttural, may be used to any extent. Here are examples of the poetic pure quality, representing, as already intimated, *gentle contemplation* with feelings, not too strong, of what may be either *joyous* or *sad*.

> All night merrily, merrily,
> They would pelt me with starry spangles and shells,
> Laughing and clapping their hands between,
> All night merrily, merrily.
> —*The Merman* : *Tennyson.*

> She sleeps : her breathings are not heard
> In palace chambers far apart.
> The fragrant tresses are not stirred
> That lie upon her charmèd heart.
> She sleeps ; on either hand upswells
> The gold-fringed pillow lightly pressed.
> She sleeps, nor dreams, but ever dwells
> A perfect form in perfect rest.
> —*The Day Dream* : *Tennyson.*

The *orotund*, as contrasted with the pure tone, has a slightly husky as well as hollow effect. Therefore its poetic form necessitates, besides the use of the long and back vowels, that of the subvowels or subtonics, like *m, n, ng, l, b, d,* and *v.* Here are examples of the poetic orotund, indicating any thing, not provoking, which stirs one to *deep feeling,* or, as was stated before, to *deep delight, admiration, courage,* or *determination,* as inspired by contemplation of the *noble* or *grand.*

> " Glory to God," unnumbered voices sung;
> " Glory to God," the vales and mountains rung;
> Voices that hailed creation's primal morn,
> And to the shepherds sung a Saviour born.
> Slowly, bare-headed through the surf we bore
> The sacred cross, and kneeling kissed the shore.
> *—Voyage of Columbus : Rogers.*

> Now is the winter of our discontent
> Made glorious summer by this son of York,
> And all the clouds that lowered upon our house
> In the deep bosom of the ocean buried.
> *—Richard III.,* i., 1 : *Shakespear.*

> Daughter of Faith, awake, arise, illume
> The dread unknown, the chaos of the tomb,
> Melt and dispel, ye spectre-doubts, that roll
> Cimmerian darkness o'er the parting soul.
> Fly, like the moon-eyed herald of Dismay,
> Chased on his night-steed by the star of day.
> The strife is o'er—the pangs of nature close,
> And life's last rapture triumphs o'er her woes.
> *—Pleasures of Hope : Campbell.*

> Peace and order and beauty draw
> Round thy symbol of light and law.
> *—Barbara Frietchie : Whittier.*

All the more *impure* qualities—the *hiss,* the *guttural,* and the *pectoral*—represent allied emotions. Therefore, in elocution, there is a tendency to combine their effects. It is the same in poetry. Notice the following:

> See with what heat these dogs of hell advance
> To waste and havoc yonder world. . . .
> * * * * * * *
> And know not that I call'd and drew them thither,
> My hell-hounds, to lick up the draff and filth,
> Which man's polluting sin with taint hath shed
> On what was pure ! till, cramm'd and gorg'd, nigh burst
> With suck'd and glutted offal, at one sling
> Of thy victorious arm, well-pleasing Son,
> Both Sin and Death and yawning Grave, at last
> Through Chaos hurled, obstruct the mouth of hell
> Forever, and seal up his ravenous jaws.
> —*Paradise Lost*, 10 : *Milton.*

> Fret till your proud heart breaks ;
> Go show your slaves how choleric you are,
> And make your bondmen tremble. Must I budge ?
> Must I observe you ? Must I stand and crouch
> Under your testy humor ? By the gods,
> You shall digest the venom of your spleen
> Tho' it do split you ; for from this day forth
> I 'll use you for my mirth—yea, for my laughter—
> When you are waspish.
> —*Julius Cæsar*, iv., 3 : *Shakespear.*

So, too, the poetic *pure* and *orotund* naturally go together; for example:

> For though the giant ages heave the hill
> And break the shore, and evermore
> Make and break and work their will ;
> Though worlds on worlds in myriad myriads roll
> Round us, each with different powers
> And other forms of life than ours,
> What know we greater than the soul ?
> On God and godlike men we build our trust.
> —*Ode on Duke of Wellington* : *Tennyson.*

Much of the representative beauty of poetry depends on a judicious alternation of these different qualities of sound. Notice this fact as exemplified in the last three quotations, as well as in the fourth and fifth lines of the following, where the poetic orotund is introduced in the midst of an aspirate passage:

> The bright sun rises to his course, and lights
> A race of slaves. He sets, and his last beams
> Fall on a slave; not such as swept along
> By the full tide of power, the conqueror leads
> To crimson glory and undying fame;
> But base ignoble slaves; slaves to a horde
> Of petty tyrants, feudal despots, lords
> Rich in some dozen paltry villages,
> Strong in some hundred spearmen, only great
> In that strange spell—a name.
> —*Rienzi's Address to Romans : Mitford.*

CHAPTER XII.

EFFECTS OF POETIC QUALITY CONTINUED.

Imitative Effects of Letter-Sounds corresponding to Aspirate Quality, representing Serpents, Sighing, Rapidity, Winds, Slumber, Conspiracy, Fear, Frightening, Checking—Guttural Quality, representing Grating, Forcing, Flowing Water, Rattling, Effort—Pectoral Quality, representing Groaning, Depth, Hollowness—Pure Quality, representing Thinness, Clearness, Sharpness, Cutting—Orotund Quality, representing Fulness, Roundness, Murmuring, Humming, Denying, etc.—These Effects as combined in Various Illustrations of Carving; Dashing, Rippling, and Lapping Water; Roaring; Clashing; Cursing; Shrieking; Fluttering; Crawling; Confusion; Horror; Spite; Scorn; etc.

LET us turn now to poetic effects produced by quality corresponding to those of *dramatic*, as distinguished from *discoursive*, elocution; and first to the aspirate. In poetry, as in elocution, the *repellant aspirate* imitates any thing that *hisses;* for example:

>   He would have spoke,
> But hiss for hiss returned with forkèd tongue
> To forkèd tongue; for now were all transformed
> Alike, to serpents all as accessories
> To his bold riot: dreadful was the din
> Of hissing through the hall, thick swarming now
> With complicated monsters, head and tail,
> Scorpion and asp, and amphisbæna dire,
> Cerastes horn'd, hydrus, and ellops drear,
> And dipsas; not so thick swarmed once the soil
> Bedropped with blood of Gorgon, or the isle
> Ophiusa.
>   —*Paradise Lost*, 10: *Milton.*

IMITATIVE EFFECTS OF LETTER-SOUNDS.

The *acquiescent aspirate* imitates any thing that *sighs;* for example :

> She gave me for my pains a world of sighs ;
> She swore.—In faith 't was strange, 't was passing strange,
> 'T was pitiful, 't was wondrous pitiful ;
> She wish'd she had not heard it ; yet she wish'd
> That heaven had made *her* such a man.
> —*Othello*, i., 3 : *Shakespear.*

But it is possible to go still more into detail than this. As Guest has pointed out in his "History of English Rhythms," developing for that purpose a suggestion made by Bacon, certain letters and combinations of them seem especially adapted for the imitation of certain specific operations. Things, for instance, that *fly rapidly*, make sounds resembling those of the sibilants. Hence the appropriateness of the following :

> How quick they wheeled, and flying behind them shot
> Sharp sleet of arrowy showers against the face
> Of their pursuers.
> —*Paradise Reg.*, 3 : *Milton.*

> Brushed with the hiss of rustling wings. As bees
> In spring-time.
> —*Paradise Lost*, 1 : *Idem.*

The *winds* make similar sounds :

> The breezy call of incense-breathing morn.
> —*Elegy : Gray.*

> By whispering winds soon lulled asleep.
> —*L'Allegro : Milton.*

So do *nurses, fountains,* and *sea-waves,* when lulling one to *sleep :*

> O Sleep, O gentle Sleep,
> Nature's soft nurse, how have I frightened thee
> That thou no more wilt weigh mine eyelids down,
> And steep my senses in forgetfulness ?
> Why rather, Sleep, liest thou in smoky cribs,
> Upon uneasy pallets stretching thee,

> And hushed with buzzing night-flies to thy slumber ;
> Than in the perfumed chambers of the great,
> Under the canopies of costly state,
> And lulled with sound of sweetest melody.
> —*2 Henry IV.*, iii., 1 : *Shakespear.*

In the following we seem to hear the *whisperings* of *conspirators :*

> Who rather had,
> Though they themselves did suffer by it, behold
> Dissentious numbers pestering streets, than see
> Our tradesmen singing in their shops and going
> About their functions friendly.
> —*Cariolanus*, iv., 6 : *Shakespear.*

And here the whisperings of *fear :*

> A hideous giant, horrible and high.
> —*Faerie Queene*, 1, 7, 8 : *Spenser.*

> Fit vessel, fittest imp of fraud, in whom
> To enter and his dark suggestions hide.
> —*Paradise Lost*, 9 : *Milton.*

When we wish to *frighten* a bird or animal, we often make a prolonged sound of *s*, and then stop it suddenly with the sound of *t*. Now, look at the use of *st* in the following to indicate motion that is checked by being frightened :

> Stern were their looks like wild amazed steers,
> Staring with hollow eyes and stiff upstanding hairs.
> —*Faerie Queene*, 2, 9, 13 : *Spenser.*

> With staring countenance stern, as one astown'd,
> And staggering steps, to weet what sudden stour
> Had wrought that horror strange.
> —*Idem*, 1, 8, 5.

> But she fast stood.
> Pallas had put a boldness in her breast
> And in her fair limbs tender fear compressed,
> And still she stood.
> —*Chapman's Tr., Odyssey.*

> Though death-struck, still his feeble frame he rears ;
> Staggering, but stemming all, his lord unharmed he bears.
> —*Childe Harold*, 1 : *Byron.*

P and *t*, because their sounds cannot be prolonged, as well as *d*, when pronounced like *t*, have also the effect of representing the *stopping* of movement ; *e. g.:*

> Sudden he stops ; his eye is fixed : away,
>   Away thou heedless boy ! prepare the spear :
> Now is thy time to perish or display
>   The skill that yet may check his mad career.
> —*Idem.*

> If thou more murmur'st, I will rend an oak,
> And peg thee in his knotty entrails, till
> Thou hast howled away twelve winters.
> —*Tempest*, i., 2 : *Shakespear.*

The poetic *guttural* imitates any thing that *grates;* for example :

> How the garden grudged me grass
>   Where I stood—the iron gate
> Ground his teeth to let me pass.
> —*A Serenade at the Villa : R. Browning.*

Besides this, it is well to notice that the chief guttural consonants, *g*, *j*, *k*, and *ch*, are all made as a result of effort, and, more than this, of effort that is internal in the sense of not being outwardly visible. They are produced by forcing the tongue against the palate, and the breath between the two. For this reason they seem to be recognized as appropriate for the representation of *effort*, especially of effort that is *internal;* for example :

> Caitiff, to pieces shake,
> That under covert and convenient seeming
> Hast practised on man's life. Close pent-up guilts,
> Rive your concealing continents, and cry
> These dreadful summoners grace.—I am a man.
> —*King Lear*, iii., 2 : *Shakespear.*

> Thou, trumpet, there 's my purse,
> Now crack thy lungs, and split thy brazen pipe:
> Blow, villain, till thy spherèd bias cheek
> Out-swell the colic of puff'd Aquilon;
> Come stretch thy chest.
> —*Troilus and Cressida*, iv., 5: *Shakespear.*

This last quotation suggests that not only the chief guttural consonants, but *b* and *p* also, though in a less degree, may represent effort. This will not seem strange from our present point of view, when we notice that they are both produced by compressing the lips precisely as we do when we are making a *strong muscular exertion:*

> And him beside sits ugly Barbarism,
> And brutish Ignorance, ycrept of late
> Out of dred darkness of the deep Abysme,
> Where being bred he light and heaven does hate.
> —*Tears of the Muses: Spenser.*

> Behemoth, biggest born of earth.
> —*Par. Lost*, 7: *Milton.*

> His bursting passion into plaints thus poured.
> —*Idem*, 9.

> Their broad bare backs upheave
> Into the clouds.
> —*Idem*, 7.

L and *r*, like the other consonants just mentioned, are formed by interrupting the flow of the breath; but in these it is not checked even for a moment, but passes outward at either side of the tongue. Both, therefore, are felt to be appropriate for imitating sounds of *flowing waters* or *liquids*, or other objects having this motion; for example:

> For a charm of powerful trouble,
> Like a hell-broth boil and bubble.
> Double, double toil and trouble,
> Fire burn, and cauldron bubble.
> —*Macbeth*, iv., 1: *Shakespear.*

> Some of serpent kind,
> Wondrous in length and corpulence, involved
> Their snaky folds.
>
> > —*Par. Lost*, 7 : *Milton.*

> The crisped brooks
> Rolling on orient pearl and sands of gold.
> * * * * * * *
> Pour'd forth profuse on hill and dale and plain.
>
> > —4, *Idem.*

> O'er which the mantling vine
> Lays forth her purple grape, and gently creeps
> Luxuriant, meanwhile murmuring waters fall
> Down the slope hills dispersed or in a lake.
>
> > —*Idem.*

R has a sound both harsher and higher than *l*, and is better adapted, therefore, for imitating grating and rattling noises; *e. g.* :

> Such bursts of horrid thunder,
> Such groans of roaring wind and rain, I never
> Remember to have heard.
>
> > —*Lear*, iii., 2 : *Shakespear.*

> ——for this day will pour down,
> If I conjecture aught, no drizzling shower,
> But rattling storm of arrows barb'd with fire.
>
> > —*Par. Lost*, 6 : *Milton.*

The brazen throat of war had ceased to roar.

> —*Idem*, 11.

> And the villainous saltpetre
> Rung a fierce discordant metre
> Round their ears.
>
> > —*The Old Continentals* : *McMaster.*

> And frighted waves rush wildly back
> Before the broadside's reeling rack.
>
> > —*The American Flag* : *Drake.*

L and *r*, too, in combination with *g*, *k*, *p*, *b*, *st*, and some other consonants, increase the effect of the noise made by stoppage in the flow of the articulating breath; and so they also represent *difficulty* or *effort ;* for example:

> Staring full ghastly like a strangled man ;
> His hair upreared, his nostrils stretched with struggling ;
> His hands abroad displayed, as one that grasp'd
> And tugg'd for life, and was by strength subdued.
> Look ! on the sheets his hair, you see, is sticking ;
> His well-proportioned beard made rough and rugged.
> —*2 Henry VI.*, iii., 2 : *Shakespear.*

The poetic pectoral imitates any thing that *groans ;* for example :

> Oh, horror, horror, horror.—Tongue nor heart
> Cannot conceive nor name thee.
> —*Macbeth*, ii., 1 : *Shakespear.*

So all *deep, hollow sounds* are supposed to be imitated, and, as we found when considering pitch, really are imitated by this class of vowels:

> All these and thousand thousands many more,
> And more deformed monsters thousand-fold,
> With dreadful noise and hollow rombling roar,
> Came rushing.
> —*F. Q.*, 2, 12, 25 : *Spenser.*

> A dreadful sound
> Which through the woods loud bellowing did rebound.
> —*Idem*, 1, 7, 7.

> So high as heav'd the tumid hills, so low
> Down sunk a hollow bottom, broad and deep.
> —*Par. Lost*, 7 : *Milton.*

> Hell at last
> Yawning received them whole and on them closed.
> —*Idem*, 6.

The poetic *pure* tones imitate any thing that sounds *thin* and *clear ;* for example :

IMITATIVE EFFECTS OF LETTER-SOUNDS. 143

> Hear the sledges with the bells, silver bells—
> What a world of merriment their melody fortells?
> How they tinkle, tinkle, tinkle in the icy air of night,
> While the stars that oversprinkle all the heavens seem to twinkle
> With a crystalline delight.
> —*The Bells : Poe.*

The vowels used in *pure* quality, especially *e* both short and long, and these especially when combined with the sibilants and the whispering consonants, *p, t,* and *f,* produce an effect which some recognized to be imitative of any thing *sharp* and *cutting;* for example :

> What 's this ? a sleeve ? 'T is like a demi-cannon ;
> What ! up and down, carved like an apple-tart ?
> Here 's snip and nip, and cut and slish and slash.
> Like to a censor in a barber's shop.
> —*Taming the Shrew*, iv., 3 : *Shakespear.*

> And thou hast talked
> Of sallies and retires ; of trenches, tents,
> Of palisadoes, frontiers, parapets ;
> Of basilisks, of cannon, culverin ;
> Of prisoners' ransom, and of soldiers slain,
> And all the current of a heady fight.
> —1 *Henry IV.*, ii., 3 : *Shakespear.*

> The clouds were fled
> Driven by a keen north wind that blowing dry
> Wrinkled the face of deluge.
> —*Par. Lost*, II : *Milton.*

> The whistler shrill that whoso hears doth die.
> —*F. Q.*, 2, 12, 36 : *Spenser.*

> And at the point two stings infixèd are,
> Both deadly sharp, that sharpest steel exceeden far.
> But stings and sharpest steel did far exceed
> The sharpness of his cruel rending claws.
> —*F. Q.*, 1, 11, 11 : *Spenser.*

The poetic *orotund* imitates any thing that sounds *full* and *round*. It is admirably alternated with pure quality in the following :

> The old song sounds hollower in mine ear
> Than thin keen sounds of dead men's speech—
> A noise one hears and would not hear ;
> Too strong to die, too weak to reach
> From wave to beach.
> —*Felise : Swinburne.*

In connection mainly with the more orotund vowels, *m, n,* and *ng* always, and *b, d, v,* and *l,* when their preliminary sounds are prolonged, produce tones resembling the *low notes* of musical instruments, or the *murmur* or *hum* of insects, men, or other objects moving at a distance ; for example :

> Married to immortal verse ;
> Such as the meeting soul may pierce,
> In notes with many a winding bout
> Of linked sweetness long drawn out,
> With wanton heed and giddy cunning ;
> The melting voice through mazes running,
> Untwisting all the chains that tie
> The hidden soul of harmony.
> —*L'Allegro : Milton.*

> —Every sound is sweet ;
> Myriads of rivulets hurrying through the lawn,
> The moan of doves in immemorial elms,
> And murmuring of innumerable bees.
> —*The Princess : Tennyson.*

> Sweet bird, that shun'st the noise of folly,
> Most musical, most melancholy.
> —*Il Pensero : Milton.*

> The bum-cock humm'd wi' lazy drone,
> The kye stood rowtin' i' the loan.
> —*The Twa Dogs : Burns.*

> Where each old poetic mountain
> Inspiration breathed around,
> Every shade and hallowed fountain
> Murmured deep a solemn sound.
> —*The Progress of Poesy : Gray.*

In his "Expression of the Emotions," Darwin taking

a suggestion from Wedgeworth's "Origin of Language," surmises that sounds of *m* and *n* found in negations like *nay* and *no* may be traced to the noises made by children when refusing food. In our own language, as in most others, the *n* especially seems to have this negative effect.

> To whom our Saviour sagely thus replied :
> " Think not but that I know these things, or think
> I know them not : nor therefore am I short
> Of knowing what I ought ; he who receives
> Light from above, from the fountain of light,
> No other doctrine needs, though granted true ;
> But these are false, or little else but dreams,
> Conjectures, fancies built on nothing firm,
> The first and wisest of them all professed
> To know this only, that he nothing knew."
> —*Paradise Reg.*, 4 : *Milton.*

> Fear naught—nay that I need not say—
> But doubt not aught from mine array.
> * * * * *
> Nor would I call a clansman's brand
> For aid against one valiant hand.
> —*Lady of Lake*, 5 : *Scott.*

> The hand of Douglas is his own,
> And never shall in friendly grasp
> The hand of such as Marmion clasp.
> —*Marmion*, 6 : *Idem.*

By combining the sounds of consonants and vowels in fulfilment of the principles just mentioned, or of others like them, all of our best poets are constantly producing effects that are distinctively imitative. For instance, hear the knife *carving* the ivory in this:

> Ancient rosaries,
> Laborious orient ivory, sphere in sphere.
> —*The Princess : Tennyson.*

And the *loud dashing* and *soft rippling* of the *waves* in these:

> Roared as when the rolling breakers boom and blanch on the precipices.
> —*Böadicea : Idem.*

> The murm'ring surge
> That on the unnumber'd idle pebbles chafes.
> —*Lear*, iv., 6 : **Shakespear.**

And the ice and rocks, resounding with the *clanging* of *armor* and *footsteps* in this :

> Dry clashed his harness in the icy caves
> And barren chasms, and all to left and right
> The bare black cliff clanged round him as he based
> His feet on juts of slipp'ry crag that rang
> Sharp smitten with the dint of armèd heels.
> —*Mort D'Arthur :* **Tennyson.**

And the *roar* and *clash* and *speed* of *warriors* and their chariots and *weapons* in this :

> ——nor stood at gaze
> The adverse legions, nor less hideous joined
> The horrid shock. Now storming fury rose
> And clamor, such as heard in heaven till now
> Was never ; arms on armor clashing bray'd
> Horrible discord, and the madding wheels
> Of brazen chariots raged ; dire was the noise
> Of conflict ; overhead the dismal hiss
> Of fiery darts in flaming vollies flew,
> And flying vaulted either host with fire.
> —*Paradise Lost*, 6 : **Milton.**

And the smooth *water, lapping* the body of the swimmer in this :

> And softlier swimming with raised head
> Feels the full flower of morning shed,
> And fluent sunrise round him rolled,
> That laps and laves his body bold
> With fluctuant heaven in water's stead,
> And urgent through the growing gold
> Strikes, and sees all the spray flash red.
> —*Epilogue :* **Swinburne.**

And the *cursing* and *shrieking*, *fluttering*, *crawling*, and generally *appalling character* of this:

> —and then again
> With curses cast them down upon the dust,
> And gnashed their teeth and howled ; the wild birds shriek'd
> And terrified did flutter on the ground,
> And flap their useless wings ; the wildest brutes
> Came tame and tremulous ; and vipers crawled
> And twined themselves among the multitude,
> Hissing but stingless—they were slain for food ;
> And War which for a moment was no more,
> Did glut himself again ;—a meal was bought
> With blood, and each sate sullenly apart
> Gorging himself in gloom ; no love was left.
> —*Darkness : Byron.*

And the climax of *confusion, overthrow*, and *horror* in almost every form, in this :

> The overthrown he raised, and as a herd
> Of goats or timorous flock together thronged
> Drove them before him thunderstruck, pursued
> With terror and with furies to the bounds
> And crystal wall of heaven, which opening wide
> Rolled inward, and a spacious gap disclosed
> Into the wasteful deep ; the monstrous sight
> Struck them with horror backward ; but far worse
> Urged them behind ; headlong themselves they threw
> Down from the verge of heaven, eternal wrath
> Burned after them to the bottomless pit.
> Hell heard th' insufferable noise, hell saw
> Heaven ruining from heaven, and would have fled
> Affrighted, but strict fate had cast too deep
> Her dark foundations, and too fast had bound.
> Nine days they fell ; confounded Chaos roared,
> And felt tenfold confusion in their fall
> Through his wild anarchy ; so huge a rout
> Incumber'd him with ruin ; hell at last
> Yawning received them whole, and on them closed,
> Hell their fit habitation, fraught with fire
> Unquenchable, the house of woe and pain.
> —*P. L.*, 6 : *Milton.*

In certain poems, as in fact in certain of the quotations already given, it is difficult to determine how far the effects correspond to those of dramatic or of discoursive elocution. We cannot clearly distinguish in them between that which is and is not strictly imitative. One of the finest examples of this kind which we have, is furnished by Robert Browning's *Holy-Cross-Day*, purporting to represent the feelings of the Jews in Rome, when forced, as was formerly the custom on that day, to attend church, and listen to an annual Christian sermon. Notice the concentrated *spite* and *scorn* represented in the qualities—mainly guttural and aspirate—of most of the sounds used. Only a part of the poem can be quoted; but the rest of it is almost equally effective :

> Higgledy piggledy, packed we lie,
> Rats in a hamper, swine in a stye,
> Wasps in a bottle, frogs in a sieve,
> Worms in a carcass, fleas in a sleeve.
> Hist! square shoulders, settle your thumbs
> And buzz for the bishop—here he comes.
>
>   *   *   *   *   *   *
>
> Aaron's asleep—shove hip to haunch,
> Or somebody deal him a dig in the paunch.
> Look at the purse, with the tassel and knob,
> And the gown with the angel and thingumbob.
> What's he at, quotha?—reading his text.
> Now you've his courtesy—and what comes next?
>
>   *   *   *   *   *   *
>
> Give your first groan—compunction's at work;
> And soft, from a Jew you mount to a Turk!
> Lo, Micah,—the self-same beard on chin
> He was four times already converted in.
> Here's a knife, clip quick—it's a sign of grace—
> Or he ruins us all with his hanging-face.
>
>   *   *   *   *   *   *
>
> Groan all together, now, whee-hee-hee!
> It's a work, it's a work, ah, woe is me!

> It began when a herd of us, picked and placed,
> Were spurred through the Corso, stripped to the waist;
> Jew-brutes, with sweat and blood well spent
> To usher in worthily Christian Lent.
>
> It grew, when the hangman entered our bounds,
> Yelled, pricked us out to this church, like hounds.
> It got to a pitch when the hand indeed
> Which gutted my purse would throttle my creed.
> And it overflows, when, to even the odd,
> Men I helped to their sins, help me to their God.
> —*Holy-Cross-Day : R. Browning.*

In the following, too, we have similar effects, partly imitative and partly not. In the last two lines of each stanza, calling for the echo, we hear the resonant poetic orotund. Aside from these, the poem begins in the first stanza with the hush of the aspirate:

> The splendor falls on castle walls
>   And snowy summits old in story;
> The long light shakes across the lakes,
>   And the wild cataract leaps in glory.
> Blow, bugle, blow, set the wild echoes flying.
> Blow, bugle; answer echoes, dying, dying, dying.

Then we have mainly the thin, clear quality of the pure tone:

> O hark, O hear! how thin and clear,
>   And thinner, clearer, farther going;
> O sweet and far, from cliff and scar,
>   The horns of Elfland faintly blowing!
> Blow, let us hear the purple glens replying;
> Blow, bugle; answer echoes, dying, dying, dying.

And, lastly, the deeper feeling indicated by the orotund:

> O love, they die in yon rich sky,
>   They faint on hill or field or river;
> Our echoes roll from soul to soul,
>   And grow forever and forever.
> Blow, bugle, blow, set the wild echoes flying,
> And answer echoes, answer, dying, dying, dying.
> —*The Bugle, from the Princess : Tennyson.*

CHAPTER XIII.

THE SACRIFICE OF SENSE TO SOUND.

Verse in which Attention to Sound prevents Representation of Thought—Violating Laws of Natural Expression or Grammatical Construction—Excellences exaggerated, the Source of these Faults—Insertion of Words, Pleonasm, Superfluity ; Transposition of Words, Inversion, Hyperbaton, tending to Obscurity—Style of the Age of Dryden—Alteration of Words in Accent ; or by Aphæresis, Front-Cut ; Syncope, Mid-Cut ; or Apocope, End-Cut—All these often show Slovenly Workmanship.

THE theory underlying all that has been said thus far is, that poetry is an artistic development of language; its versification, of the pauses of natural breathing; its rhythm and tune, of the accents and inflections of ordinary conversation ; and the significance in its sounds, of ejaculatory and imitative methods actuating the very earliest efforts of our race at verbal expression. The inference suggested has been that these effects produced by sound are legitimate in poetry, because, like language, and as a part of it, and far more significantly than some forms of it, they represent thought. This inference necessarily carries with it another, which it seems important to emphasize before we leave this part of our subject. It is this,—that no effects produced by sound are legitimate in poetry, which fail in any degree to represent thought. If a man's first impression on entering a picture-gallery comes from a suggestion of paint, he may know that he is not in the presence of the masters. So if his first impression on beginning to read verse comes from a suggestion of jingle, of sound or of form of any kind not connected in some most intimate way with an appeal to his higher æsthetic nature, he may be sure that the lines before him do not entitle their author to a high poetic rank. As I intend to show further on, all artistic poetry must produce the effects of form, but these include impressions recognized not only by the outer ear, but also by the inner mind. It is because of the exceeding difficulty of perfectly adjusting sound to thought and thought to sound, till, like perfectly attuned strings of a perfect instrument, both strike together in all cases so as to form a single chord of a perfect harmony, that there are so few great poets. Before we pass on, therefore, let us notice a few of the more prominent ways in which writers, because of their endeavor to conform their expressions to the requirements of mere versification, fail to make them conform to the requirements of language, fail to make them represent thought.

In making this examination, we shall be compelled to take for our standard the language of ordinary intercourse. Poetic form necessitates a peculiar selection and arrangement of words and phrases. But if these violate the laws of natural expression or of grammatical construction, as exemplified in the language of prose, their meanings may be obscured entirely, or, if not so, will, at least, be conveyed through forms that seem artificial. It was for these reasons that Wordsworth argued that there should be no difference between the language of poetry and of prose. In his own practice he sometimes carried out his theory only too faithfully; but a truth underlay it, which always needs to be borne in mind. The problem in connection with all versification is, how to arrange words at once metrically and naturally. We all recognize that certain poets are able to do this, and that this fact tends to increase their popularity. It is one of the chief charms of the poetry of Longfellow. Notice this for instance:

> Lives of great men all remind us
>   We can make our lives sublime,
> And, departing, leave behind us
>   Footprints on the sands of time.
> —*Psalm of Life.*

Lines like these seem very easy to write; yet a book filled with lines like these is very difficult to write. Few poets could arrange vowels and consonants so as to produce such rhythmical and musical effects, without impairing, somewhat, the naturalness of their phraseology. Their departures from the latter, in order to satisfy the demands of the former, usually manifest themselves in one of five different ways, viz.: in the *insertion*, the *transposition*, the *alteration*, the *omission*, or the *misuse* of words.

All these, as we shall find, are exaggerations of tendencies, which, kept in due subordination, or used to increase the effect of the thought and not of the sound alone, are excellences. The first fault mentioned, for instance, the *insertion* of words not needed for the sense, termed also *pleonasm*, or *superfluity*, grows out of a legitimate endeavor to enhance the impressiveness of what is presented. In the following, the very fact that the prayer is made the chief object of observation, makes it proper, not only, but desirable, to bring in an otherwise useless *he*, in order to represent rightly the order of the thought:

> His prayer he saith, this patient holy man.
> —*Eve of St. Agnes : Keats.*

So, in these lines, the author's putting the words *wind*

SACRIFICE OF SENSE TO SOUND. 153

and *ship* before the apparently superfluous pronouns, really adds as much to the thought as if he had written a separate sentence, calling our attention to these objects. In reading his words, we think first of the objects as existing, and then of what they did:

> The wind it blew, and the ship it flew
> And it was "Hey for hame."
>   *   *   *   *   *
> And then the good ship, she lay to
>   *   *   *   *   *
> The skipper, he louted to the king.
> —*The Earl o' Quarterdeck*: George MacDonald.

Even actual repetition, in certain cases the worst form of pleonasm, is not always a defect. Who does not perceive how much of the impressiveness of these lines depends on the repetition of the word red?

> The light that seemed a twinkling star
> Now blazed portentous, fierce and far,
> Dark-red the heaven above it glowed,
> Dark-red the sea beneath it flowed,
> Red rose the rocks on ocean's brim,
> In blood-red light her islets swim.
> —*Lord of the Isles* 5: Scott.

Or who could wish to have the second of these lines omitted?

> They glide like phantoms into the wide hall;
> Like phantoms, to the iron porch they glide,
> —*Eve of St. Agnes*: Keats.

But when the words producing the pleonasms merely fill out the form of the phraseology, and help the metre without amplifying or aiding the thought, then, like verbosity in prose, they weaken the passage in which they occur. Notice how the same thought is repeated in different lines of the following:

> The spacious firmament on high
> With all the blue ethereal sky,
> And spangled heavens, a shining frame,
> Their great Original proclaim.
> —*Hymn: Addison.*

Notice too the italicized words, evidently placed in this merely to make out the line and rhyme:

> Here he lives in state and bounty,
> Lord of Burleigh, *fair and free;*
> Not a lord in all the country
> Is so great a lord as he.
> —*Lord of Burleigh: Tennyson.*

To condemn *fair and free* for the reason given, may seem hypercritical; but probably all will recognize that at least in the two following stanzas, there are many words used for no higher purpose than the one just mentioned. If so, what is it that they represent?—the poet's thought?—Why not rather his lack of thought?

> Across a deep swift river, and the door
> Shut fast against him, did he see therein,
> Where through with trembling steps he passed before,
> That happy life above all lives to win,
> And round about him the sharp grass and thin
> Covered low mounds that here and there arose,
> For to his head his forerunners were close.
>
> Then with changed voice he moaned, and to his feet
> Slowly he gat, and 'twixt the tree-boles gray
> He 'gan to go, and tender words and sweet
> Were in his ears, the promise of a day
> When he should cast all troublous thoughts away.
> He stopped and turned his face unto the trees
> To hearken to the moaning of the breeze.
> —*The Man Who Never Laughed Again: W. Morris.*

The *transposition* of words, called too *inversion* and *hyperbaton*, is also, like the insertion of them, a development of a tendency not only legitimate but essential to the highest excellence, wherever the thought can be thus more strikingly represented; as, for instance, in the following, where the phraseology pictures the influence described in the order of its course from its beginning to its end :

> From harmony, from heavenly harmony
>   This universal frame began :
>   From harmony to harmony
> Through all the compass of the notes it ran,
> The diapason closing full in man.
>   —*Song for St. Cecilia's Day : Dryden.*

Or in the opening lines of the *Paradise Lost*, in which Milton, following the examples of Homer and Virgil and Dante in their great epics, transposes the clauses of the introductory sentence so that the thought which is to form the theme of the poem, and to which he wishes to attract the reader's first attention, shall be read first :

> Of man's first disobedience, and the fruit
> Of that forbidden tree, whose mortal taste
> Brought death into the world, and all our woe, . . .
> Sing heavenly Muse.
>   —*Paradise Lost, I.*

Keats opens his *Hyperion* in a similar way :

> Deep in the shady sadness of a vale,
> Far sunken from the healthy breath of morn,
> Far from the fiery noon and eve's one star,
> Sat gray-eyed Saturn, quiet as a stone.

And we all can recall the arrangement for analogous reasons of Shakespeare's description of the death of Cæsar.

> Then burst his mighty heart.
>   —*Julius Cæsar*, iii., 2.

But transposition of the words for the sake of the thoughts in them is one thing, and for the sake of the sounds in them, is another. In the latter case, it may become a very serious fault, rendering the phraseology not only obscure but artificial. The following, for instance, is obscure:

> "But reason thus : 'If we sank low,
> If the lost garden we forego,
> Each in his day, nor ever know
>   But in our poet-souls its face ;
> Yet we may rise until we reach
> A height untold of in its speech—
> A lesson that it could not teach
>   Learn in this darker dwelling-place.'
>
> "And reason on ; 'We take the spoil ;
> Loss made us poets and the soil
> Taught us great patience in our toil,
>   And life is kin to God through death.
> Christ was not one with us but so,
> And if bereft of Him we go ;
> Dearer the heavenly mansions grow,
>   His home, to man that wandereth.'"
>
> —*Scholar and Carpenter* : *Jean Ingelow.*

The following, illustrating the same fault, is a good example of the artificial, stilted, heroic couplet, which was the fashion in the times when it was written. It was against this style that Wordsworth was arguing when he asserted that poetic language from Pope's *Translation of Homer* to Darwin's *Temple of Nature* could "claim to be poetic for no better reason than that it would be intolerable in conversation or in prose."

> For while he mischief means to all mankind,
> Himself alone the ill effects does find ;
> And so like witches justly suffers shame,
> Whose harmless malice is so much the same.
> False are his words, affected is his wit ;
> So often he does aim, so seldom hit ;
> To every face he cringes while he speaks,
> But when the back is turned the head he breaks.
>
> —*Essay upon Satire* : *Dryden.*

The chief characteristic of this style is evidently a determination to produce rhyme and a sort of metrical balance in the lines, no matter how unnatural the effects may seem, as compared with the language of prose. What is remarkable, too, is that, with all this preponderating devotion to the supposed requirements of form, there appears to be, both in Pope and Dryden, a marked absence of any desire to produce the finer qualities of sound, like those of assonance, phonetic syzygy and gradation, which make poetry really musical. With all their transpositions, they never succeeded in producing the purely melodious effects of Tennyson and Longfellow.

By the *alteration* of words is meant either the changing of their conventional accents, or the adding to them or taking from them of letters or syllables. In some cases, these changes may augment the effect of the thought. On account of their real or supposed resemblance to archaic, dialectic, or colloquial uses of language, and for the very reason that the words are not in the highest sense elegant, they emphasize the fact that the style is natural for the circumstances; and the very quaintness of it, like the rustic air and dress of an otherwise pretty maiden, adds to its attractiveness. Thus Thomas Chatterton, in *Bristowe Tragedy*, in connection with many changes in spelling which need not be noted here, alters *parts*, *crows*, *spectacle*, and *noble*; *e. g.*:

   The bloody axe his body fair
    Into four parties cut ;
   And every part and eke his head,
    Upon a pole was put.

   One part did rot on Kynwulft hill,
    One on the minster tower,
   And one from off the castle gate,
    The crowen did devour ;

> The other an St. Powle's good gate,
>   A dreary spectacel ;
> Its head was placed on the high cross,
>   In high street most nobel.

As we should expect from a dialect writer, the poems of Burns are full of examples of this.

> For a' that and a' that,
>   Their tinsel show and a' that,
> The honest man, though e'er sae poor,
>   Is king o' men for a' that.
> 						—*Is there for honest Poverty.*

> Heard ye o' the tree o' France,
> I watna what 's the name o' 't.
> 						—*Tree of Liberty.*

And Shakespear, in this single sentence, shortens one word and lengthens another.

> I 'gin to be a-weary of the sun.
> 						—*Macbeth*, v., 5.

Notwithstanding cases in which these alterations are appropriate, it is easy to see that the tendency causing them may be carried too far. For every legitimate effect produced by them, there are scores of instances in which nothing better can be said of them than that they represent slovenly workmanship. This is true sometimes of forms so familiar to us that the altered words seem scarcely to be altered at all; as, for instance, in cases of *aphæresis* or *front-cut*, like *I 'll, he 's, 't is, 'neath, 'tween;* of *syncope* or *mid-cut*, like *o'er, e'en, e'er;* and of *apocope* or *end-cut*, like *o', wi'*, and *i'*. Whatever may be thought of these cases, however, there is no doubt about the effects of less familiar changes. Notice the following:

> But peaceful was the night
> Wherein the Prince of Light

His reign of peace upon the earth began ;
　The winds with wonder whist
　Smoothly the waters kist,
Whispering new joys to the mild oceàn.
　　　　　　　　—Hymn on the Nativity : Milton.

　　I joyless view thy rays adorn
　　The faintly markèd distant hill.
　　　　　　　　　—Lament : Burns.

　　And at his side by that same tide
　　Came bar and beam alsò.
　　　　　　　— Winstanley : Jean Ingelow.

And so sepùlchred in such pomp dost lie,
That kings for such a tomb would wish to die.
　　　　　　　　—On Shakespear : Milton.

　　Shall my foolish heart be pined
　　'Cause I see a woman kind ;
　　Or a well disposèd nature
　　Joinèd with a lovely feature ?
　　　　　　　　—The Manly Heart : G. Wither.

　　A shield that gives delight
　　Even to the enemies' sight,
Then when they're sure to lose the combat by 't.
　　　　　　　　—To Mr. Hobbes : Cowley.

Slowly he gat and 'twixt the tree-boles gray
He 'gan to go.
　—The Man Who Never Laughed Again : Wm. Morris.

　　I stand 'mazèd in the moonlight.
　　　　　　　　—The Unbeloved : Massey.

Yet are 'ware of a sight, yet are 'ware of a sound.
　　　—A Rhapsody of Life's Progress : Mrs. Browning.

　　O perfect love that 'dureth long.
　　　—Afternoon at a Parsonage : Jean Ingelow.

　　And 'plaineth of love's disloyalties.
　　　　　　　　—Divided : Jean Ingelow.

The fact that some of these latter words were once used in English without prefixes, does not excuse these

elisions. Most readers feel that this had nothing to do with their appearance in the particular places where we find them, and that they were used here solely because their writers did not exercise the skill needed in order to construct their lines so as to contain words like *amazed, aware, endureth,* and *complaineth.*

If nothing else can show us the inappropriateness of these changes in serious poetry, the way in which they are used for comic effects should do it ; for example :

> Stick close to your desks, and never go to sea,
> And you all may be rulers of the queen's navee.
> —*Pinafore : Gilbert.*

> I du believe in prayer an' praise
>   To him—that hez the grantin'
> O' jobs ; in every thin' thet pays ;
>   But most of all in cantin' ;
> This doth my cup with marcies fill,
>   That lays all thought o' sin to rest ;
> I don't believe in princerple,
>   But, O ! I du in interest.
> —*Bigelow Papers : Lowell.*

CHAPTER XIV.

SACRIFICE OF SENSE TO SOUND CONTINUED.

Omission of Words or Ellipsis indicating Crudeness—Leading to Obscurity because Meanings are conveyed by Phrases as well as by Words—Misuse of Words, Enallage—Poetic Sounds are Artistic in the Degree in which they really represent Thought and Feeling.

THE alteration of words leads to results far less serious than the *omission* of them, which is the fault that we have next to consider; for while the former makes the style less natural, and, so far as art is to be judged by the standards of nature, less artistic, the latter makes it less useful, at times, indeed, well-nigh unintelligible. Omission or *ellipsis* is an exaggeration of terseness in style, which is often a great excellence. In all kinds of writing, but especially in that appealing to the imagination, it is a fault to express too much. Those to whom poetry is naturally addressed derive their main satisfaction and therefore interest, from that which influences them in the way of suggestion, leaving their fancies free to range where and as they will. Notice in the following how much the ellipses—and there are many of them—add to the vivaciousness of the effect, and at the same time how little they detract from its clearness.

Coriolanus.—Hear'st thou, Mars?
Aufidius.—Name not the god, thou boy of tears—
Coriolanus.—Ha!
Aufidius.—No more.

Coriolanus.—Measureless liar, thou hast made my heart
Too great for what contains it.   Boy !—O slave !—
Pardon me lords, 't is the first time that ever
I was forced to scold.   Your judgments, my grave lords,
Must give this cur the lie . . .
Cut me to pieces, Volsces ; men and lads,
Stain all your edges on me !—Boy !   False houna,
If you have writ your annals true, 't is there
That like an eagle in a dove-cote, I
Fluttered your Volscians in Corioli :
Alone I did it—Boy !
                              —*Coriolanus* v., 6 : *Shakespear.*

    Beside its embers, red and clear,
    Basked, in his plaid, a mountaineer ;
    And up he sprung with sword in hand,—
    " Thy name and purpose ! Saxon, stand ! "
    " A stranger."—" What dost thou require ? "
    " Rest and a guide, and food and fire.
    My life 's beset, my path is lost,
    The gale has chilled my limbs with frost."
    " Art thou a friend to Roderic ? "—" No."—
    " Thou darest not call thyself a foe ? "
    " I dare ! to him and all the band
    He brings to aid his murderous hand."—
    " Bold words !—but, though the beast of game
    The privilege of chase may claim,
    Though space and law the stag we lend,
    Ere hound we slip, or bow we bend,
    Who ever recked, where, how, or when,
    The prowling fox was trapped or slain ?
    Thus, treacherous scouts—yet sure they lie,
    Who say thou comest a secret spy ! "
              —*Lady of the Lake*, 4 : *Scott.*

In using ellipses, however, there is always danger, as is suggested here in the last line but one, that the poet, in trying not to express his thoughts too fully, will fail to express them adequately, especially when he is beset by the additional temptation of omitting certain of his words in order to make his phraseology fit his metres. If he yield to this temptation, his style will manifest, if nothing worse, a crudeness and lack of skill inconsistent with the best artistic effects. Here are instances of this, in which the article is omitted:

> As frozen drop of wintry dew.
> —*Lady of the Lake*, 5 : *Scott.*
>
> The near approach of dreaded foe.
> —*Idem.*
>
> While Porphyro upon her face doth look,
> Like puzzled urchin on an aged crone
> Who keepeth clos'd a wondrous riddle-book,
> As spectacled she sits in chimney nook.
> —*Eve of St. Agnes : Keats.*

Here a pronoun is omitted:

> No foot Fitz-James in stirrup stayed.
> —*Lady of Lake*, 5 : *Scott.*
>
> Jumped from the wreck upon the reef to catch
> The hands that strained to reach (them) but tumbled back.
> —*Wreck of Grace of Sunderland : Jean Ingelow.*
>
> Though mixed with most unhallowed leven,
> That proved to those who foolishly partook (of it)
> Eternal bitterness.
> —*Course of Time*, 2 : *Pollock.*

Here a preposition and article:

> Right hand, they leave thy cliffs.
> —*Lady of Lake*, 5 : *Scott.*

Here a preposition:

> Made to look me and light me to heaven.
> —*A Poor Man's Wife : Massey.*

Here verbs are omitted: the whole stanza is quoted:

> No grasping at love, gaining a share
> O' the sole spark from God's life at strife
> With death, so, sure of range above
> The limits here ? For us and love,
> Failure ; but, when God fails, despair.
> —*Le Byron de nos Jours : R. Browning.*

This stanza shows the worst feature in these omissions,—their tendency to obscurity. In conventional language we derive ideas not only from words but from phrases; and we must hear the phrase as a whole, or its words may not only fail to convey clearly their intended meaning but may misrepresent it. The phrase *a girl of age*, for instance, used in the next quotation, means a girl who has arrived at her majority, and not at all the same as *a girl of an age*, which, presumably, is what the poet intended to say. So the phrases *in part, under way, by way*,—and a like truth might be affirmed of hundreds of others,—do not mean the same as *in the part, under the way*, or *by the way*. Hence we see that the omission of even an occasional article, apparently the least important of our words, may make a most important difference in the ideas communicated. Let us examine, now, another passage from that great master of the ellipsis, Robert Browning, and notice, again, how he drifts into obscurity, and this, too, where there is no occasion for it in the sense, nor gain from it in the effect. In order to express fully the meaning of the following lines, according to the methods of ordinary prose, one would be obliged to supply, of words that are omitted, seven pronouns, three articles, two prepositions, one adverb, two conjunctions, one factor of a comparison, three auxiliary and four principal verbs, as well as to change the mood and tense of another verb, and to transpose many of the words and phrases:

> So I said and did
> Simply. As simply followed, not at first
> But with the outbreak of misfortune, still
> One comment on the saying and doing—what?
> No blush at the avowal you dared buy
> A girl of age beseems your granddaughter,
> Like ox or ass?
> —*The Ring and the Book; Count Guido: R. Browning.*

Here is what this means, expressed in ordinary language:

>So I said, and did
>Simply. As simply *as I did it, there* followed,
>Not at first but with the outbreak of *the* misfortune, still
>One comment on the saying and doing *of it, which was*—
>   What *does this mean?*
>*Do you show* no blush at the avowal *that* you dared *to* buy
>Like *an* ox or ass,—
>A girl of *an* age *that might* beseem your granddaughter?

Of course it would not be necessary actually to insert all these words into this passage, to make plain prose of it. But they would all have to be *understood*, as grammarians express it. That is to say, in order to get at the meaning of Browning's forty-six words, it would be necessary for the reader to supply twenty-two words more. We all believe that poetry should appeal to the imagination. But is not this rather over-doing the appeal? Does it not involve too much of a stretch of the imagination for ordinary mortals? Is it a wonder, therefore, that some fail to catch all of this poet's meanings? Is it their fault or his that he feels impelled to write:

>Well, British public, ye who like me not,
>(God love you) and will have your proper laugh
>At the dark question, laugh it! I laugh first.
>   —*The Ring and the Book, Introduction.*

The *misuse* of words is the last of the faults that we have to consider in this connection; and it is the most objectionable, because while the others misrepresent the thought indirectly, this does so directly. Nevertheless, it, too, springs from the exaggeration of a tendency which, kept within bounds, may enhance the effect of the thought. It appears in its mildest form when by *enallage*, as it is called, one part of speech or one modification of a part of speech, like its number, mood, or tense, is used for another. Probably all of us can recall cases in which the thought to be expressed is made much more graphic and therefore distinct in its appeal to the mind through the use of this figure. Here, for example, a noun is used for a verb:

> I 'll queen it no inch further,
> But milk my ewes and weep.
> —*Winter's Tale*, iv., 3 : *Shakespear.*

Here an adjective for a verb:

> Be he ne'er so vile,
> This day shall gentle his condition.
> —*Henry V.*, iv., 3 : *Idem.*

Here adverbs for nouns:

> Full of all the tender pathos
> Of the Here and the Hereafter.
> —*Song of Hiawatha : Longfellow.*

Here a preposition for an adjective:

> I will fight
> Against my canker'd country with the spleen
> Of all the under fiends.
> —*Coriolanus*, iv., 5 : *Shakespear.*

Here a preposition for a noun:

> Yet long'st,—
> But in a fainter kind :—O not like me,
> For mine 's beyond beyond.
> —*Cymbeline*, iii., 2 : *Idem.*

Here one number for another:

> And see the lovely ladies gay,
> Step on in velvet gown.
> —*Winstanley : Jean Ingelow.*

Here an intransitive for a transitive verb:

> It yearns me not if men my garments wear.
> —*Henry V.*, iv., 3 : *Shakespear.*

And here one tense for another, by what is termed *metastasis*, and in this particular use of it, the *historical present*.

> Sudden a thought came like a full-blown rose,
> Flushing his brow, and in his pained heart
> Made purple riot ; then doth he propose
> A stratagem, that makes the beldame start.
> —*Eve of St. Agnes : Keats.*

The occasional use of these methods, however, in order to make the representation of the ideas more graphic, scarcely justifies that kind of poetic license which violates the laws of grammar and of lexicography, merely for the sake of form. Notice a few examples of this :

> *Sudden* his steed his leader rein'd.
> —*Lady of the Lake*, 5 : *Scott.*

> Who *instant* to his stirrup sprung.
> —*Idem.*

> You are one of many, the old Mayor said,
> That *on* the rock complain [for *of*].
> —*Winstanley : Jean Ingelow.*

> More *ruddier* too than is the rose
> Within her lovely face.
> —*The Portrait : Heywood.*

> And there was naught of *strange beside.*
> —*High Tide : Jean Ingelow.*

> I fell flooded with a *Dark*
> In the silence of a swoon.
> —*Bertha in the Lane : Mrs. Browning.*

> Do you know our voices
> Chanting down the *Golden ?*
> —*Drama of Exile : Idem.*

The worst thing that can be said of some of these, perhaps, is that they sound a little like slang. Here there is an ungrammatical arrangement of tenses:

> At last surrounds their sight
> A globe of circular light
>   That with long beams the shamefaced night *arrayed;*
> The helmèd Cherubim,
> And sworded Seraphim,
>   Are seen in glittering ranks with wings displayed.
>   —*Hymn on the Nativity : Milton.*

Graver instances of this fault occur, however, where, in order to produce sounds supposed to be desirable, words are used with little reference to their meanings, calculated, therefore, if interpreted literally, to convey ideas absurd or false. In this stanza, for instance, few can fail to suspect that the poet uses the word *countenance* because it alliterates with *decorum*, and contains a vowel-sound that goes well with *decorum* and *wore;* that he uses *ancient* because it forms an assonance with *raven*, and also *shorn and shaven*, because the latter word rhymes with *raven*. That is to say, these words seem to be used, and the number of them might be multiplied even in this stanza, not because they are the best through which to express the sense, but on account of their sounds.

> Then this ebony bird, beguiling my sad fancy into smiling,
> By the grave and stern decorum of the countenance it wore,
> "Though thy crest be shorn and shaven, thou," I said, "art sure no
>   craven;
> Ghastly, grim, and ancient raven, wandering from the nightly shore,
> Tell me what thy lordly name is on the night's Plutonian shore."
>   Quoth the raven, " Nevermore."
>   —*The Raven : Poe.*

Poe is given to such faults as these. Notice the incorrectness of words like *fully* and *distinctly*, as used in the following.

>   Yet the ear it fully knows,
>   By the twanging
>   And the clanging
>   How the danger ebbs and flows ;
>   Yet the ear distinctly tells,
>   In the jangling
>   And the wrangling
>   How the danger sinks and swells,
>   By the sinking or the swelling in the anger of the bells,—
>   Of the bells,—
>   Of the bells, bells, bells, bells,
>   Bells, bells, bells,—
>   In the clamor and the clangor of the bells.
>
>   —*The Bells.*

The same fault is apparent in Swinburne, another great master of the music of verse, who occasionally allows the music to master him. Opening his *Studies in Song*, I turn to these stanzas. Am I to blame that, while reading them, I find myself instinctively asking: " Desire and require *what ?* What are the daysprings of *fire,* and how are they *beneath* him? How can harps *approve?* What sort of an appearance could descend through *darkness* to *grace* any thing? How does *breath* set free? And what possible connection can there be between most of the deeds detailed and the effects attributed to them? Of course a little reflection may enable me to make out the poet's meanings here. But they do not lie on the surface. His words do not clearly picture his thoughts. They are not distinctly representative. They are not in the highest sense, therefore, poetic.

>   There are those too of mortals that love him,
>   There are souls that desire and require,
>   Be the glories of midnight above him
>   Or beneath him the daysprings of fire :
>   And their hearts are as harps that approve him,
>   And praise him as chords of a lyre,

> That were fain with their music to move him
>   To meet their desire.
>
> To descend through the darkness to grace them
>   Till darkness were lovelier than light :
> To encompass and grasp and embrace them
>   Till their weakness were one with his might.
> With the strength of his wings to caress them,
>   With the blast of his breath to set free,
> With the mouths of his thunders to bless them
>   For sons of the sea.
>
> —By the North Sea.

The same lack of an exact and, therefore, of a distinctly representative and graphic use of terms is apparent in words like *frank, bounteous,* and others too in this stanza, further on in the same poem ; and why did the poet obscure his meaning by using *of* and *for* in the third line ?

> Rose triumphal, crowning all a city,
>   Roofs exalted once with prayer and psalm,
> Built of holy hands for holy pity,
>   Frank and fruitful as a sheltering palm.
> Church and hospice wrought in faultless fashion,
>   Hall and chancel bounteous and sublime,
> Wide and sweet and glorious as compassion,
>   Filled and thrilled with force of choral chime.
>
> —Idem.

It is not strange that one who has thoroughly at command the resources of the music of verse like Swinburne, or of suggestive ellipses like Browning, or of picturesque details like Morris, should occasionally, in the heat and exuberance of his creative moods, push his peculiar excellence altogether beyond the limits of legitimate art ; but it is strange that the critics who make it their business to form cool and exact estimates of literary work, should so seldom have sufficient insight to detect, or courage to reveal, wherein lie the faults that injure the style of each, and how they may be remedied. How can criticism be of any use except so far as in a kindly way it can aid in the perfecting of that on which it turns its scrutiny? And yet it is doubtful whether, amid all the eulogy and abuse which have greeted all the works of Robert Browning, any one, in private or in print, has ever told him plainly what those faults are—all so easy to correct,—but for which the man with the greatest poetic mind of the age would be—what now he is not—its greatest poet. And if criticism of this kind is needed by authors who have attained his rank, how much more by those who, with the imitative methods of inexperience, are always prone to copy unconsciously, and usually to exaggerate, the weak rather than the strong points of the masters! Many a young writer, doing this at that critical period of his life when a lack of stimulus and appreciation may wholly check one's career, has failed, notwithstanding great merits. All his ability in other directions has not compensated for his ignorance of the requirements of poetic technique. It was largely with a hope of aiding such, that this work was first conceived.

The conclusions that have been reached thus far concur in serving to prove that poetry as an art must have form, the very sounds of the single and consecutive words of which must represent the phases and movements, physical, intellectual, or emotional, of which they are supposed to be significant; and it has been shown that great poets like Shakespear, Spenser, and Milton are great masters of representative expression in this sense. It follows from these facts that no poet is artistically justified in producing effects of sound through any insertion, transposition, alteration, omission, or other use of words, that by violating the laws of grammar or lexicography obscures the meaning. "Like the organs of seeing and hearing," says Veron, in his "Æsthetics," "our intellectual powers are only able to expend a very limited amount of energy at one time. . . . If we be called upon to expend three quarters of our mental energy in disentangling and interpreting the symbols, it is obvious that we shall have but one quarter left for the appreciation of the ideas of the poet." This statement agrees not only with the most recent deductions of physiological æsthetics, but also with those of common-sense. The test of form in every case is its fitness to represent, at least clearly, if not, as it sometimes should, brilliantly, every line and color, every phase and movement, every fact and suggestion of the ideas to be expressed. If this test be borne in mind, there can still be plenty of poetic failures from lack of poetic ideas, but no failures from a mere lack of the very easily obtained knowledge of the rudimentary principles of poetic technique.

CHAPTER XV.

MEANINGS OF WORDS AS DEVELOPED BY ASSOCIATION AND COMPARISON.

Instinctive Ejaculatory Sounds, and Reflective Imitative Sounds, becoming words by Agreement, in Fulfilment of the Principle of Association or Comparison, can represent but a few Ideas—Other needed Words may be due to Agreement in using Arbitrary Symbols; it is Philosophical to suppose them largely developed by Tendencies underlying the Formation of Primitive Words—How these Tendencies lead to the Use of the same Word in Different Senses—In the case of Words whose Meanings depend on Association—How what refers to the Material comes to refer to the Immaterial—Words whose Meanings depend on Comparison—What refers to the Material is by Comparison used for the Immaterial—Great Varieties of Meanings are developed from the same Word by Continued Processes of Association and Comparison—A Knowledge of this fact, and its Results are Necessary to an Intelligent Use of Language.

IN the former part of this work we have considered ejaculatory and imitative sounds and the influence of the methods of their formation and arrangement upon poetic form, so far as sounds determine this. We have found that it is reasonable to suppose that by associating certain utterances with certain circumstances in which they are used, or by comparing them with the sounds of objects to which they refer, men in primitive ages learn what the utterances mean, and, consciously or unconsciously, agree to accept them as representative of similar meanings whenever or wherever heard. How to produce at will these representative sounds solves the first problem of all language. But it requires no proof to show that no large number of the objects that engage our thoughts can be represented either by their own peculiar ejaculations or by imitative sounds. For this reason it is held by some that perhaps the majority of our words are merely arbitrary symbols, by which they mean that agreement which is undoubtedly a chief factor in giving definite meanings to sounds is also a chief factor in giving us the sounds themselves. While there are reasons for this theory, it may be pushed too far, and hardly seems to accord with what we know of the action of the mind with reference to other analogous matters. It seems more philosophical to attribute the enlargement of the primitive vocabulary mainly to further developments of mental processes in some way analogous to those to which the formation of the very earliest words is attributable. Facts, too, so far as they are known, sustain this view.

To show that this is so, let us recall for a moment the methods of forming a word from an ejaculatory or imitative sound. This will start us in the right place from which to observe how continuous operations of the same method necessarily lead to the formation from the same sound, or the same slightly modified, of a multiplicity of words. Attention was directed in the former part of this work to the fact that the organs of speech are so constructed that usually the earliest articulated sounds made by the babe are *mama* and *papa;* and that the earliest persons to whom they are addressed are the mother and father; and that, for this reason, people speaking in scores of different languages have come to associate *mama*, which, as a rule, is uttered first, with an appeal to the mother; and *papa* with an appeal to the father. In a similar way, but attributed to comparison rather than association, it was said that imitative sounds become words. A man says *whiz* because the sound that he makes compares, at least sufficiently for his purpose, with one that he has heard; and when he and others have uttered it many times, it comes, by common consent, to mean what it does, and nothing else.

Now, with these facts in view, can we not perceive that, after a few words have been formed, the formation of others from them is inevitable? It is so, in the first place, because of the tendency of the mind to carry further in the same direction the same processes of association and comparison that have led to the formation of these earliest words; and, in the second place, because of the mind's tendency to economize labor. After men have accumulated a stock of primitive words, and have begun to reflect upon them, and to perceive the relations which they sustain to other things, they seem to recognize, in some subtle way, that they can save themselves the trouble of originating new sounds by using the terms already in vogue in more than one sense. A word applying to one thing can be made to apply to an altogether different thing, if only the two are similar in certain of their features or relations. If the principle connecting the two is merely one of association, if they are merely allied, then the new term is produced by a continuation of the process underlying the formation of words from ejaculations. If the principle connecting the two is one of comparison, if they are really alike, then the process continues that of forming words from imitative sounds.

Very often the two are only associated. Thus, a man is named after his employment, a Baker, a Smith, George a husbandman, Edward a protector of property; or after his country, York or Lancaster. Thus, a town or city is named after a man, like Columbus or America. Thus, things very subtle in their nature are named after others easily apprehended. Take, for instance, one of the earliest terms used to indicate that in man, which, as immaterial, cannot be adequately represented by any thing ejaculatory or imitative. "When," says Max Müller, " man wished for the first time to grasp and express a distinction " (and it will be noticed that he could never have wished to do this until he had entirely passed the period of the formation of the very earliest words) " between the body and something else within him distinct from the body, an easy name that suggested itself was breath. The breath seemed something immaterial and almost invisible; and it was clearly connected with the life that pervaded the body, for as soon as the breath ceased the life of the body became extinct. Hence the Greek name ψυχή, which originally meant breath, was chosen to express at first the principle of life as distinguished from the decaying body, and afterwards the incorporeal, the immaterial, the undying, the undecaying, the immortal part of man, his soul, his mind, his self."

There are other cases, however, in which the two things for which the same term is used may be compared; and in these cases, as has been said, there is a process analogous to that of forming words by imitation. As in imitation, a sound produced by the mouth is made to refer to an object producing a similar sound, because the two sounds are alike; so here a term used for one conception is made to refer to another, because the two conceptions are alike. Trench's "Study of Words," contains a large number of exemplifications of this. Notice, for instance, the way in which the word *kind* is derived from the word *kin*. In olden times, all were supposed to be enemies, except those belonging to the same tribe or of the same *kin;* only these therefore were *kind* to one another. But after a while all whose actions could be compared to those of kinned-men were called *kind*. Again, for centuries subsequent to the time when Christianity had been accepted by the cities of the Roman Empire, the inhabitants of the villages, or the *pagani* as they were termed, remained heathen; after a while all those who could be compared to the *pagani*, on account of their religious beliefs, were termed *pagans*. Later, in Europe the disciples of the great theologian Duns Scotus, were called Dunses. After a while all who might be compared with these, in that their views differed from those held ordinarily, were called *dunces*.

In forming words by comparison, as by association, terms applicable literally only to material conceptions come to refer after a time to those that are immaterial. Take words, for instance, describing the operations of the mind. We say that a man's thoughts are *pure*, *clear*, *mixed*, *muddled*, or *clouded*, and that he *expresses* and *impresses* them upon others; but only to material things like water, wine, or the atmosphere, can the former class of terms be applied literally; and only *into* or *out of* a material thing can another, and this only a material thing, be literally *pressed*. Evidently terms of this kind are used as a result of comparing the mental to the material process, to which in some regards it is analogous. Were it not possible to symbolize the one process in the other, it is obvious that many things which we desire to communicate, would remain forever unexpressed. We see, therefore, how essential to the very existence of language is this power which enables us to figure or picture an object or operation through referring to something which, though like it in some respects, is wholly different from it in others; as different from it as the paint and canvas of a portrait are from the flesh and blood of the person portrayed. We see, too, how the element of representation, which is essential to all art, is a factor in the very constitution of language from which poetic art is developed. We see also how the means of representation are furnished mainly by the objects and operations of nature; and this not only by those appealing to the ear, the sounds of which can be imitated, but also by those appealing to the eye, the appearance of which suggests words like *express* and *impress*. In fact, the uses to which the sights and sounds of nature are thus constantly put, make literally true a statement like this of Wordsworth:

>   I have learned
> To look on nature, not as in the hour
> Of senseless youth, but hearing oftentimes
> The still, sad music of humanity.
> —*Lines Composed above Tintern Abbey.*

Were it not for nature, where would be the music, the voice, the language, the symbolism, through which only thought can be represented?

It is superfluous to point out to those at all acquainted with this subject, how through continuing the kinds of comparisons that have been mentioned, one word may often come to have a large number of very different meanings. The noun stock, for instance, as Trench reminds us in his " Study of Words," is the old past participle of the verb *to stick*, and indicates any thing that is fixed in its character. Hence we speak of railway stock, family stock, gunstocks, stock in trade, live stock, stocks that ships are built on, etc. So from the word post, meaning placed, we get the terms, military post, official post, posting a ledger and a letter, a post-office, post-haste, etc.

Though all languages are largely composed of words, the meanings of which can be traced with comparative ease to causes similar to the ones just mentioned, these words are so familiar to us, we have become so accustomed to their conventional significance, that we seldom pause to inquire how they came to mean what they do. I can remember distinctly the moment when, as a boy, it flashed upon my mind that a term, having so obvious an origin as the Fourth of July, was not a grandiloquent word of many syllables, originated for the purpose of necessarily suggesting gunpowder and fireworks; but merely a phrase indicative of the fourth day of the seventh month. A similar revelation is constantly awaiting the mind that makes a study of other words. Similar revelations, multiplied by almost the whole number of words employed, must flash light through all the hidden depths that underlie the surface forms of one's vernacular, before he can understand them, and use them with absolute appropriateness. Especially is this so in the case of the words with which we are now dealing,—the words formed as a result of comparison; because these contain, far more decidedly than those derived from association, a representative or picturesque—what grammarians term a figurative—element. But before we go on to exemplify this statement, and in doing so, to trace out further than has yet been done how naturally the representative language of poetry is developed from ordinary language, let us consider the subject in another aspect.

CHAPTER XVI.

MEANINGS OF PHRASES AS DETERMINED BY ASSOCIATION OR COMPARISON.

Language, a Process in which Words and Ideas represented by them are used consecutively—How Words in Progression can represent Mental Processes—How Acts in Progression do this in Pantomime—How this is done when Words, as Symbols, are substituted for the Acts in Pantomime—How Subject, Predicate, and Object are put together—Subject, Predicate, and Object of a Complete Sentence, are the Beginning, Middle, and End of a Complete Process, of which all the Parts of Speech are Logical Parts—Examination of Certain Sentences—How the Meanings of them, considered as Wholes, depend on the Principle of Association or of Comparison.

AS was said, when treating of the representative nature of sounds, language is a form for thought, and thought implies mental activity, a process, a series of sensations and experiences, all of them exerting more or less influence upon one another. A single idea might be represented in a single word, but a series of ideas necessitates a series of words. How, now, can these series of words represent, with any thing like accuracy, internal processes of the mind, together with the necessary relationships and interactions that must exist between their constituting elements? Or, to begin at the right place, how can any series of external and material elements, even though they do represent a process, represent a process that takes place in thought? If we can come to understand this, it will be easy for us to understand how, according to a similar analogy, series of words can do the same.

Those of us who have been in countries with the languages of which we were not familiar, have, perhaps, improved our powers of origination, as well as started original conceptions in the minds of those about us, through presenting our internal processes of thought to men who had not ears to heed our English, in the form of pantomime. What other resource could we have, when thirsty or sleepy or wishing to hire a hack or take a sail? But suppose that we had been shut out from pantomime, and shut in to sound, how, according to the same analogy, could we have expressed our processes of thought through the latter medium? Had we possessed the power of rendering intelligible to others our references to our internal sensations, as well as to external objects and operations, by the use of exclamations, imitative sounds, and words derived from them by association and comparison,—how could we have combined all these elements in such a way as to represent in sound a process of thought? Is not the answer simple? Instead of taking two objects and joining or separating them, could we not have taken two names for these objects, and joined or separated these? or, if we wished to make our meaning still more intelligible, joined the names by putting between them an intervening exclamation expressive of assimilation; or separated them by putting there an expression of aversion? Could we not thus have represented in words what circumstances had prevented us from representing in pantomime? Instead of emphatically flinging ourselves on the floor, or pathetically resting our heads upon our hands, when, tired out in the evening, we desired to show our wish to go to bed why might we not have exclaimed "I—bed," or "I—oh—

bed"? Is not this precisely what, though put in different forms, we have heard the foreigner do, a hundred times, perhaps, when trying to express in sound the thought which his ignorance of our language prevented him from expressing fully? Is not this precisely the method through which every child begins the difficult process of conversation—*i. e.*, by placing two words together, which thus constitute a compound word; or by uniting the two, one of which is used for the subject of a sentence and the other for its object, by a third, which serves the purpose of a predicate? And it is well to notice, too, in this connection, that, whether used by a foreigner or a child, the predicate is always the last essential factor of a perfect sentence to be used with accuracy. "I seen him," cried a street-boy under my window the other day; "and I throw'd a stone at him."

While on this subject, in order to show that the use of the exclamation for the verb in the illustration of a sentence just given, though fanciful, is not entirely out of analogy with what is really done in language, it may be interesting to recall what Max Müller says of one of our most common grammatical forms—*it is*. He tells us that this sound can be traced back almost as far in language as we can go. The German says *ist*, the Roman *est*, the Slave *yeste*, the Greek *esti*, and the Hindoo *asti*. But *asti* is a compound of the pronoun *ti* and the verb *as*, the root of which signifies to breathe. Whatever breathes exists or is; so that in the oldest language in which we find the verb, it seems to be only an expression representative of the fact, and, very probably, of the act of aspiration or breathing.

But, to return from theory to fact, we have found how it is possible to put words together in such a way as to indicate a process. Indeed, whenever we put them together in the right way, they necessarily do indicate this; for in such cases we put together sentences, and sentences invariably represent, if not physical, at least mental, processes, the subject, as a rule, indicating the beginning of them, the predicate the continuation of them, and the object, if there be one, the end of them. In fact, all the different grammatical parts of speech and modifications of them, viewed in one light, are merely methods of representing dependencies and relationships of different parts of whole processes, which, with more or less completeness, are represented by the sentences.

That we may perceive this and, at the same time, the degree in which all the different factors of the phraseology may be made to augment the force of the figures used in single words, let us examine a few sentences. As we do so, we shall find it possible to class all combinations of words under two heads, corresponding to those under which we have already grouped single words. The first class includes those depending for their meaning upon the principle of *association*, and the second, those depending upon the principle of *comparison*.

To get our bearings here, let us recall briefly that it has been said, with reference to the first class of words, that the emergencies or circumstances in which a certain exclamatory sound like *mama* or *papa* is used, cause men, on account mainly of its associations, to accept it as a word, meaning what it does; and that later, after a vocabulary has been partly formed, the same principle of association causes them to ally something for which they have a name with some other thing, and to use the same name for both, as when they call towns or implements after their founders or inventors. It has been said, again, with reference to the second class of words, that a certain sound proceeding from an object perceived by men is imitated by their vocal organs, and, on account of the *comparison* between the two sounds, the one that they have produced is accepted as a name for that which originally produced it, as when *cuckoo* is adopted as a term of designation for a certain bird; and that later, after a vocabulary has been partly formed, the same principle of comparison causes them to perceive that some conception for which they have a term, is like some other conception, and to apply the same term to it also, as when they use the word *clear* to refer both to the atmosphere and to the mind.

In accordance with the analogy of these two methods of determining the meanings of words, when used singly, we shall find that we determine also their meanings when used conjointly, *i. e.*, either by the *associations* which, when combined in phrases and sentences, the words suggest, or by the *comparisons* which they embody. To illustrate this, suppose that one says: "Their cultivated conversation and attire interfered with the effects of their depravity." The sentence, so far as concerns its meaning, is perfectly intelligible, and this because we have learned to *associate* with each of the words used, cultivated, conversation, attire, etc., a certain definite conception; and this conception comes up before the mind the moment that we hear them. But now, suppose the same thought is expressed, as in this sentence of Goldsmith: "Their finery threw a veil over their grossness." In this latter case, neither the word *finery*, nor *threw*, nor *veil*, nor *grossness*, has precisely the meaning that we are accustomed to associate with it. We do not understand the sentence precisely, until we consider it as a whole, and then not until we consider that the whole expresses a comparison. In other words, the sentence means what it does, not mainly on account of the ordinary associations of its words, but on account of the comparison which it embodies. Take another pair of sentences which perhaps will illustrate this difference more clearly. Let one wish to express an unfortunate change in the character of a man hitherto honest. He may say that " His integrity is impaired by severe temptation"; and in this case his meaning will be obvious, because men associate definite meanings with the words *integrity, impaired, severe,* and *temptation.* Instead of using this language, however, the man may select words indicating a comparison, and a series of comparisons. He may make a picture of his idea, representing the process of the change in character, by describing the process of an analogous change in nature. He may say: "His uprightness bends before some pressing blast." Notice how much more definitely we perceive the comparison, the picture, in *uprightness* than in *integrity,* in *bends* than in *impaired,* in *pressing* than in *severe,* in *blast* than in *temptation.* In this last sentence, we perceive at once, as in a picture, the character that stood straight up, the clouds that gathered, the storm that burst, and the ruin that ensued. The immaterial process is represented literally in the material one, and only in connection with this latter have words like *bends, pressing,* and *blast* any relevancy.

CHAPTER XVII.

POETIC AND UNPOETIC WORDS.

Words depending for their Meanings on Association not necessarily Prosaic; nor those depending on Comparison necessarily Poetic—The Latter necessitate Imagination to originate, and, at first, to interpret them, but after being used become Conventional—This the Natural Tendency of all Words—Poets can always cause Words to seem Poetic. First, by selecting those representing Poetic Associations—This applies to Conventional Words—Second, by arranging Words imaginatively so as to suggest New Comparisons or Pictures—Why English of Anglo-Saxon Origin is preferred by our Poets—Have Familiar Associations—Sounds fit Sense—Are used by us in Different Senses—Figures represented in Compound Words Apparent—In General more Significant—Why the English Language is fitted to remain Poetic.

IT is natural that some may suppose that the principles unfolded in the last chapter would carry with them the inference that series of words and sentences like " Their cultivated conversation and attire interfered with the effects of their depravity," or " His integrity is impaired by severe temptation," the meanings of which, as has been said, are determined by the *associations* which we have with the terms used, would be classed as prose; and that series of words and sentences like " Their finery threw a veil over their grossness," and " His uprightness bends before some pressing blast," the meanings of which are determined by the *comparisons* embodied in the expressions, would be classed as poetry. In fact, when men speak of poetic language, do they not almost invariably refer to language of the latter kind, *i. e.*, to words and phrases full of comparisons and figures? Let us weigh this question carefully and detect, if we can, just how much truth and how much error is in the idea underlying it.

In contrasting the sentences quoted above, two things claim our notice; first, that expressions of the *comparative* kind, like "His uprightness bends before some pressing blast," call forth a greater effort of the imagination both to compose and to interpret them; and second, that these expressions call forth a greater effort of the imagination when first produced or heard than afterwards. In fact, if often used to represent the same idea, there comes to be a time when any number of terms like *uprightness, pressing, bends,* and *blast* suggest no pictures whatsoever, except to one in search of them. They become at last no more significant than words depending for their meanings on *association;* and often less so. In reading them, we are conscious of no more than could be gained from unsuggestive arbitrary symbols. Even, therefore, though in the main poetic language were confined to these words embodying *comparisons,* this of itself would not suffice to keep the words in such a condition that men would recognize the pictures in them.

When words pass thus from the language of imagination where they start, into that of mere conventionality, they move according to a natural tendency exemplified in every phase of intellectual development. The unfamiliar never can be understood by us till classified on the ground of likeness to some other thing that we have known before. The earliest name assigned to the unfamiliar object represents this fact. The Indian's "horse that breathes forth fire," the "iron horse," the "locomotive,"— all, at first, present the mind with pictures. But after a little, men select and agree to use some single term for the object, and, when the term is uttered, it calls to mind this object and no other. In this way, words in every language are constantly becoming more exact in meaning, and not only so, but they are constantly accumulating. Different shades of meaning are perpetually assuming definite shape in forms of thought; as, indeed, is needed where the thought of each succeeding age is constantly becoming more complex as well as comprehensive. Of course, as words become exact in meaning, they have less in them suggestive of a different meaning. So, as a language grows conventional and scientific, it loses much of its imaginative and poetic force. When men have arbitrary symbols to express precisely what they wish to say, their fancies do not search for others to suggest what, at best, can but vaguely picture it. We hear them speak of engines and of locomotives, not of "horses breathing fire."

The question now arises: Amid circumstances like these must poetry succumb? If not, in what way can the poet overcome them? Certainly in one way only—by recognizing his conditions, and making the most of the material at his disposal. He must use a special poetic diction. In doing this two things are incumbent on him. The first is to choose from the mass of language words that have *poetic associations*. All our words convey definite meanings not only, but accompanying suggestions; and some of these are very unpoetic. Particular sights or sounds in the material world, or concepts in the mind, are instantly represented to the imagination, as well as presented to the understanding, when these words are heard. For this reason, therefore, though they do not in themselves embody *comparisons*, they are sufficiently representative, for a part, at least, of the purposes of poetry.

It is words like these, though not suggested in a like connection, that Grant Allen mentions in his "Physiological Æsthetics," when, carrying out his theory that "the purpose of poetry" is "the production of massive pleasurable emotion," because it "depends for its effect upon the unbroken succession of beautiful ideas and images," he says that terms like *violet, palfrey*, and *ruby*, because suggesting what is more pleasing, are more poetic than terms like *cabbage, donkey*, and *chalk;* and terms, in the sphere of light, like *scarlet, crimson, pink, orange, golden, green, blue, azure, purple*, and *violet*, are more poetic than *gray, brown, dun, black, bay*, and *drab*. So *brilliant, sparkling, sheeny, polished, lustrous, luminous, twinkling, glancing, silvery, pearly*, are more poetic, he says, than *dull, dingy, rough, turbid;* and *rounded, curling, graceful, lithe, flowing*, are more poetic than *straight, stiff, awkward*, and *upright;* and, in the sphere of sound, terms like *clear, ringing, silvery, musical, sweet, melodious, mellow, rich, low*, are more poetic than *shrill, hoarse, grating, harsh, loud*, and *croaking;* and, in the sphere of touch, terms like *soft, waxen, fleecy, smooth, delicate, slender*, are more poetic than *hard, rough, harsh, tough*, and *coarse;* and, in the sphere of smell, terms like *fragrant, sweet, perfumed, scented, odorous*, are more poetic than *stench* and *stinking;* and, in the sphere of taste, terms like *luscious, melting, honeyed, sugared*, are more poetic than *bitter, sour, biting, acid, acrid;* and, in the sphere of organic sensations, terms like *cool, fresh, buoyant, warm, easy, pure*, are more poetic than *hot, close, weary, cold*, and *chilly.*

Most of the words thus instanced,—only a small proportion of those in Mr. Allen's lists,—depend but little for their poetic or unpoetic effects, on any comparison suggested by their origin or expressed in the passage in which they are placed. They depend for these mainly upon the ideas that they conventionally represent—ideas invariably *associated* with them, whenever they are heard. This fact is enough to show us that the distinction between poetry and prose lies deeper than can be determined solely by the etymological character of the phraseology.

But there is a second thing incumbent on the poet in view of the present unpoetic tendencies of language. He must choose from the mass of language words that embody *poetic comparisons*,—choose them not only negatively, by excluding terms too scientific or colloquial, which, with material and mean associations, break the spell of the ideal and spiritual; but positively, by going back in imagination to the view-point of the child, and (either because arranging old words so as to reveal the pictures in them, or because originating new expressions of his own) by substituting for the commonplace that which is worthy of an art which should be æsthetic. Wordsworth did not exclude the unpoetic, disenchanting *comparison*, when in his otherwise beautiful, *She was a Phantom of Delight*, he wrote of his love:

> And now I see with eye serene
> The very pulse of the *machine*.

And Shelley did go back to the view-point of the child, when he wrote:

> And multitudes of dense, white, fleecy clouds
> Were *wandering* in thick *flocks* along the mountains,
> *Shepherded* by the slow, unwilling wind.
> —*Prometheus Unbound*, ii., 1.

Only a moment's thought will reveal to us that the principles just unfolded are closely related—in connection, however, with one or two other considerations—to that preference which almost all English poets exhibit for words of native or Anglo-Saxon origin, as distinguished from those derived from foreign sources, especially from the Latin through the French. "Remuneration?" says Shakespear's clown Costard[1]; "O that's the Latin word for three farthings." "Are you aware," says the author[2] of the "Strange Adventures of a Phaeton" to his heroine, "that, at a lecture Coleridge gave in the Royal Institution in 1808, he solemnly thanked his Maker that he did not know a word of that frightful jargon, the French language?" From the few contrasted expressions considered a little while ago, we can understand what Coleridge with his fine poetic conceptions probably felt. *Concealed, threw a veil over,*—*depravity, grossness,*—*integrity, uprightness,*—*impaired, bends,*—*severe, pressing,*—and others might be added to the list, *intelligence, understanding,*—*defer, put off,*—*divest, strip off,*—*retire, go to bed.* No one can fail to see how much more capacity for producing representative effects there is in the latter words of these pairs than in the former. This is so for several reasons. To begin with, as Herbert Spencer suggests in his "Essay on Style," the words of Anglo-Saxon origin include most of those used in our youth, in connection with which, therefore, through long familiarity with them, we have the most definite possible associations; whenever we hear them, therefore, they seem preëminently representative.

Then, too, we hear in the Anglo-Saxon derivatives, to a greater extent than in the foreign, the sounds which, when originally uttered, were meant to be significant of their sense. In fact, almost all the words instanced in another place as having sounds of this kind were Anglo-

---

[1] *Love's Labor Lost*, iii., 1.   [2] William Black.

Saxon. On the contrary, almost all our words derived from the Latin through the French have suffered a radical change in sound, both in the French language and in our own. Therefore their sounds, if ever significant of their meanings, can scarcely be expected to be so now.

Again, we know, as a rule, the history of our Anglo-Saxon terms, inasmuch as we still use them in their different meanings and applications, as developed by association and comparison. But foreign words are usually imported into our language in order to designate some single definite conception, and often one very different from that which they designated originally. All of us, for instance, can see the different meanings of a word like *way* or *fair* and the connections between them; but to most of us words like *dunce* and *pagans*, from the Latin *Duns* and *pagani*, have only the effects of arbitrary symbols.

One other reason applies to compound words. If the different terms put together in these exist and are in present use in our own language, as is the case with most of our native compounds, then each part of the compound conveys a distinct idea of its separate meaning; so that we clearly perceive in the word its different factors. For instance, the terms *uprightness, overlook, underwriter, understanding, pastime,* all summon before the mind both of the ideas which together make up the word. We recognize, at once, whatever comparison or picture it represents. In compound words of entirely foreign origin, on the contrary, it is almost invariably the case that, at least, one of the factors does not exist at present in our own tongue. *Integrity* meant a picture to the Roman. But none of us use the word from which its chief factor is derived. So we fail to see the picture. Nor do we use either factor of the words *depravity, defer, retire.*

For reasons like these our words of Anglo-Saxon origin are more representative of their sense, and hence more forcible and expressive, than our words of foreign extraction, even if, at times, less elegant and more homely. Homeliness, however, is not a wholly unpleasant characteristic. " Who can enjoy a chat with a man," says a writer in one of the old numbers of the *London Saturday Review*, " who always talks of women as *females*, and of a man as an *individual;* with whom things are never *like*, but *similar;* who never *begins* a thing, but *commences* it ; who does not *choose*, but *elects;* who does not *help*, but *facilitates;* nor *buy*, but always *purchases;* who calls a *beggar* a *mendicant;* with whom a *servant* is always a *domestic* when he is not a *menial;* who calls a *house* a *residence*, in which he does not *live* but *resides;* with whom a *place* is always a *locality*, and things do not *happen* but *transpire*. The little girl working in the brick-fields, who told the commissioners, ' We swills the spottles off us faces before we has us dinners,' made them understand exactly the degree of cleansing she went through. If the time ever comes when she will say instead, ' We perform our ablutions before we dine,' more will be left to guess-work. The cook-maid of the future may count up the dishes she has to wash, and expatiate on the toil of her task in pedantic English ; but when the char-woman of the present day says : ' He fouled a matter o' six plates,' there is a protest against luxury in the use of a verb that conveys more than the simple numbers would do if twice told."

The lack of representative power in the majority of words introduced from foreign languages, is probably one reason why, from Homer to Shakespear, poets have ranked highest who have written at an early stage in the history of a nation's language, before it has become corrupted by the introduction of foreign words and phrases. It may furnish one reason, too, why Dante, near the end of his life, thought fit to deliver lectures to the people of Ravenna upon the use of their vernacular. It may explain why Goethe, at the beginning of his career, turned his back upon the fashionable French language, and gave himself to the cultivation of the neglected tongue of his fatherland. At any rate, it does explain, as has been said before, why most of the great poets of England, from Chaucer to Tennyson, have been distinguished among other things for their predominating use of words derived from the Anglo-Saxon. These words still exist in our tongue; and fortunately, notwithstanding the natural tendency of all words to grow less poetic, they have lost little of their original significance and force; because side by side with them there exist other words, almost synonymous, derived mainly from Latin sources. The fact that these latter by common consent are used almost exclusively for the technical purposes of science, philosophy, and trade, thus leaving the Anglo-Saxon terms to the slighter changes and deteriorations that take place in literature, may furnish the best reason that we have for hoping that this composite language of ours will continue to be for centuries in the future, as it has been in the past, perfectly fitted to give form to the grandest poetry.

CHAPTER XVIII.

PLAIN AND FIGURATIVE LANGUAGE.

Two Kinds of Language used in Poetry, that depending for its Meaning on Association and that depending on Comparison—Distinction between the Term Figurative Language, as applied to Poetry and as used in ordinary Rhetoric—Figures of Rhetoric containing no Representative Pictures: Interjection, Interrogation, Apostrophe, Vision, Apophasis, Irony, Antithesis, Climax—Figures of Rhetoric necessitating Representative Language: Onomatopœia, Metonymy, Synecdoche, Trope, Simile, Metaphor, Hyperbole, Allegory—Laws to be observed, and Faults to be avoided, in using Similes and Metaphors—When Plain Language should be used—And when Figurative.

FROM the facts noticed in the last chapter, we may infer that two kinds of language—whether we apply this term to single words or to consecutive ones—can be used in poetry: that which depends for its meaning upon the *associations* which the words suggest, and that which depends upon the *comparisons* which they embody. The former corresponds in most of its features, but not in all of them, to what is ordinarily called plain language, and its words have a tendency to appeal to us like arbitrary symbols. The latter corresponds in a similar way to what is called *figurative* language, and its words have a tendency to appeal to us like pictures.

A distinction needs to be drawn, however, between the term figurative language as it is generally applied to poetic phraseology, and the same term as used in rhetoric. Many of the so-called "figures of rhetoric" scarcely necessitate using any actual figure at all, in the sense of representing one phase or process through mentioning another to which it is compared. They are little more than modifications of plain language. The moment we recall some of them, this fact will be apparent. Take, for instance, what is termed *Interjection*, the using of an interjection for a verb, as in, "Oh for a lodge in some vast wilderness"; or take *Interrogation*, the using of a question for a direct statement, as in, "Who then is Paul, and who is Apollos, but ministers by whom ye believed?" or take *Apostrophe*, the turning of a statement into an invocation, as in, "O death, where is thy sting? O grave, where is thy victory?" or take *Vision* or *Imagery*, the representation of what is in the past through the use of the historical present, as in "Cæsar leaves Gaul, crosses the Rubicon, and enters Italy," instead of "left Gaul," etc.; or take *Apophasis*, *Paralipsis*, or *Omission*, the pretended suppression of what one is all the time mentioning, as in, "I say nothing of the notorious profligacy of his character, nothing of the reckless extravagance with which he has wasted an ample fortune"; or take *Irony*, the statement of a fact or idea through using words which literally interpreted mean the opposite of what is intended, as in, "Oh yes, you are honest, you are, your actions show it!" or take *Antithesis*, the placing of opposite thoughts in juxtaposition so as to heighten the effect of each by contrast, as in, "Though grave yet trifling, zealous yet untrue"; or take *Climax*, the arrangement of a series of words, clauses or sentences in such a way that each, to the end of the passage, is of greater importance than the one preceding it, as in, "He not only spared his enemies, but continued them in employment; not only continued them in employment, but advanced them";—all these "figures of rhetoric" can be used, as will be recognized, without any very apparent exercise of the principle of representation.

There are others, however, of which this is not true. One of these, *Onomatopœia*, under the head of imitative sounds, as also several "figures of syntax" rather than "of rhetoric," have been considered in the former part of this work, and do not immediately concern us here, where we are dealing with the representation of one phase or process through employing words that refer to another. Of the figures that do concern us, it may be said, in general, that they all have a tendency to present the thought in some picturesque way. In all of them some special phase or process, which can be perceived, is used in order to bring vividly before the mind some other like it, which cannot be perceived,—at least, as easily. Ordinarily they are used in order to illustrate some general principle more or less abstract in its nature, and of wide applicability, as where Jacob in the Scriptures is made to say: "Judah is a lion's whelp," or Paul to say: "For me to live is Christ," each statement putting into the concrete form of a picture what it would take pages to express in full.

These figures, in which the pictures are perceptible, can be classified under two heads, corresponding to those already used in classifying words; they may be said to depend for their meaning largely upon the principle of *association*, or entirely upon that of *comparison*. The chief of the former class of figures—that, in fact, of which all of the class are varieties—is *Metonymy*. By this is meant a change of names between things related: as, *e. g.*, between *cause* and *effect*, as in: "When every rood of ground maintained its man," instead of "all the products of the ground," and "Gray hairs should be respected," instead of "old age"; between *place* and its *inhabitants*, as in:

"America is disgraced by speculators," instead of "the people of America"; between the *sign* and the *thing signified*, as in: "The sceptre shall not depart from Judah," instead of "the royal succession"; between *subject* and its *attribute*, as in: "A sleighful of youth and health," instead of "the young and healthy"; between *progenitor* and *posterity*, as in: "Hear, O Israel," instead of "descendants of Israel"; between *container* and thing *contained*, as in: "Our ships opened fire," instead of "the sailors" in them; between the *possessor* and the *thing possessed*, as in: "Drove the bristled lips before him," instead of "the man with the lips"; or between the *material* and the *thing made from it*, as in: "His steel gleamed on high," instead of his "sword."

A special form of metonymy is termed *Synecdoche*, which means the using of the name of a part for that of the whole, or the name of the whole for that of a part, or of a definite number for an indefinite, as in these: "The sea is covered with sails," instead of "ships"; "Our hero was gray," instead of "his hair"; "and "Ten thousand were on his right hand," instead of "a large number."

Trope is usually considered to be a general term applying to all *turns* of expression made through the use of single words, whether in the way of metonymy, synecdoche, or metaphor. But some hold that the trope embodies the principle of metonymy applied not, as that figure is, to nouns but to adjectives. Thus by a trope, according to Macbeth's "Might and Mirth of Literature," an adjective describing *one operated on* is assigned to the *cause*, as in, "the weary way" or "the merry bells"; an adjective *belonging to a subject* is bestowed on *one part or member of it*, as in, "religious footsteps"; an adjective true of an *agent* is applied to *his instrument*, as in, "coward sword"; an **adjective** belonging to the *possessor* is applied to the *thing possessed*, as in, "The gentleman with foolish teeth"; an adjective descriptive of a *season, place,* or *person* is assigned to an *object connected with it*, as in, "Winding its sultry horn"; an adjective proper to the *cause* is joined to *its effect*, as in, "the sweet load"; and an adjective qualifying the *thing worn* is made to qualify the *wearer* of it, as in, "The dogs far kinder than their purple masters."

We now come to the figures based directly and entirely on the principle of *comparison;* and, as they are the most clearly figurative, and as it is in using them that mistakes in imagery are most likely to occur, and as, if correctly used, they involve the correct use of all imagery of this kind,—in short, as they are typical of every form of representative expression, it is to these mainly that attention will be confined in our further discussions of this subject. The first of these is the *Simile*. In this, the comparison between one entity and another is made explicitly, and the two are usually joined by the words *like, as,* or *so,* as in, "He shall be like a tree planted by the rivers," "Christ is like a life-boat." The second is the *Metaphor*. In this, the comparison is made implicitly; it is taken for granted that the reader will supply the missing links, and no connecting *like, as,* or *so* is used. "He shall be a tree planted by the rivers," and "Christ is a life-boat," are metaphors. Here are others:

> And when the lark, the laureate of the sun,
> Doth climb the east, eager to celebrate
> His monarch's crowning.
> —*A Life Drama*, 2: *Alex. Smith.*

> I 've learned to prize the quiet lightning deed;
> Not the applauding thunder at its heels,
> Which men call fame.
> —*Idem*, 13.

The third figure is *Hyperbole*, which need not, but, as a fact, usually does, involve comparison. In the latter case, it is merely a simile with one of its factors exaggerated, as in, "They were swifter than eagles, they were stronger than lions." The fourth figure is *Allegory*. This is an extended simile, in which, however, only one of the two things compared is described at length, as in "Thou hast brought a vine out of Egypt, thou has cast out the heathen and planted it. Thou preparedst room before it, and didst cause it to take deep root, and it filled the land. The hills were covered with the shadow of it, and the boughs thereof were like the goodly cedars." It will be noticed that the last two figures involve no principles that do not apply equally to the first two. For this reason, our discussion of figurative language, as used in poetry, can practically be narrowed down to little more than a treatment of the uses and abuses of the simile and the metaphor.

Certain laws, with reference to the employment of these figures, have been determined by the criticism of the past, and are recorded as accepted principles in every ordinary Rhetoric. It may be well to refresh our memories by recalling these laws, as preliminary to what is to be said hereafter. The truth underlying them all is the fact, well understood with reference to both the simile and the metaphor, that nothing is gained by any use of these which does not add to the effect of the thought to which they give expression. For this reason, they are acknowledged to be faulty when the resemblance between the things compared is too *slight* to render the picture apparent, as in this:

> Give me thy crown.—Here, Cousin, seize the crown ;
> On this side, my hand ; and on that side, thine.

> Now is the golden crown like a deep well,
> That owns two buckets, filling one another ;
> The emptier ever dancing in the air,
> The other down unseen and full of water ;
> That bucket down and full of tears am I,
> Drinking my griefs whilst you mount up on high.
> —*Richard II.*, iv., 1 : *Shakespear.*

Or too *trite* to render the picture striking, as in repetitions of old, familiar, often-noticed resemblances, like these :

> Hearts *firm as steel*, as *marble hard*,
> 'Gainst faith and love and pity barred,
> Have *quaked like aspen leaves* in May
> Beneath its universal sway.
> —*Rokeby*, 2 : *Scott.*

Or too *apparent* to need mention, as in this, because all women are so much alike that the picture is not helped by directing attention to more than one :

> To Pales, or Pomona, thus adorn'd
> Likest she seem'd—Pomona when she fled
> Vertumnus—or to Ceres in her prime,
> Yet virgin of Proserpina from Jove.
> —*Paradise Lost*, 9 : *Milton.*

Or too *unintelligible*, as in this, because one of the things compared is not well known :

> What, dullard ? we and you in smothery chafe,
> Babes, baldheads, stumbled thus far into Zin
> The Horrid . . .
> . . . Potsherd him, Gibeonites !
> —*Sordello*, 3 : *Browning.*

Or too *unequal*, either because the subject illustrated is too great and dignified for that which is compared to it, as in this :

> And now I see with eye serene
> The very pulse of the *machine ;*

> A Being breathing thoughtful breath,
> A Traveller between life and death.
> —*She Was a Phantom of Delight: Wordsworth.*

Or because the subject illustrated is too small and insignificant for that which is compared to it, as in this:

> Loud as a bull makes hill and valley ring,
> So roared the lock when it released the spring.
> —*Odyssey*, 21 : *Pope's Trans.*

The above principles need only to be mentioned to have their reasonableness recognized. To some of them reference will be made hereafter; but attention will be confined chiefly to the two following, because in poetic representation it is these that chiefly interfere with excellence. The first is the "far-fetched" simile or metaphor, as it is called. In this, minor points of resemblance are sought out and detailed to such an extent that the main thought is liable to be forgotten, while attention is concentrated on subjects that really are of no importance except so far as they illustrate it. This fault and its effects will be amply treated in Chapter Twenty-sixth.

The second fault, to which special attention will be directed, is the "blending" and "mixing" of similes or metaphors. Both are manifestations of one tendency. The "blending" occurs when plain and figurative expressions are used with reference to the same object in the same clause or sentence. It is this fault, introduced into the text without warrant by the words used in the translation, that causes Homer in the following to speak of having a *column* torn from one's *embrace* without a kind *adieu*. Of course the picture here is not true to life, and in this sense is not representative:

> Now from my fond *embrace* by tempests torn,
> Our other *column* of the state is borne,
> Nor took a kind *adieu* nor *sought consent*.
> —*Odyssey*, 4 : *Pope's Trans.*

The "mixing" occurs when two different figures applying to the same object are used in immediate connection; as where Tennyson says, as if one had to *dip* in order to *see*, or could *see* with a *dipper:*

> For I dipt into the future far as human eye could see.
> —*Locksley Hall.*

Or Addison, as if he could *bridle* a *ship*, or *launch* a *horse:*

> I *bridle* in my struggling muse with pain,
> That longs to *launch* into a bolder strain.
> —*Letter from Italy.*

A still more important consideration with reference to these figures, and one that underlies the entire use of the language embodying them, is to determine in what circumstances thought and feeling should be expressed in them rather than in plain language. Fortunately, as an aid to our answer, both forms of language are natural to conversation; and by finding out their uses here, we may come to understand the principles that should control their use in poetry. To begin with, we must bear in mind that the object of language is to cause others to share our mental processes, to communicate to them the substance of our ideas and their associated feelings. In doing this, it represents both what a man has observed in the external world and what he has experienced in his own mind—not either one or the other, but invariably both of them. If a man, for instance, show us a photograph of something that he has seen, he holds before our eyes precisely what has been before his own eyes; but if he describe the scene in words, he holds before our mind only those parts of it that have attracted his attention; and not only so, but added to these parts many ideas and emotions of his own that were not in the scene but occurred to him when viewing it.

A similar added element from the man's mind accompanies every endeavor of his to tell what he has heard, or even, at some other time, thought or felt. From these facts, it follows that the aim of language, so far as this can be determined by what it actually and necessarily does, is to cause the same effects to be produced in the hearer's mind that are experienced in the speaker's mind. Now if one, when talking, conceive that this is an easy aim to attain; that what he has heard or seen or thought or felt, needs only to be told in clear, intelligible phraseology, in order to produce in another the same effects as in himself, then he will be content with conventional modes of expression; he will use in the main plain language, whether referring to what he has heard, as in this:

> And there was mounting in hot haste : the steed,
> The mustering squadron, and the clattering car,
> Went pouring forward with impetuous speed,
> * * * * * * *
> And near, the beat of the alarming drum
> Roused up the soldier ere the morning star ;
> While thronged the citizens with terror dumb,
> Or whispering, with white lips,—" The foe ! they come ! they come !
> —*Childe Harold*, 3 : *Byron.*

Or to what he has seen, as in this :

> Then from the shining car
> Leaped Hector with a mighty cry, and seized
> A ponderous stone, and, bent to crush him, ran
> At Teucer, who had from his quiver drawn
> One of his sharpest arrows, placing it
> Upon the bowstring. As he drew the bow,
> The strong-armed Hector hurled the jagged stone,
> And smote him near the shoulder, where the neck
> And breast are sundered by the collar-bone,—
> A fatal spot. The bowstring brake ; the arm
> Fell nerveless ; on his knees the archer sank,
> And dropped the bow. Then did not Ajax leave

His fallen brother to the foe, but walked
Around him, sheltering him beneath his shield,
Till two dear friends of his—Menestheus, son
Of Echius, and Alastor nobly born—
Approached, and took him up and carried him,
Heavily groaning, to the hollow ships.
—*Iliad*, 8 : *Bryant's Tr.*

Or to what he has thought, as in this :

By the world,
I think my wife be honest, and think she is not ;
I think that thou art just, and think thou art not.
I 'll have some proof.
—*Othello*, iii., 3 : *Shakespear.*

Ay, you did wish that I would make her turn ;
Sir, she can turn, and turn, and yet go on ;
And turn again ; and she can weep, sir, weep ;
And she 's obedient, as you say,—obedient,—
Very obedient.
—*Idem*, iv., 1.

Or to what he has felt, as in this :

Six feet in earth my Emma lay ;
And yet I loved her more,
For so it seemed, than till that day
I e'er had loved before.

And turning from her grave, I met,
Beside the churchyard yew,
A blooming girl whose hair was wet
With points of morning dew.

A basket on her head she bare ;
Her brow was smooth and white ;
To see a child so very fair,
It was a pure delight !

*   *   *   *   *

There came from me a sigh of pain
Which I could ill confine ;
I looked at her, and looked again,
And did not wish her mine !
—*Two April Mornings : Wordsworth.*

On the other hand, however, if a man conceive that the end at which he is aiming is difficult to attain; that what he has heard, or seen, or thought, or felt, either on account of its own nature, or of the nature of those whom he is addressing, is hard for them to realize in its full force, and with all its attendant circumstances, then, as his object is to convey not merely an apprehension but a comprehension, both complete and profound, of that of which he has to speak, he will dwell upon it; he will repeat his descriptions of it; he will tell not only what it is, but what it is like; in other words, he will try to produce the desired effect, by putting extra force into his language, and, in order to do this, inasmuch as the force of language consists in its representative element, he will augment the representation by multiplying his comparisons; his language will become figurative. It will be so for the same reason that the language of a savage or a child, even when giving utterance to less occult ideas, is figurative,—because he feels that the words at his command are inadequate to express or impress his meaning completely. Notice the exemplifications of these statements in the following, referring to what has been heard:

> A cry that shivered to the tingling stars,
> And as it were one voice, an agony
> Of lamentation, like a wind that shrills
> All night in a waste land where no one comes.
> —*Mort d'Arthur* : Tennyson.

> And the wide hum of that wild host
> Rustled like leaves from coast to coast,
> As rose the Muezzin's voice in air
> In midnight call to wonted prayer;
> It rose, that chanted mournful strain,
> Like some lone spirit's o'er the plain;
> 'T was musical, but sadly sweet,
> Such as when winds and harp-strings meet,

        And take a long, unmeasured tone,
        To mortal minstrelsy unknown.
                        —*The Siege of Corinth : Byron.*

To what has been seen :

        As when the ocean billows, surge on surge,
        Are pushed along to the resounding shore
        Before the western wind, and first a wave
        Uplifts itself, and then against the land
        Dashes and roars, and round the headland peaks
        Tosses on high and spouts its spray afar,
        So moved the serried phalanxes of Greece
        To battle, rank succeeding rank, each chief
        Giving command to his own troops.
                        —*Iliad*, 4 : *Bryant's Tr.*

To what has been thought :

        I had rather be a kitten, and cry mew,
        Than one of these same metre ballad-mongers ;
        I had rather hear a brazen can'stick turn'd,
        Or a dry wheel grate on the axle-tree ;
        And that would set my teeth nothing on edge,
        Nothing so much as mincing poetry.
        'Tis like the forc'd gait of a shuffling nag.
                        —1 *Henry IV.*, iii., 1 : *Shakespear.*

        She moves as light across the grass
          As moves my shadow large and tall ;
        And like my shadow, close yet free,
        The thought of her aye follows me,
          My little maid of Moreton Hall.
                        —*A Mercenary Marriage : D. M. Mulock.*

And to what has been felt :

        Oh, what a noble mind is here o'erthrown !
        The courtier's, scholar's, soldier's eye, tongue, sword ;
        Th' expectancy and rose of the fair State,
        The glass of fashion, and the mould of form,
        Th' observed of all observers, quite, quite down !
        And I, of ladies most deject and wretched,
        That suck'd the honey of his music vows,
        Now see that noble and most sovereign reason,
        Like sweet bells jangled, out of tune and harsh.
                        —*Hamlet*, iii., 1 : *Shakespear.*

CHAPTER XIX.

PROSE AND POETRY; PRESENTATION AND REPRESENTATION IN ITS VARIOUS FORMS.

Tendencies of Plain Language toward Prose, and of Figurative toward Poetry—Plain Language tends to Present Thought, and Figurative to Represent it—All Art Representative—But Plain Language may represent, and Figurative may present—Poetic Representation depends upon the Character of the Thought—If a Poet thinks of Pictures, Plain Language describing them will represent according to the Method of Direct Representation—If not of Pictures, he may illustrate his Theme by thinking in Pictures, and use Figurative Language according to the Methods of Indirect Expressional or Descriptive Representation—Pure Representation is solely Representative—Alloyed Representation contains some Presentation.

THERE is a subtle feeling in the minds of many, but especially of those who, with strong imaginations and delicate æsthetic sensibilities, have not improved their critical faculties by a wide acquaintance with the best poetry, that figurative language only is in the highest sense poetic. Whenever a feeling like this exists, it should be treated with respect; we may be sure that there is a reason for it. The feeling in the particular case before us, leads to an erroneous inference, as we must conclude from considerations already noticed, and this conclusion will be confirmed as we go on. But how about the origin of the feeling? It springs, as seems most likely, from the fact that plain and figurative language are judged less from the effects that they produce when actually used in poetry, than from the principles that appear to be exemplified in their formation. If carried to an extreme, the tendencies that lead to plain language move unmistakably toward prose, as those that lead to figurative language move toward poetry. The error just mentioned lies in mistaking tendencies for a consummation of them.

These tendencies, however, are important in their bearings upon the real distinction that separates prose from poetry. Let us for a little consider them.

Plain language, as we have traced it, is a development of the instinctive methods of expression used in natural ejaculations. These, by being *associated* with the circumstances in which they are uttered, come to be used as words; and, in a broad way of generalizing, there is a sense in which all words, no matter how originated, whenever they come to mean what they do on account of this principle, can be put in this class. But now, if we think a little, we shall recognize that, from the moment of the utterance of the first ejaculation to the use of the latest sound which means what it does merely because conventionally *associated* with an idea to which it stands in the relation of an arbitrary symbol, the tendency exemplified is a desire to *present* rather than to *represent* the thought or feeling.

Just the contrary, however, is true of *figurative* language. We have traced it to a development of the reflective methods of expression which arise when one hears and imitates for a purpose the sounds about him. The same tendency is carried out when he puts these sounds together, after they have become conventional words, so as to represent the relations between the sights about him, as in the terms *express, understand;* in fact, it is carried out in every case in which there is a use of imaginative or figurative language. This latter language, then, from its earliest source to its utmost development, exemplifies a tendency to *represent* rather than merely to *present* the thought or feeling.

This work has constantly maintained that art is representative ; and, bearing this in mind, we shall begin to get a glimmer of the reason why poetry, which is the artistic form of language, is associated in many minds with only these representative words or figurative modes of expression. But we have not yet reached the whole truth with reference to the matter.

It must be remembered that thus far we have been dealing mainly with single words or with a few of them arranged in single sentences. Each of these words or sentences may be supposed to express some single phase or process of the mind's experiences. But to express a series of these processes, as words usually do when used at all, we need a series of words and sentences. Now it is conceivable that, though each factor of the series when taken by itself, should merely *present* some single phase, all the factors when taken together should *represent* a series of these phases ; and it is equally conceivable that though each factor of the series when taken by itself should *represent* a mental phase, all the factors when taken together should merely *present* a series of these phases. In other words, it is conceivable that owing to the artistic use, not of single words but of series of them, plain language should *represent* the thought and feeling, and therefore be poetic; and it is equally conceivable that figurative language should merely *present* these, and therefore be prosaic ; prose, so far as it is determined by the mode of communicating thought, being the *presentative* form of that of which poetry is the *representative*.

These conditions which we have considered conceivable, we shall find to be true in fact; and for this reason poetic methods of communicating thought, considered as a whole, must be judged, precisely as was said in another place of poetic sounds, by the degree in which they *represent* the thought or feeling to which they give expression. Now what, in the last analysis must determine the method of the communication?—what but the method in which the thought itself is conceived in the mind of the writer? If he think in pictures, his words, whether or not picturesque or figurative in themselves, will describe pictures Otherwise they will not. Moreover, if we reflect a moment, we shall recognize that there are many times when he can think *in* pictures, even when he is not thinking *of* pictures; as, for instance, when he is impressing a truth upon the mind through using a story, a parable, or an illustration, as we call it. In this case, his method, if it accurately convey to us that which is passing before his own mind, must be *representative,* and not merely *presentative.*

Accordingly we find, when we get to the bottom of our subject, that the figurative or the representative element in poetry may exist in the conception as well as in the phraseology. If it exist in only the conception, we have representation in *plain* language, or *direct* representation; if in the phraseology, by which is meant now the words or expressions illustrating the main thought, we have representation in *figurative* language, or *illustrative* representation, which, in turn, as will be shown presently, it is possible, but not practicable, to divide again into the *expressional* and the *descriptive.* If, in any of these ways, all the significance expressed in a passage be *represented*, the form of the representation will in this work be termed *pure ;* if a part of the significance be merely *presented*, the representation will be termed *alloyed ;* and in the degree in which this is the case, it will be shown by and by that the whole is prosaic.

Pure representation is pictorial in character, as we should expect from the pictorial tendency of which we have found it to be an outgrowth, and its methods are not wholly unlike those of painting. When composing in accordance with them, the poet indicates his thought by using words referring to things that can be perceived; and in this way he causes the imaginations of those whom he addresses to perceive pictures. Alloyed representation, while following in the main the methods of that which is pure, always contains more or less of something which cannot be supposed to have been perceived, at least not in connection with circumstances like those that are being detailed. For this reason, that which is added to the representation is like alloy, interfering with the pureness and clearness of the pictures presented to the imaginations of those addressed. It appeals to them not according to the methods of poetry, but of science or philosophy, or of any kind of thought addressed merely to the logical understanding.

The distinction between pure and alloyed representation lies at the basis of all right appreciation of poetic effects. Yet a man is more fortunate than most of his fellows, if among all his literary friends he finds one who really understands the difference between the two. Because, therefore, of the general ignorance with reference to this distinction, as also of its intrinsic subtlety, both forms of representation will now be explained and illustrated in full.

CHAPTER XX.

PURE DIRECT REPRESENTATION.

In what sense, and how far, Thought and Feeling can be Communicated Representitively—Pure Representation, as used by Tennyson—Hunt, etc.—Pure Direct Representation, as used by Homer, Milton, Shakespear, Morris, Heine, Tennyson, Arnold, Burns, Gilbert, etc.—Extensive Use of this Method in all Forms of Poetry.

IT has been maintained all along in this work that the forms of art represent partly that which is passing in the mind of the artist at the time of composition, and partly that which he has perceived in nature. The art products —to state in a single expression all that they can do— symbolize the thoughts and feelings of the artist through an arrangement of the phenomena of nature which represents them. If we are to approach the subject before us in a logical way, therefore, it seems appropriate that we should first determine in what sense and to what extent thoughts and feelings can be expressed at all in any definite way according to the methods of representation. Afterwards we can go on and ask how a man desirous of representing his own thoughts and feelings would use the phenomena of nature in order to do this.

In considering the first of these questions, attention will be directed only to examples of pure representation. This will enable the reader to notice not only in what sense and how far thoughts and feelings can be represented as a possibility; but also, in connection with this, how they actually are represented when poetry is at its best. Under these circumstances, as has been said, the poetry contains nothing except representation; and for this reason, if for no other, it is very properly termed pure. Its composer, when producing it, confines himself to his legitimate work. Poetry, as we have found, is an art; and art does not consist of thoughts, explanations, or arguments concerning things, but of images or pictures representing them; and there can be no legitimate image or picture, except of what may be supposed to be perceived. If, for instance, certain persons are doing certain things, one will probably draw some inferences from their actions with reference to their motives, and he will have a right to tell his inferences—in prose; but not, as a rule, in poetry. In this, he must picture what he has observed, and leave others, as free as he himself has been, to infer what they choose. At the same time, in the degree in which he is an artist, his picture will be of such a character as to impel others to draw from it the same inference that he himself has drawn. To illustrate how a genuine artist can make his product influence others thus, let me quote Tennyson's description of what followed the reading, by the poet Hall, of his epic on the "Death of Arthur." The reader will remember, perhaps, that when Hall began to read, he described the poem as being "nothing worth." The mention of this fact will explain the use of the phrase "There, now,—that's nothing," in the quotation.

>   Here ended Hall, and our last light, that long
>   Had winked and threatened darkness, flared and fell;
>   At which the Parson, sent to sleep with sound,
>   And waked with silence, grunted "Good!" but we
>   Sat rapt; it was the tone with which he read—
>   Perhaps some modern touches here and there

> Redeemed it from the charge of nothingness,—
> Or else we loved the man, and prized his work ;
> I know not ; but we sitting, as I said,
> The cock crew loud : as at that time of year
> The lusty bird takes every hour for dawn :
> Then Francis, muttering, like a man ill-used,
> "There, now,—that 's nothing !" drew a little back,
> And drove his heel into the smouldered log,
> That sent a blast of sparkles up the flue ;
> And so to bed.
> <div align="right">—<i>Mort d'Arthur</i> : Tennyson.</div>

Is not this simple tale of what was done, much more expressive than would have been a long prosy description of what was felt? This example shows, therefore, that poetry may be strictly representative of external sights and sounds,—may confine itself to that which reproduces for the imagination a picture ; and yet may be equally and in the highest sense representative also of those ideas and feelings which exist only in the mind.

Nor must it be supposed that this kind of representation is unfitted for clear and forcible communication of thought. Notice in the following how effectively Leigh Hunt *represents* his moral :

> Abou Ben Adhem (may his tribe increase !)
> Awoke one night from a deep dream of peace,
> And saw within the moonlight in his room,
> Making it rich and like a lily in bloom,
> An angel writing in a book of gold :
> Exceeding peace had made Ben Adhem bold,
> And to the presence in the room he said :
> "What writest thou ?"—the vision raised its head,
> And, with a look made of all sweet accord,
> Answered : "The names of those who love the Lord."
> "And is mine one ?" said Abou. "Nay, not so,"
> Replied the angel. Abou spake more low,
> But cheerly still, and said : "I pray thee, then,
> Write me as one that loves his fellow-men."

> The angel wrote and vanished. The next night
> It came again with a great wakening light,
> And showed the names whom love of God had blessed,—
> And lo! Ben Adhem's name led all the rest!
>
> *—Abou Ben Adhem.*

Equally successful in indicating their thoughts were the authors of the following:

> Jack brags he never dines at home,
>   With reason, too, no doubt—
> In truth, Jack never dines at all
>   Unless invited out.
>
> *—Elegant Extracts.*

> The golden hair that Galla wears
>   Is hers—who would have thought it?—
> She swears 't is hers, and true she swears,
>   For I know where she bought it.
>
> *—Harrington: Idem.*

It has been said that pure representation may be either direct or illustrative. Let us look now at some examples of it in both forms. After doing so, we shall be better prepared to pass on and compare with them the various departures from it exemplified in alloyed representation. Direct pure representative poetry, as has been intimated, pictures to the mind, without the use of figurative language, a single transaction or series of transactions in such a way as to influence the thoughts of him who hears the poetry, precisely as they would have been influenced had he himself perceived the transaction or series of transactions of which the poetry treats. The works of Homer, as in fact of all the classic writers, are filled with examples of this kind of representation. Here are some of them, with an occasional exceptional expression in illustrative representation, indicated by italics:

> Then, from the fleet, illustrious Hector led
> The Trojans, and beside the eddying stream,

In a clear space uncumbered by the slain,
Held council. There, alighting from their cars,
They listened to the words that Hector spake,—
Hector beloved of Jove. He held a spear,
In length eleven cubits, with a blade
Of glittering brass, bound with a ring of gold.
On this he leaned, and spake these *winged* words :
" Hear me, ye Trojans, Dardans, and allies.
But now I thought that, having first destroyed
The Achaian host and fleet, we should return
This night to wind-swept Ilium. To their aid
The darkness comes, and saves the Greeks, and saves
Their galleys ranged along the ocean side.
Obey we then the dark-browed night ; prepare
Our meal, unyoke the steeds with flowing manes,
And set their food before them . . ."

* * * * * * *

So Hector spake, and all the Trojan host
Applauded ; from the yoke forthwith they loosed
The sweaty steeds, and bound them to the cars
With halters ; to the town they sent in haste
For oxen and the fatlings of the flock,
And to their homes for bread and pleasant wine,
And gathered fuel in large store. The winds
Bore up the fragrant fumes from earth to heaven.
— *The Iliad*, 8 : *Bryant's Tr.*

Notice in these descriptions of contests in battle, how the directness and exactness of the language used augment its representative power.

Beneath the collar bone
It pierced him and passed through ; the brazen point
Came out upon the shoulder ; to the ground
He fell, his armor clashing with his fall.
Then Ajax smote the valiant Phorcys, son
Of Phœnops, in the navel. Through the mail
The brazen weapon broke, and roughly tore
The entrails. In the dust he fell, and clenched
The earth with dying hands.
—*Idem*, 17.

> The sharp stone smote his forehead as he held
> The reins, and crushed both eyebrows in ; the bone
> Resisted not the blow ; the warrior's eyes
> Fell in the dust before his very feet.
>
> * * * * * * *
>
>   He spake and set his heel
> Upon the slain, and from the wound drew forth
> His brazen spear and pushed the corpse aside,
> And with the weapon hurried on.
> <div align="right">—<i>Idem</i>, 16.</div>

In the last paragraph of " Paradise Lost," too, we have a fine example of direct representation :

> In either hand the hastening angel caught
> Our lingering parents, and to the eastern gate
> Led them direct, and down the cliff as fast
> To the subjected plain ; then disappeared.
> They looking back, all the eastern side beheld
> Of paradise, so late their happy seat,
> Waved over by that flaming brand, the gate
> With dreadful faces thronged and fiery arms.
> Some natural tears they dropped, but wiped them soon.
> The world was all before them, where to choose
> Their place of rest, and Providence their guide.
> They, hand in hand, with wandering steps and slow,
> Through Eden took their solitary way.
> <div align="right">—<i>P. L.</i>, 12.</div>

There are many instances of the same in Shakespear also. Here are some :

> You all do know this mantle ; I remember
> The first time ever Cæsar put it on ;
> 'T was on a summer's evening in his tent
> That day he overcame the Nervii.
> Look ! in this place ran Cassius' dagger through ;
> See what a rent the envious Casca made ;
> Through this the well-beloved Brutus stabb'd ;
> And, as he plucked his cursed steel away,
> Mark how the blood of Cæsar followed it.
> <div align="right">—<i>Julius Cæsar</i>, iii., 2.</div>

> A figure like your father,
> Arm'd at all points, exactly, cap-à-pié,
> Appears before them, and with solemn march
> Goes slow and stately by them.
> —*Hamlet*, i., 2.

Among the writers of the present day, William Morris, perhaps, has been the most successful in this kind of representation. Notice the following from his story of "Cupid and Psyche":

> They ceased, and Psyche, pondering o'er their song,
> * * * * * * *
> About the chambers wandered at her will,
> And on the many marvels gazed her fill,
> Where'er she passed still noting everything;
> Then in the gardens heard the new birds sing,
> And watched the red fish in the fountains play,
> And at the very faintest time of day
> Upon the grass lay sleeping for a while
> 'Midst heaven-sent dreams of bliss that made her smile;
> And, when she woke, the shades were lengthening,
> So to the place where she had heard them sing
> She came again, and through a little door
> Entered a chamber with a marble floor,
> Open atop unto the outer air,
> Beneath which lay a bath of water fair,
> Paved with strange stones and figures of bright gold,
> And from the steps thereof could she behold
> The slim-leaved trees against the evening sky
> Golden and calm, still moving languidly.
> So for a time upon the brink she sat,
> * * * * * * *
> And then arose and slowly from her cast
> Her raiment, and adown the steps she passed
> Into the water, and therein she played,
> Till of herself at last she grew afraid,
> And of the broken image of her face,
> And the loud splashing in that lonely place.
> —*The Earthly Paradise.*

And, lest any should think that this kind of representation is confined to epic and dramatic art, here is one of Heine's lyrics. Could any thing illustrate better than this does, the fact that, under certain circumstances, poetry and painting can be made to have the same effects? Although a changing series of scenes is pictured in this beautiful little poem, as is proper where the medium of representation is a series of words, the feelings suggested by it are almost identical with those which would be awakened by the single scene of a painting.

> We sat by the fisher's cottage,
>   And looked at the stormy tide;
> The evening mist came rising,
>   And floating far and wide.
>
> One by one in the lighthouse
>   The lamps shone out on high;
> And far on the dim horizon
>   A ship went sailing by.
>
> We spoke of storm and shipwreck,—
>   Of sailors, and how they live;
> Of journeys 'twixt sky and water,
>   And the sorrows and joys they give.
>
> We spoke of distant countries,
>   In regions strange and fair,
> And of the wondrous beings
>   And curious customs there;
>
> Of perfumed lamps on the Ganges,
>   Which were launched in the twilight hour;
> And the dark and silent Brahmins,
>   Who worship the lotus flower.
>
> Of the wretched dwarfs of Lapland,—
>   Broad-headed, wide-mouthed, and small,—
> Who crouch round their oil-fires cooking,
>   And chatter, and scream, and bawl.

>   And the maidens earnestly listened,
>   Till at last we spoke no more:
>   The ship like a shadow had vanished,
>   And darkness fell deep on the shore.
>   —*The Fisher's Cottage: Tr. by C. G. Leland.*

This is all that there is to the poem; yet, after reading it, we could sit and muse for hours, as we could before a painting, recalling what people talk about under such circumstances,—how little things make imagination wander off to the ends of the earth,—and of how little account it all is when the wandering is over.

Here, too, is another lyric, a celebrated one, and of the most effective type; yet it contains nothing but direct representation:

>   Break, break, break,
>   On thy cold, gray stones, oh Sea!
>   And I would that my tongue could utter
>   The thoughts that arise in me.
>
>   O well for the fisherman's boy
>   That he shouts with his sister at play!
>   O well for the sailor lad,
>   That he sings in his boat on the bay!
>
>   And the stately ships go on
>   To their haven under the hill;
>   But oh for the touch of a vanished hand,
>   And the sound of a voice that is still!
>
>   Break, break, break,
>   At the foot of the crags, oh Sea!
>   But the tender grace of a day that is dead
>   Will never come back to me.
>   —*Break, Break, Break: Tennyson.*

Notice these also:

>   Each on his own strict line we move,
>   And some find death ere they find love;
>   So far apart their lives are thrown
>   From the twin soul that halves their own.

    And sometimes, by still harder fate,
    The lovers meet, but meet too late.
    —Thy heart is mine !—*True, true ! ah, true !*
    —Then, love, thy hand !—*Ah, no ! adieu !*
          —*Too Late :* **Matthew Arnold.**

    Of a' the airts the wind can blaw
     I dearly like the west,
    For there the bonnie lassie lives,
     The lassie I lo'e best ;
    There wild woods grow, an' rivers flow,
     An' mony a hill between ;
    But day an' night my fancy's flight
     Is ever wi' my Jean.

    I see her in the dewy flowers,
     I see her sweet an' fair ;
    I hear her in the tunefu' birds,
     I hear her charm the air :
    There 's not a bonnie flow'r that springs
     By fountain, shaw, or green,
    There 's not a bonnie bird that sings,
     But minds me o' my Jean.
          —*I Love my Jean :* **Burns.**

  The following also may be classed as direct representation. It is humorous, too, for the very reason that it is direct, confessing to a kind of pride very common, but very seldom recognized to be irrational and absurd, because not expressed in such a straightforward, unequivocal way.

      He is an Englishman,
       For he himself has said it,
       And it 's greatly to his credit
      That he is an Englishman.
       For he might have been a Roosian,
       A French, or Turk, or Proosian,
      Or perhaps Ital-i-an ;
       But in spite of all temptations
       To belong to other nations,
      He remains an Englishman.
          —*Pinafore,* 2 : **Gilbert.**

Much of Gilbert's fun is of this same sort. Probably many an old maid has had thoughts like the following; but ordinarily, if not ashamed of them, she is too bashful to acknowledge them. They appear ridiculous only when bawled out at the top of the voice of a stalwart contralto into the ears of hundreds.

> Sad is the woman's lot who, year by year,
> Sees one by one her beauties disappear.
> * * * * * *
> Silvered is the raven hair,
>   Spreading is the parting straight,
> Mottled the complexion fair,
>   Halting is the youthful gait,
> Hollow is the laughter free,
>   Spectacled the limpid eye ;
> Little will be left of me
>   In the coming by and by.
>
> Fading is the taper waist,
>   Shapeless grows the shapely limb,
> And, although severely laced,
>   Spreading is the figure trim ;
> Stouter than I used to be,
>   Still more corpulent grow I,
> There will be too much of me
>   In the coming by and by.
>
> —*Patience*, 2 : *Gilbert.*

Those whose attention has never been directed to the fact, will be surprised upon examination to find how many poems contain nothing but this direct representation. Among them can be included almost all those that in the true sense of the term are ballads, like Scott's "Lochinvar," and its models in Percy's Reliques. Not only so, but as this form of representation may reproduce that which may be supposed to have been heard or said, as well as seen or done, in this class may be included a large number of more reflective poems, like Tennyson's *May Queen*, and *Northern Farmer*. It must be borne in mind, however, that when this style is used there is special need that the ideas to be expressed be picturesque in themselves, or else concentrations in concrete form illustrating much poetic truth that is generic and universal in its applicability. For poems fulfilling perfectly the first condition, notice Kingsley's *Three Fishers*, and *O Mary Go and Call the Cattle Home*, quoted in Chapter Twenty-seventh of this work. For a poem fulfilling the second, Burns' *Address to the Louse on a Lady's Bonnet*, is as good as any. He ends that, as will be remembered, passing, however, in order to do it, from pure into alloyed representation, in this way :

> O wad some power the giftie gi'e us
> To see oursels as ithers see us !
> It wad frae monie a blunder free us
> And foolish notion :
> What airs in dress an' gait wad lea'e us,
> And e'en devotion !

When either condition just mentioned is fulfilled, the conception itself is representative, and often all that is needed, for the highest poetry is a literal and therefore a direct statement of that which is perceived in consciousness. But this fact, in connection with further examples of direct representation, will be considered hereafter.

CHAPTER XXI.

PURE INDIRECT OR ILLUSTRATIVE REPRESENTATION.

Illustrative in Connection with Direct Representation enables a writer to express almost any Phase of Thought representatively or poetically—Examples—Representation, if Direct, must communicate mainly what can be seen or heard—Inward Mental Processes can be pictured outwardly and materially only by Indirect Representation—Examples of this Fact from Longfellow—From Arnold—From Whittier—From Smith—From Tennyson, Aldrich, and Bryant—Two Motives in using Language, corresponding respectively to those underlying Discoursive and Dramatic Elocution, namely, that tending to the Expression of what is within the Mind, and that tending to the Description of what is without the Mind—Examples from Longfellow of Poetry giving Form to these two different Motives—Careful Analysis might give us here, besides Indirect or Figurative Representation used for the purpose of Expression, the same used for the purpose of Description, but as in Rhetoric and Practice Expressional and Descriptive Illustration follow the same Laws, both will be treated as Illustrative Representation— Similes, ancient and modern—From Homer—From Morris—From Milton—From Shakespear—From Moore—From Kingsley—Metaphors, ancient and modern—Used in Cases of Excitation—Examples.

LET us pass on now to the illustrative forms of pure representation. The plain language used in direct representation is a development, as has been said, of the instinctive modes of expression, primarily exemplified in ejaculatory sounds; and figurative language, now to be considered, springs from the reflective modes primarily exemplified in imitative sounds. Behind imitation (see page 8) there is always an intellectual purpose, a plan, a desire to impress, if not to convince. This motive would make a prose writer didactic and argumentative. The poet it drives to illustrations, each of which in genuine poetry must be representative or picturesque, although his main thought—differing in this particular from that which must be behind direct representation—need not be so.

A moment's reflection will show us that this fact with reference to figurative or illustrative representation, renders it possible for a writer to express almost any thought or feeling whatever in a representative and poetic way. A noise, for instance, whether slight or great, is not in itself poetic; if great, one would suppose that it would be the opposite, yet see how it may become poetic on account of the way in which it is represented:

>   And now and then an echo started up,
>   And, shuddering, fled from room to room, and died
>   Of fright in far apartments.
>   —*The Princess: Tennyson.*

>   Immediate in a flame,
>   But soon obscured with smoke, all heaven appear'd,
>   From those deep-throated engines belched, whose roar
>   Embowel'd with outrageous noise the air,
>   And all her entrails tore, disgorging foul
>   Their devilish glut, chained thunderbolts, and hail
>   Of iron globes, which on the victor host
>   Level'd with such impetuous fury smote,
>   That whom they hit none on their feet might stand.
>   —*Paradise Lost*, 6: *Milton.*

That human beings often misunderstand one another is a commonplace fact of ordinary observation. But see what representation may do with the expression of the fact:

>   We are spirits clad in veils;
>   Man by man was never seen;
>   All our deep communing fails
>   To remove the shadowy screen.

PURE ILLUSTRATIVE REPRESENTATION. 227

>   Heart to heart was never known ;
>   Mind with mind did never meet ;
>   We are columns left alone
>   Of a temple once complete.
>
>   Like the stars that gem the sky,
>   Far apart, though seeming near,
>   In our light we scattered lie ;
>   All is thus but starlight here.
>   —*Thought: Cranch.*

To say that the murder of a good man will cause many to mourn, does not involve the utterance of a profound or beautiful thought, but the thought may be represented so as to seem both, as in this:

>   Besides this, Duncan
>   Hath borne his faculties so meek, hath been
>   So clear in his great office, that his virtues
>   Will plead like angels, trumpet-tongued, against
>   The deep damnation of his taking off ;
>   And pity, like a naked new-born babe,
>   Striding the blast, or Heaven's cherubim, horsed
>   Upon the sightless couriers of the air,
>   Shall blow the horrid deed in every eye,
>   That tears shall drown the wind. I have no spur
>   To prick the sides of my intent ; but only
>   Vaulting ambition, which o'erleaps itself
>   And falls on the other.——
>   —*Macbeth*, i., 7 : *Shakespear.*

So one might go through the whole catalogue of possible thoughts and feelings, and it is a question whether a man, if enough of an artist, could not express every one of them in such words, or arrange it in such connections or balance it by such antitheses, or trail after it such suggestions, or put it into the mouths of such characters, placed in such positions, induced by such communications, stirred by such surroundings, as to make it, although in itself most trivial, common, disagreeable, and mean, a part of a representation which, considered as a whole, would produce an æsthetic effect.

It must be borne in mind, however, that this statement is true only because it is possible for the poet to use a kind of representation in addition to that which is direct. The latter, as we have found, must always give expression to thoughts or feelings which can be legitimately inferred from simple, straightforward accounts of certain real or imaginary events. It is all that is needed, therefore, when communicating conclusions derived from what has been seen or heard; but not so always, when communicating that which, aside from any immediate outward influence, has been inwardly thought or felt. In the latter case, the mind, if it would represent rather than present what it has to say, must resort to figures. In using these as has been shown, it simply carries out a tendency exemplified in all language, from the time of the first imitative sounds to that of words like *express*, *impress*, and *understand*. In accordance with this tendency, unseen mental relations or processes are represented by referring to others resembling them, which are perceptible in the visible or material world. Instead of saying, "His integrity is impaired by severe temptation," one may say, "His uprightness bends before some pressing blast." In other words, instead of using conventional language, which simply presents an idea, one may assume the attitude of the first framers of language, and represent his idea, making it, in a sense, tangible, visible, graphic. An endeavor to do this, as applied to thoughts and feelings that cannot be directly represented, is the motive underlying the primitive use of figurative language, or *indirect* representation, which might be termed also *metaphorical*, in the sense of being constructed according to the methods of the metaphor, though all actual metaphors do not exemplify it, and some similes and allegories do. Longfellow, for instance, starts out to say that the examples of great men often encourage and stimulate others; but he ends by representing his thought thus:

> Lives of great men all remind us
> We can make our lives sublime,
> And, departing, leave behind us
> Footprints on the sands of time;
>
> Footprints, that perhaps another,
> Sailing o'er life's solemn main,
> A forlorn and shipwrecked brother,
> Seeing, shall take heart again.
> —*A Psalm of Life.*

Here a plain statement would be that the poet is not one of those constantly encouraged and guided by cheering thoughts, but his words are these:

> The thoughts that rain their steady glow
> Like stars on life's cold sea,
> Which others know or say they know—
> They never shine for me.
>
> Thoughts light, like gleams, my spirit's sky,
> But they will not remain;
> They light me once, they hurry by,
> And never come again.
> —*Despondency: Matthew Arnold.*

Here the declaration is made that care and trial, when passed, do not seem painful to the soul; that they are means of developing its powers harmoniously, and increasing its inward satisfaction; and that this fact causes the writer to submit cheerfully to the divine influence; but what he really says is that he has learned:

> That care and trial seem at last,
> Through memory's sunset air,

> Like mountain ranges overpast,
>   In purple distance fair ;—
>
> That all the jarring notes of life
>   Seem blending in a psalm,
> And all the angles of its strife
>   Slow rounding into calm.
>
> And so the shadows fall apart,
>   And so the west winds play ;
> And all the windows of my heart
>   I open to the day.
>
> *—My Psalm : Whittier.*

And here, once more, the writer wishes to describe in their order the effects upon the soul of sin, faith, aspiration, and love.

> Soon a trembling, naked figure, to the earth my face was bowed,
> For the curse of God gloomed o'er me like a bursting thunder-cloud.
> Rolled away that fearful darkness, past my weakness, past my grief,
> Washed with bitter tears I sat full in the sunshine of belief.
> Weary eyes are looking eastward, whence the golded sun upsprings,
> Cry the young and fervid spirits, clad with ardor as with wings :
> Life and soul make wretched jangling, they should mingle to one Sire,
> As the lovely voices mingle in a holy temple choir.
>
> *—A Life Drama*, 2 : *Alex. Smith.*

In Chapter Twenty-seventh will be found several poems illustrating this kind of representation, constructed from beginning to end according to the method of a single simile or allegory. Notice, especially, *The Deserted House*, by Tennyson, the *Nocturne*, by Aldrich, and *The Wind and Stream*, and *The Tides*, by Bryant.

We have noticed elsewhere in this work, that there are two motives in using language, corresponding respectively to those underlying discoursive and dramatic elocution (see page 33). One motive is to *express* what is within the mind; the other is to *describe* what is outside it. In poetic *direct* representation, these two motives are always combined. A man cannot *express* himself poetically in *plain* language without also *describing* some scene. But the *indirect* representation of *figurative* language may be poetic or descriptive in itself; and, therefore, in using it, the poet need think only of expressing thought so that the hearer may appreciate it, *e. g*:

>   And all my thoughts sail thither,
> Freighted with prayers and hopes, and forward urged
> Against all stress of accident, as, in
> The Eastern Tale, against the wind and tide,
> Great ships were drawn to the Magnetic Mountains.
> 			—*Spanish Student: Longfellow.*

But here the same form of representation is used in order to *describe* a scene so that the hearer may imagine it:

>   And the moon rose over the city,
>   Behind the dark church-tower.
>   I saw her bright reflection
>   In the waters under me,
>   Like a golden goblet falling
>   And sinking into the sea.
>   Along the long black rafters
>   The wavering shadows lay,
>   And the current that came from the ocean
>   Seemed to lift and bear them away.
>   —*The Bridge: Idem.*

Evidently, therefore, a complete analysis would give us, besides *indirect* or *figurative* representation used for the purpose of *expression*, the same used for the purpose of *description*. But in rhetoric no discrimination is made between expressional and descriptive purposes; and, as the same principles apply to both, no practical advantage can be derived from separating them in our present discussion.

All that is to be said in the following chapters, therefore, of either way of using figurative language will be treated under the general head of illustrative representation.

For reasons already explained, the two principal figures used for the purposes of illustration—and this is true whether representation be expressional or descriptive—are the *simile* and the *metaphor*. The former is of most frequent occurrence in the earliest poems. Notice the number of similes in this single passage from Homer:

> As when a forest on the mountain top
> Is in a blaze with the devouring flame,
> And shines afar, so, while the warriors marched,
> The brightness of their burnished weapons flashed
> On every side, and upward to the sky.
> And as when water-fowl of many tribes—
> Geese, cranes, and long-necked swans—disport themselves
> In Asia's fields beside Cayster's streams,
> And to and fro they fly with screams, and light,
> Flock after flock, and all the fields resound;
> So poured, from ships and tents, the swarming tribes
> Into Scamander's plain, where fearfully
> Earth echoed to the tramp of steeds and men;
> And there they mustered on the river's side,
> Numberless as the flowers and leaves of spring.
> And as when flies in swarming myriads haunt
> The herdsman's stalls in spring-time, when new milk
> Has filled the pails,—in such vast multitudes
> Mustered the long-haired Greeks upon the plain,
> Impatient to destroy the Trojan race.
> Then, as the goatherds, when their mingled flocks
> Are in the pastures, know, and set apart
> Each his own scattered charge, so did the chiefs,
> Moving among them, marshal each his men.
> —*Iliad*, 2 : *Bryant's Trans.*

In modern poetry the extended simile is much less of a favorite than the metaphor. Yet we find many instances of the former. Here is a fine simile from *The Lovers of Gudrun*, by Morris:

> As a gray dove, within the meshes caught,
> Flutters a little, then lies still again,
> Ere wildly beat its wings with its last pain,
> So once or twice her passion, as she spake,
> Rose to her throat, and yet might not outbreak
> Till that last word was spoken ; then, as stung
> By pain on pain, her arms abroad she flung,
> And wailed aloud.
> —*The Earthly Paradise.*

Here is one of Milton's similes, highly commended by Herbert Spencer in his essay on "The Philosophy of Style," as affording " a fine instance of a sentence, well arranged alike in the priority of the subordinate members, in the avoidance of long and numerous suspensions, and in the correspondence between the order of the clauses and the sequence of the phenomena described, which, by the way, is a further prerequisite to easy comprehension, and therefore to effect."

> As when a prowling wolf,
> Whom hunger drives to seek new haunt for prey,
> Watching where shepherds pen their flocks at eve,
> In hurdled cotes amid the fields secure,
> Leaps o'er the fence with ease into the fold :
> Or as a thief bent to unhoard the cash
> Of some rich burgher, whose substantial doors,
> Cross-barred and bolted fast, fear no assault,
> In at the window climbs, or o'er the tiles :
> So clomb the first grand thief into God's fold ;
> So since into his church lewd hirelings climb.
> —*Paradise Lost*, 4.

And here is one from Shakespear in which metaphors also are included. Notice the graphic example of pure representation in the third and fourth lines :

> This battle fares like to the morning's war,
> When dying clouds contend with growing light ;
> What time the shepherd, blowing of his nails,
> Can neither call it perfect day nor night.

> Now sways it this way like a mighty sea,
> Forced by the tide to combat with the wind;
> Now sways it that way like the self-same sea,
> Forced to retire by fury of the wind:
> Sometimes the flood prevails: and then the wind:
> Now one the better, then another best;
> Both tugging to be victors, breast to breast,
> Yet neither conqueror nor conquered:
> So is the equal poise of this fell war.
>
> —3 *Henry VI.*, ii., 5.

Illustrative representation forms the substance of much of our lyric poetry, both serious and comic, as in the following containing only a single simile:

> The bird let loose in eastern skies,
>   When hastening fondly home,
> Ne'er stoops to earth her wing, nor flies
>   Where idle warblers roam;
> But high she shoots through air and light,
>   Above all low delay,
> Where nothing earthly bounds her flight,
>   Nor shadow dims her way.
>
> So grant me, God, from every care
>   And stain of passion free,
> Aloft through Virtue's purer air,
>   To hold my course to thee!
> No sin to cloud, no lure to stay
>   My soul,—as home she springs;
> Thy sunshine on her joyful way,
>   Thy freedom in her wings!
>
> —*The Bird Let Loose*: Thomas Moore.

Here again is a very felicitous use of figures, which it may prove interesting to compare with the same author's method in direct representation, as employed in his *O Mary Go and Call the Cattle Home*, and *The Fishermen*, quoted in Chapter Twenty-seventh.

> There sits a bird on every tree;
>   Sing heigh-ho.

There sits a bird on every tree ;
And courts his love as I do thee ;
  Sing heigh-ho and heigh-ho.
Young maids must marry.

There grows a flower on every bough ;
  Sing heigh-ho.
There grows a flower on every bough ;
Its petals kiss—I 'll show you how :
  Sing heigh-ho and heigh-ho.
Young maids must marry.

From sea to stream the salmon roam ;
  Sing heigh-ho.
From sea to stream the salmon roam ;
Each finds a mate and leads her home ;
  Sing heigh-ho and heigh-ho.
Young maids must marry.

The sun 's a bridegroom, earth a bride ;
  Sing heigh-ho.
They court from morn to eventide ;
The earth shall pass, but love abide ;
  Sing heigh-ho and heigh-ho.
Young maids must marry.

—*Sing Heigh-Ho* : Kingsley.

Metaphors, to most readers, do not appear to be as frequent or as fine in the most ancient as in modern verse. This seems to be so, first, because what is once a metaphorical use of a word comes, after a time, to be accepted as an ordinary use of it, if not as a secondary meaning for it. Homer may have originated the meanings given to the words *pillar* and *shoulder* in the following passages, and to his contemporaries each may have appeared to be a very significant metaphor. But the same words, or their equivalents in our language, used in the same senses, are so familiar to us to-day, that many, without having their attention drawn to the fact, do not recognize them to be metaphors at all.

> The slain, though stranger born,
> Had been a *pillar* of the realm of Troy.
> —*Iliad* 16 : *Bryant's Translation.*

> Thrice Patroclus climbed
> A *shoulder* of the lofty wall.
> —*Idem.*

A second reason is that the metaphor, inasmuch as it depends for its force upon its suggestiveness, necessarily requires some sympathy on the part of the reader with the conditions of knowledge, thought, and feeling in the age to which it is addressed. We can imagine a time, for instance, in which the following passages, even if they could be conceived, would not be received with much favor. Yet they represent the forms of expression which, at the present time, are the most stirring and popular.

> Ignorance is the curse of God.
> —*2 Henry VI.*, iv., 7 : *Shakespear.*

> I tell thee, Jack Cade, the clothier, means to dress the commonwealth, and turn it, and set a new nap upon it.
> —*2 Henry VI.*, iv., 2 : *Idem.*

> One touch of nature makes the whole world kin.
> —*Troilus and Cressida*, iii., 3 : *Idem.*

> Here once the embattled farmers stood,
> And fired the shot heard round the world.
> —*Hymn Sung at Completion of the Concord Monument : Emerson.*

> They take the rustic murmur of their bourg
> For the great wave that echoes round the world.
> —*Idyls of the King, Geraint and Enid : Tennyson.*

> Autels que la raison en montant submergea
> —*La Temple, in La Légend des Siècles : Hugo.*

A third reason is that, while the ancient figures of speech were prompted often by a desire to express thought adequately, the modern are prompted mainly by a desire to express it æsthetically. For this reason, inasmuch as an end aimed at is usually the end attained, modern metaphors like modern paintings are, more often than ancient ones, results of the highest degree of artistic care and skill. Notice the following:

> Still as a slave before his lord,
> The ocean hath no blast ;
> *His great bright eye* most silently
> Up to the moon is cast.
> —*The Ancient Mariner :* Coleridge.

> I should make very *forges* of my cheeks,
> That would to *cinders burn up modesty,*
> Did I but speak thy deeds.
> —*Othello,* iv., 2 : *Shakespear.*

> I sate upon the deck and watched all night,
> And *listened through the stars* for Italy.
> . . . . Thus my Italy
> Was stealing on us. Genoa broke with day ;
> The Doria's long pale palace striking out,
> From green hills in advance of the white town,
> *A marble finger* dominant to ships,
> Seen glimmering through the uncertain gray of dawn.
> —*Aurora Leigh,* 7 : *Mrs. Browning.*

The simile is used mainly when there is only a moderate degree of excitation. When this is great, the mind flies naturally to the metaphor, as a more concentrated form of expression, representing many thoughts in a few words. So Macduff, in the second act of *Macbeth,* on seeing the dead Duncan, cries out :

> Confusion now hath made his masterpiece.
> Most sacrilegious murther hath broke ope
> The Lord's anointed temple and stole thence
> The life o' the building !
>
> * * * * * *
>
> Approach the chamber, and destroy your sight
> With a new Gorgon. . . .
> Shake off this downy sleep, death's counterfeit,

> And look on death itself! up, up, and see
> The great doom's image!—Malcolm! Banquo!
> As from your graves rise up, and walk like sprites
> To countenance this horror! Ring the bell.
>
> * * * * * *
>
> *Macb.:* Had I but died an hour before this chance
> I had lived a blessed time; for from this instant
> There's nothing serious in mortality;
> All is but toys; renown and grace is dead;
> The wine of life is drawn, and the mere lees
> Is left this vault to brag of.
>
> —*Macbeth*, ii., 1 : *Shakespear*.

The same abundant use of metaphorical language will be found in most of Shakespear's scenes representing quarrelling and love, like those, for instance, in *Romeo and Juliet*. This form, too, as we know, is that adopted in impassioned love lyrics.

> From the meadow your walks have left so sweet
> That whenever a March-wind sighs
> He sets the jewel-print of your feet
> In violets blue as your eyes,
> To the woody hollows in which we meet
> And the valleys of Paradise.
>
> * * * * * *
>
> Queen rose of the rosebud, garden of girls,
> Come hither, the dances are done,
> In gloss of satin and glimmer of pearls,
> Queen lily and rose in one;
> Shine out, little head, sunning over with curls,
> To the flowers, and be their sun.
>
> * * * * * *
>
> She is coming, my own, my sweet;
> Were it ever so airy a tread,
> My heart would hear her and beat,
> Were it earth in an earthy bed;
> My dust would hear her and beat,
> Had I lain for a century dead;

> Would start and tremble under her feet,
>   And blossom in purple and red.
> —*Maud: Tennyson.*

Illustrative, like direct, representation may be used, of course, for wit and humor.

> When Loveless married Lady Jenny,
> Whose beauty was the ready penny;
> "I chose her," says he, "like old plate,
> Not for the fashion but the weight."
> —*Elegant Extracts.*

> You beat your pate, and fancy wit will come;
> Knock as you please, there's nobody at home.
> —*Epigram: Pope.*

CHAPTER XXII.

PURE REPRESENTATION IN THE POETRY OF HOMER.

How the Phenomena of Nature should be used in Representation—Homer as a Model—His Descriptions are Mental, Fragmentary, Specific, Typical—The Descriptions of Lytton, Goethe, Morris, Southey, etc—Homer's Descriptions also Progressive—Examples—Dramatic Poems should show the same Traits—Homer's Illustrative Representation.

HAVING found now how poetry through pure representation, whether direct or illustrative, *is able* to give definite expression to thoughts and feelings, let us take up the second question proposed in Chapter Twentieth, and try to find *how* an artist desirous of representing his own thoughts and feelings must use the phenomena of nature in order to do this in the most effective way. In answering this question, it is essential that we start with a proper standard. Fortunately, we can get one universally acknowledged to be sufficient for our purpose, in the works of Homer, and this too—to say much less than is deserved—in a sufficiently accurate English translation. So far at least as concerns the passages to be quoted in this discussion, all have been verified by comparing them with the original text. These poems of Homer have stood the tests of centuries, and there are reasons why they have survived them. The consideration which should interest us most in the present connection, is the fact that the poems were produced by a man who spoke directly from the first promptings of nature; a man upon whom the methods of representation in other arts, and of presentation as used in science and philosophy, had had the least possible influence. In his works, therefore, better than in any others with which, in our day, we can become acquainted, we can study the tendencies of poetry in its most spontaneous and unadulterated form. Let us begin here, therefore, by examining some of the poetry of Homer, and trying to find out how he dealt with the phenomena of nature.

As we pursue our inquiry, one feature with reference to his methods should impress us immediately, and it may as well be mentioned before we take up any particular passages, because it is apparent in all of them. It may be indicated by saying that the Homeric representations are all *mental*. They fulfil in this respect the requirement already mentioned many times in this work—that the products of art should represent both man and nature. By saying that the Homeric descriptions are mental, it is meant that they show that there is a mind between the phenomena of nature and the account of them that we get in the poetry—a mind addressing our minds. Not that this mind distorts the objects which it has perceived and describes; the fact is just the opposite. Homer's representations are pure in the highest sense; yet they are not like those of a guide-book or map. He suggests his picture by telling us about those features of it that have had an effect upon him as a thinking being, or,—what is the same thing—that he expects will have an effect upon us. What he tells us is true to nature, but not, by any means, all the truth concerning it. Certain parts of the scenes presumably witnessed have arrested his attention, and suggested certain inferences to him. These parts, consciously or unconsciously, he selects and arranges in ways that arrest our attention as they have arrested his. In this sense it is that his descriptions are mental. Let us look now at some of them. Here is one of his accounts of a man, and another of a homestead, both very simple, but for this very reason admirably adapted to our present purpose.

> And first, Æneas, with defiant mien
> And nodding casque, stood forth. He held his shield
> Before him, which he wielded right and left,
> And shook his brazen spear.
> —*Iliad*, Book 20: *Bryant's Trans.*

> He wedded there
> A daughter of Adrastus, and he dwelt
> Within a mansion filled with wealth ; broad fields
> Fertile in corn were his, and many rows
> Of trees and vines around him ; large his flocks,
> And great his fame as one expert to wield,
> Beyond all other Greeks, the spear in war.
> —*Iliad*, 14 : *Bryant's Trans.*

Notice now, in the second place, that these descriptions are *fragmentary*, the items mentioned in them being few. They present us with just such incomplete glimpses as one would obtain or remember amid circumstances in which the persons or objects observed would form parts of larger objects of consideration, while at the same time all of them, or, perhaps, he himself might be in motion.

Notice, in the third place, that the descriptions are *specific*. Of the few items that are mentioned, we have a very definite account in the "defiant mien," the "nodding casque," the shaking "shield" and "spear," the "mansion filled with wealth," the "broad fields fertile in corn," the "rows of trees," the "vines," the "large flocks," and the "expert" in wielding "the spear." There is no uncertainty of outline here, and therefore there is no doubt in the mind of the reader as to whether or not the author has taken his descriptions from nature. The whole impression conveyed is that he is describing the appearance of some particular man and homestead, and of no other.

Notice also, in the fourth place, that the descriptions, while specific, are also *typical.* The features spoken of are such as to indicate the genus or kind of person or thing that is represented. So fully is this the case, that the few specific items mentioned, like the few bold outlines of a painter's sketch, suggest every thing that the imagination really needs in order to make out a complete picture. This fact makes it possible for them to be few and definite, and yet distinctly representative. They do not include all the objects that might be seen, all that might be photographed, but only a few of them. At the same time, they are those which in the circumstances would be likely to attract any one's eye, those from which, and from which only, even if one saw the scene, he would be likely to draw his impressions with reference to the whole of it. Some of my readers may remember that Timothy Titcomb,[1] in giving advice to young men intending to go into ladies' society, does not bid them attend mainly to that which shall make them appear intelligent or moral. Not at all. He writes from the view-point of a man of common-sense, understanding human nature. He advises them to attend to their neckties. The truth is, that our first view of a person always lights upon some one or two prominent features, the eyes, lips, smile, hand, gait, coat, or necktie, as the case may be, which, by absorbing our attention, causes us to overlook every thing else. In fact, we always remember people, and houses, and localities, by these single and simple, often very ab-

---
[1] Timothy Titcomb's Letters : J. G. HOLLAND.

surd, things, which are instantly suggested whenever our minds recur to that for which, so far as concerns our recollection of it, they stand. It is mainly this fact with reference to memory that Robert Bulwer Lytton illustrates in his touching little poem, *Aux Italiens*.

* * * * * * *

Meanwhile I was thinking of my first love
   As I had not been thinking of aught for years ;
Till over my eyes there began to move
   Something that felt like tears.

I thought of the dress that she wore last time
   When we stood 'neath the cypress trees together,
In that lost land, in that soft clime,
   In the crimson evening weather ;

Of that muslin dress (for the eve was hot),
   And her warm white neck, in its golden chain,
And her full soft hair, just tied in a knot,
   And falling loose again.

And the jasmine flower in her fair young breast,
   (O, the faint, sweet smell of that jasmine flower !)
And the one bird singing alone to his nest ;
   And the one star over the tower.

I thought of our little quarrels and strife,
   And the letter that brought me back my ring ;
And it all seemed then, in the waste of life,
   Such a very little thing !

For I thought of her grave below the hill,
   Which the sentinel cypress-tree stands over ;
And I thought " Were she only living still,
   How I could forgive her and love her !"

And I swear as I thought of her thus in that hour,
   And of how, after all, old things are best,
That I smelt the smell of that jasmine flower
   Which she used to wear in her breast.

It smelt so faint, and it smelt so sweet,
   It made me creep, and it made me cold,

> Like the scent that steals from the crumbling sheet
>   Where a mummy is half unrolled.
>
> And I turned and looked : she was sitting there,
>   In a dim box over the stage ; and drest
> In that muslin dress, with that full soft hair,
>   And that jasmine in her breast.
>
> * * * * * * *
>
> My thinking of her, or the music's strain,
>   Or something which never will be exprest,
> Had brought her back from the grave again,
>   With the jasmine in her breast.
>
> * * * * * * *
>
> But O, the smell of that jasmine flower,
>   And O, that music ! and O, the way
> That voice rang out from the dunjon tower :
>   Non ti scordar di me,
>   Non ti scordar di me !

It is in accordance with the workings of observation and memory illustrated here, that the poet, if he desire to describe persons or things precisely as they would be recalled by a narrator who had perceived them, must be careful to mention but a few items in his representation, and these very specifically, so that they will seem to have been seen by him, and not merely imagined. He must choose these items too, so that they will be characteristic or typical of the whole nature of the objects or transactions of which they form parts. He must dwell upon those features which would naturally attract the attention of a spectator and impress him. These principles are so important, and so frequently illustrated in the poetry of Homer, that, before dismissing the subject, it will not be out of place to give several examples of them. Notice every thing in the following, but especially the italicized phrases :

>   The helm
> Of massive brass was vain to stay the blow :
> The weapon pierced it and the bone, and stained
> The brain with blood ; it felled him rushing on.
> The monarch stripped the slain, and, leaving them
> *With their white bosoms bare,* went on to slay
> Isus and Antiphus, King Priam's sons.
>
> <div align="right">—<i>Iliad</i>, 11 : <i>Bryant's Trans.</i></div>

>   Meanwhile
> Antilochus against his charioteer,
> Mydon, the brave son of Atymnias, hurled
> A stone that smote his elbow as he wheeled
> His firm-paced steeds in flight. He dropped the reins,
> *Gleaming with ivory as they trailed in dust.*
> Antilochus leaped forward, smiting him
> Upon the temples with his sword. He fell
> Gasping amidst the sand, *his head immersed
> Up to his shoulders*—for the sand was deep,—
> And there remained till he was beaten down
> Before the horses' hoofs.
>
> <div align="right">—<i>Iliad</i>, 5 : <i>Idem.</i></div>

> And now the mighty spearman, Phyleus' son,
> Drew near and smote him with his trenchant lance
> Where meet the head and spine, and pierced the neck
> Beneath the tongue ; and *forth the weapon came
> Between the teeth.* He fell, and in the fall
> *Gnashed with his teeth* upon the *cold, bright blade.*
>
> <div align="right">—<i>Iliad</i>, 5 : <i>Idem.</i></div>

>   Their beloved wives meanwhile,
> And their young children, stood and watched the walls,
> With aged men among them, while the youths
> Marched on, with Mars and Pallas at their head,
> Both wrought in gold, with golden garments on,
> Stately and large in form, and over all
> Conspicuous in bright armor, as became
> The gods ; the rest were of an humbler size.
>
> <div align="right">—<i>Iliad</i>, 18 : <i>Idem.</i></div>

>   Meantime the assembled Greeks
> Sat looking where the horses scoured the plain
> And filled the air with dust. Idomeneus,

> The lord of Crete, descried the coursers first,
> For on the height he sat above the crowd.
> He heard the chief encouraging his steeds,
> And knew him, and he marked before the rest
> A courser, chestnut-colored, *save a spot*
> Upon the *middle* of the *forehead, white,*
> And *round as the full moon.* And then he stood
> Upright, and from his place harangued the Greeks.
>
> —*Iliad*, 23 : *Idem.*

The following is a very different kind of description, but notice in it the same characteristics—what an air of reality is given to the whole by the specificness with which a few features only, and these the typical features likely to impress the spectator, are mentioned. Speaking of Hecamede it is said:

> First she drew forth a table fairly wrought,
> Of polished surface, and *with steel-blue feet,*
> And on it placed a brazen tray which bore
> A thirst-provoking onion, honeycomb,
> And sacred meal of wheat. Near these she set
> A noble beaker which the ancient chief
> Had brought from home, embossed with studs of gold.
> Four were its handles, and each handle showed
> Two golden turtles feeding, while below
> Two others formed the base. Another hand
> Could scarce have raised that beaker from its place,
> But Nestor lifted it with ease. The maid,
> Fair as a goddess, mingled Pramnian wine,
> And grated o'er it, with a rasp of brass,
> A goat's-milk cheese, and, sprinkling the white flour
> Upon it, bade them drink. With this they quenched
> Their parching thirst, and then amused the time
> With pleasant talk. Patroclus to the door
> Meantime, a god-like presence, came, and stood.
> The old man, as he saw him, instantly
> Rose from his princely seat and seized his hand,
> And led him in and bade him sit ; but he
> Refused the proffered courtesy, and said :
>
> —*Iliad*, 11 : *Idem.*

William von Humboldt, in his criticism of Goethe's *Hermann and Dorothea*, directs attention to a similar characteristic in the passage in which Goethe makes his hero describe his first meeting with the heroine. Here are Hermann's words :

> Now my eyes, as I made my way along the new street there,
> Happen'd to light on a wagon, built of the heaviest timber,
> Drawn by a pair of steers of the largest breed and stoutest.
> By their side a maid with vigorous step was walking,
> Holding a long staff up to guide the strong pair onward,
> Starting them now, then stopping them, deftly did she guide them.

One who was less of an artist, instead of revealing in a single glance the sturdy swinging gait and deftly wielded staff, which were enough to account for the young peasant's falling in love with Dorothea, would have given us a lengthy description of the color of her hair and eyes, the crook of her nose, the pout of her lips, the whiteness of her teeth, the number of the dimples on her cheeks, with a minute enumeration probably of all the articles of her wearing apparel, as in the following from *The Lovers of Gudrun*, by William Morris :

> That spring was she just come to her full height,
> Low-bosomed yet she was, and slim and light,
> Yet scarce might she grow fairer from that day ;
> Gold were the locks wherewith the wind did play,
> Finer than silk, waved softly like the sea
> After a three days' calm, and to her knee
> Wellnigh they reached ; fair were the white hands laid
> Upon the door-posts where the dragons played ;
> Her brow was smooth now, and a smile began
> To cross her delicate mouth, the snare of man ;
> For some thought rose within the heart of her
> That made her eyes bright, her cheeks ruddier
> Than was their wont, yet were they delicate
> As are the changing steps of high heaven's gate ;
> Bluer than gray her eyes were, somewhat thin

> Her marvellous red lips ; round was her chin,
> Cloven and clear wrought ; like an ivory tower
> Rose up her neck from love's white-veiled bower.
> But in such lordly raiment was she clad
> As midst its threads the scent of southlands had,
> And on its hem the work of such-like hands
> As deal with silk and gold in sunny lands.
> Too dainty seemed her feet to come anear
> The guest-worn threshold-stone. So stood she there
> And rough the world about her seemed to be,
> A rude heap cast up from the weary sea.
> —*The Earthly Paradise.*

In a similar strain he describes Olaf :

> Great-limbed was Olaf Hauskuldson, well knit,
> And like a chief upon his horse did sit ;
> Clear-browed and wide-eyed was he, smooth of skin
> Through fifty rough years ; of his mother's kin,
> The Erse king's daughter, did his short lip tell,
> And dark-lashed, gray-blue eyes ; like a clear bell
> His voice was yet, despite of waves and wind, etc., etc.
> —*Idem.*

Imagine a man telling a story in natural conversation, and going into these minute particulars. Imagine him noticing them in the presence of the characters described. To conceive of his doing it is almost impossible. Therefore the detailing of them imparts an air of unreality to the narrative ; and for this reason makes it also uninteresting. There is much excellence, however, in these lines of Morris, aside from that which is here criticised. To recognize just how uninteresting this kind of description can be, as well as how much less it really tells us about the persons described than the kind of representation exemplified in Homer and in Hermann's glimpse of Dorothea, let us take a passage less excellent in other regards than that of Morris. It is from Southey's *Thalaba*, by many considered his best poem :

> The stranger was an ancient man,
>   Yet one whose green old age
> Bore the fair characters of temperate youth ;
> So much of manhood's strength his limbs retained,
>   It seemed he needed not the staff he bore.
> His beard was long and gray and crisp ;
>   Lively his eyes and quick,
>   And reaching over them
>   The large broad eyebrow curled.
> His speech was copious, and his winning words
> Enriched with knowledge that the attentive youth
>   Sat listening with a thirsty joy.

Notice this also :

> Black were his eyes and bright ;
>   The sunny hue of health
> Glowed on his tawny cheek ;
> His lip was darkened by maturing life ;
> Strong were his shapely limbs, his stature tall,
>   Peerless among Arabian youths was he.
>   —*Idem.*

All that is given us in these descriptions might be said of a thousand men that everybody meets in a lifetime. Notice, too, in the same poem, this microscopic description of a locust :

> The admiring girl surveyed
>   His outspread sails of green ;
>   His gauzy underwings,
> One closely to the grass-green body furled,
> One ruffled in the fall, and half unclosed.
>   She viewed his jet-orbed eyes,
>   His gossy gorget bright,
>   Green glittering in the sun ;
>   His plumy pliant horns,
>   That nearer as she gazed
> Bent tremblingly before her breath.
> She marked his yellow-circled front
>   With lines mysterious veined.

This passage suggests a fifth characteristic of the Homeric descriptions, which probably is the underlying and determining cause of the last three. It is that they are *progressive*,—the fact that they always represent what is in motion. They are constructed in fulfilment of that principle of nature first noticed by Lessing in his celebrated criticism on "The Laocoön," in accordance with which words represent ideas, feelings, events,—whatever it may be to which they give expression—that follow one another in the order of time. In the last passage quoted from Homer we are not told what Hecamede found on the table; the poet pictures the maid in the act of spreading the table and putting the different articles of food on it. So in the following we are not told how Patroclus or Juno looked when dressed; but we are told how they dressed themselves. The successive words in the descriptions are all made to represent successive acts.

> He spake: Patroclus, then in glittering brass,
> Arrayed himself; and first around his thighs
> He put the beautiful greaves, and fastened them
> With silver clasps; around his chest he bound
> The breastplate of the swift Æacides,
> With star-like points, and richly chased; he hung
> The sword, with silver studs and blade of brass,
> Upon his shoulders, and with it the shield,
> Solid and vast; upon his gallant head
> He placed the glorious helm with horsehair plume,
> That grandly waved on high. Two massive spears
> He took, that fitted well his grasp, but left
> The spear which great Achilles only bore,
> Heavy and huge and strong, and which no arm
> Among the Greeks save his could poise.
> —*Iliad*, 16: *Bryant.*

> She entered in
> And closed the shining doors; and first she took
> Ambrosial water, washing every stain

> From her fair limbs, and smoothed them with rich oil,
> Ambrosial, soft, and fragrant, which, when touched
> Within Jove's brazen halls, perfumed the air
> Of earth and heaven.   When thus her shapely form
> Had been anointed, and her hands had combed
> Her tresses, she arranged the lustrous curls,
> Ambrosial, beautiful, that clustering hung
> Round her immortal brow.   And next she threw
> Around her an ambrosial robe, the work
> Of Pallas, all its web embroidered o'er
> With forms of rare device.   She fastened it
> Over the breast with clasps of gold, and then
> She passed about her waist a zone which bore
> Fringes an hundred-fold, and in her ears
> She hung her three-gemmed ear-rings, from whose gleam
> She won an added grace.   Around her head
> The glorious goddess drew a flowing veil,
> Just from the loom, and shining like the sun ;
> And, last, beneath her bright white feet she bound
> The shapely sandals.   Gloriously arrayed
> In all her ornaments, she left her bower.
> —*Iliad*, 14 : *Idem.*

So when Homer describes a camp, he connects it with action; we are told of a process of building or of demolition.

> And ere the morning came, while earth was gray
> With twilight, by the funeral pile arose
> A chosen band of Greeks, who, going forth,
> Heaped round it from the earth a common tomb
> For all, and built a wall and lofty towers
> Near it,—a bulwark for the fleet and host.
> And in the wall they fitted massive gates,
> Through which there passed an ample chariot-way ;
> And on its outer edge they sank a trench,—
> Broad, deep,—and planted it with pointed stakes.
> So labored through the night the long-haired Greeks.
> —*Iliad*, 7 : *Idem.*

> For those
> Trusting in portents sent from Jupiter,
> And their own valor, labored to break through

> The massive rampart of the Greeks ; they tore
> The galleries from the towers, and levelled down
> The breastworks, heaved with levers from their place
> The jutting buttresses which Argive hands
> Had firmly planted to support the towers,
> And brought them to the ground ; and thus they hoped
> To force a passage to the Grecian camp.
>
> —*Iliad*, 12 : *Idem.*

Even in Homer's references to natural scenery, we find every thing in constant motion. Notice these traits in his description of the fire kindled by Vulcan in order to save the Greeks from the flood.

> The ground was dried ; the glimmering flood was staid.
> As when the autumnal north-wind, breathing o'er
> A newly watered garden, quickly dries
> The clammy mould, and makes the tiller glad,
> So did the spacious plain grow dry on which
> The dead were turned to ashes. Then the god
> Seized on the river with his glittering fires.
> The elms, the willows, and the tamarisks
> Fell, scorched to cinders, and the lotus-herbs,
> Rushes, and reeds, that richly fringed the banks
> Of that fair-flowing current, were consumed.
> The eels and fishes, that were wont to glide
> Hither and thither through the pleasant depths
> And eddies, languished in the fiery breath
> Of Vulcan, mighty artisan. The strength
> Of the greatest river withered.
>
> —*Iliad*, 21 : *Idem.*

So a snow-storm seems interesting to him mainly because it is doing something, and can be used as an illustration of something else that is doing something ; *e. g.*,

> As when the flakes
> Of snow fall thick upon a winter-day,
> When Jove the Sovereign pours them down on men,
> Like arrows, from above ;—he bids the wind
> Breathe not : continually he pours them down,

> And covers every mountain-top and peak,
> And flowery mead, and field of fertile tilth,
> And sheds them on the havens and the shores
> Of the gray deep; but there the waters bound
> The covering of snows,—all else is white
> Beneath that fast-descending shower of Jove;—
> So thick the shower of stones from either side
> Flew toward the other.
>
> —*Iliad,* 12: *Idem.*

Notice also the account of the action of the water in this,—how he portrays the struggle of Achilles with it, in such a way as to make the whole living and graphic. Here, too, the mental quality appears again. The water itself seems interesting to the narrator, mainly because of its connection with the actions of a man with whom he sympathizes.

> And then Achilles, mighty with the spear,
> From the steep bank leaped into the mid-stream,
> While, foul with ooze, the angry River raised
> His waves, and pushed along the heaps of dead,
> Slain by Achilles. These, with mighty roar
> As of a bellowing ox, Scamander cast
> Aground; the living with his whirling gulfs
> He hid, and saved them in his friendly streams.
> In tumult terribly the surges rose
> Around Achilles, beating on his shield,
> And made his feet to stagger, till he grasped
> A tall, fair-growing elm upon the bank.
> Down came the tree, and in its loosened roots
> Brought the earth with it; the fair stream was checked
> By the thick branches, and the prostrate trunk
> Bridged it from side to side. Achilles sprang
> From the deep pool, and fled with rapid feet
> Across the plain in terror. Nor did then
> The mighty river-god refrain, but rose
> Against him with a darker crest. . . .
> . . . . Askance
> He fled; the waters with a mighty roar
> Followed him close. As when a husbandman

> Leads forth, from some dark spring of earth, a rill
> Among his planted garden-beds, and clears
> Its channel, spade in hand, the pebbles there
> Move with the current, which runs murmuring down
> The sloping surface and outstrips its guide,—
> So rushed the waves where'er Achilles ran,
> Swift as he was ; for mightier are the gods
> Than men. As often as the noble son
> Of Peleus made a stand, in hope to know
> Whether the deathless gods of the great heaven
> Conspired to make him flee, so often came
> A mighty billow of the Jove-born stream
> And drenched his shoulders. Then again he sprang
> Away ; the rapid torrent made his knees
> To tremble, while it swept, where'er he trod,
> The earth from underneath his feet. He looked
> To the broad heaven above him and complained.
> —*Iliad*, 21 : *Bryant's Trs.*

Look now at the way in which Homer describes the scenes by which some of his heroes pass in flight. How few comparatively are the objects that are noticed, yet how specifically do they indicate the typical features, which in such circumstances one would see and remember, and from which, in the rapid glance that he would have of every thing, he would derive all his impressions.

> They passed the Mount of View,
> And the wind-beaten fig-tree, and they ran
> Along the public way by which the wall
> Was skirted, till they came where from the ground
> The two fair springs of eddying Xanthus rise,—
> One pouring a warm stream from which ascends
> And spreads a vapor like a smoke from fire ;
> The other even in summer, sending forth
> A current cold as hail, or snow, or ice.
> And there were broad stone basins, fairly wrought,
> At which in time of peace before the Greeks
> Had landed on the plain, the Trojan dames

And their fair daughters washed their sumptuous robes.
Past these they swept ; one fled and one pursued,—
A brave man fled, a braver followed close,
And swiftly both.
—*Iliad*, 22 : *Idem.*

Meantime the Trojans fled across the plain
Toward the wild fig-tree growing near the tomb
Of ancient Ilus, son of Dardanus,—
Eager to reach the town ; and still the son
Of Atreus followed, shouting, and with hands
Blood-stained and dust-begrimmed. And when they reached
The Scæan portals and the beechen tree,
They halted, waiting for the rear, like beeves
Chased panting by a lion who has come
At midnight on them, and has put the herd
To flight, and one of them to certain death.

* * * * * * *

Thus did Atrides Agamemnon chase
The Trojans ; still he slew the hindmost ; still
They fled before him. Many by his hand
Fell from their chariots prone, for terrible
Beyond all others with the spear was he.
But when he now was near the city wall,
The Father of immortals and of men
Came down from the high heaven, and took his seat
On many-fountained Ida.
—*Iliad*, 11 : *Idem.*

Now contrast with these the following description. It is not a poor one of its kind ; but all must perceive that a poem characterized by many passages like it, could not be in the highest degree interesting. Such descriptions, on account of their lack of the qualities noticed in those of Homer, tend to interrupt the plot and the interest felt in its characters. Besides this, of the many items mentioned here, few are described with sufficient specificness to make us feel that they were really perceived, and not merely fancied.

It was broad moonlight, and obscure or lost
The garden beauties lay;
But the great boundary rose distinctly marked.
These were no little hills,
No sloping uplands lifting to the sun
Their vineyards with fresh verdure, and the shade
Of ancient woods, courting the loiterer
To win the easy ascent; stone mountains these,
Desolate rock on rock,
The burdens of the earth,
Whose snowy summits met the morning beam
When night was in the vale, whose feet were fixed
In the world's foundations.   Thalaba beheld
The heights precipitous,
Impending crags, rocks unascendible,
And summits that had tired the eagle's wing:
"There is no way!" he said.
Paler Oneiza grew,
And hung upon his arm a feebler weight.

But soon again to hope
Revives the Arabian maid,
As Thalaba imparts the sudden thought.
"I passed a river," cried the youth,
"A full and copious stream.
The flowing waters cannot be restrained;
And where they find or force their way,
There we perchance may follow; thitherward
The current rolled along."
So saying, yet again in hope
Quickening their eager steps,
They turned them thitherward.

Silent and calm the river rolled along,
And at the verge arrived
Of that fair garden o'er a rocky bed,
Toward the mountain base
Still full and silent, held its even way.
But farther as they went, its deepening sound
Louder and louder in the distance rose,
As if it forced its stream
Struggling through crags along a narrow pass.

  And lo! where, raving o'er a hollow course,
  The ever-flowing flood
  Foams in a thousand whirlpools. There adown
  The perforated rock
  Plunge the whole waters; so precipitous,
  So fathomless a fall,
  That their earth-shaking roar came deadened up
  Like subterranean thunders.
         —*Thalaba*, 7: *Southey.*

The following description, similar in general character, is more interesting, because it is more specific and shorter:

  Onward amid the copse 'gan peep,
  A narrow inlet, still and deep,
  Affording scarce such breadth of brim,
  As served the wild-duck's brood to swim.
  Lost for a space, through thickets veering,
  But broader when again appearing,
  Tall rocks and tufted knolls their face
  Could on the dark-blue mirror trace;
  And farther as the hunter strayed,
  Still broader sweep its channels made.
  The shaggy mounds no longer stood,
  Emerging from entangled wood,
  But, wave-encircled, seemed to float,
  Like castle girdled with its moat;
  Yet broader fields extending still
  Divide them from their parent hill,
  Till each, retiring, claims to be
  An islet in an inland sea.
        —*Lady of the Lake*, 1: *Scott.*

But this is still more interesting, because it represents action that is closely connected with the plot.

  Then did Apollo and the god of sea
  Consult together to destroy the wall
  By turning on it the resistless might
  Of rivers. . . .
  . . . nine days against the wall
  He bade their currents rush, while Jupiter
  Poured constant rain, that floods might overwhelm

> The rampart ; and the god who shakes the earth,
> Wielding his trident, led the rivers on.
> He flung among the billows the huge beams
> And stones which, with hard toil, the Greeks had laid
> For the foundations. Thus he levelled all
> Beside the hurrying Hellespont, destroyed
> The bulwarks utterly, and overspread
> The long, broad shore with sand.
>
> *—Iliad*, 12 : *Bryant's Trs.*

The principles that apply to these representations of persons and scenes in nature, apply also to conversations in dramatic poems. All lengthy descriptions or declamatory passages that have nothing to do directly with giving definiteness, character, and progress to the plot, detract from the interest of the poem, considered as a whole. The effect of these things upon the form is the same as that of rubbish thrown into the current of a stream—it impedes the movement, and renders the water less transparent. This is the chief reason why the works of the dramatists of the age of the history of our literature commonly called classical, like Dryden, Addison, Rowe, Home, and Brooke, notwithstanding much that is excellent in their writings, have not been able to maintain their popularity. Ordinary audiences do not go to the theatre to be preached at in this style :

> These are all virtues of a meaner rank—
> Perfections that are placed in bones and nerves.
> A Roman soul is bent on higher views :
> To civilize the rude, unpolished world,
> And lay it under the restraint of laws ;
> To make man mild and sociable to man ;
> To cultivate the wild, licentious savage
> With wisdom, discipline, and liberal arts,
> The embellishments of life ; virtues like these
> Make human nature shine, reform the soul,
> And break our fierce barbarians into men.
>
> *—Cato*, 1, 4 : *Addison.*

Some may suppose that the chief reason why such passages as these, and those quoted from Southey, are not popular, is because they manifest so few evidences of the work of constructive imagination, by which is meant mainly that they contain so little figurative language.

Yet, we have seen that some of Homer's descriptions are equally lacking in figures. It is not merely this that renders a description inartistic. It is its failure to be truly representative. For this reason the mere addition to it of figurative language would not remedy its defects.

This fact, however, will be considered at full in other chapters. The present chapter will be closed with a few quotations exemplifying, beyond what has been done in the preceding passages, how Homer carries the principles now under consideration into his *illustrative* representation. In the descriptions used in order to *exemplify* the main thought in the following, will be found the same characteristics as in those making up the main thought in most of the preceding quotations. It will be noticed that the items forming the features of every separate figure, mentioned for the sake of comparison, are presented in the same mental, fragmentary, specific, typical and progressive way with which we may now be supposed to have become familiar.

> The hero was aroused
> To fury fierce as Mars when brandishing
> His spear, or as a desolating flame
> That rages on a mountain-side among
> The thickets of a close-grown wood. His lips
> Were white with foam; his eyes from underneath
> His frowning brows streamed fire; and as he fought,
> Upon the hero's temples fearfully
> The helmet nodded. . . .
>   Through the serried lines
> He could not break; the Greeks in solid squares

Resisted, like a rock that huge and high
By the gray deep abides the buffetings
Of the shrill winds and swollen waves that beat
Against it. Firmly thus the Greeks withstood
The Trojan host, and fled not. In a blaze
Of armor, Hector, rushing toward their ranks,
Fell on them like a mighty billow raised
By the strong cloud-born winds, that flings itself
On a swift ship, and whelms it in its spray.
—Iliad, 15 : *Bryant's Trs.*

Then Pallas to Tydides Diomed
Gave strength and courage, that he might appear
Among the Achaians greatly eminent,
And win a glorious name. Upon his head
And shield she caused a constant flame to play,
Like to the autumnal star that shines in heaven
Most brightly when new-bathed in ocean tides.
Such light she caused to beam upon his crest
And shoulders, as she sent the warrior forth
Into the thick and tumult of the fight.
—Iliad, 5 : *Idem.*

All the Greeks
Meanwhile came thronging to the appointed place.
As swarming forth from cells within the rock,
Coming and coming still the tribe of bees
Fly in a cluster o'er the flowers of spring,
And some are darting out from right to left.
So from the ships and tents a multitude
Along the spacious beach in mighty throngs
Moved toward the assembly.
—Iliad, 2 : *Idem.*

CHAPTER XXIII.

ALLOYED REPRESENTATION : ITS GENESIS.

>Alloy introduces Unpoetic Elements into Verse—All Classic Representation Pure—Tendencies in Poetic Composition leading to Alloyed Representation—In Direct Representation—In Illustrative Representation—Lawful to enlarge by Illustrations an Idea Great and Complex or Small and Simple—Descriptions of a Meal—Sunset—Peasant—Sailor—How these Tendencies may introduce Alloy that does not represent—Exaggerations in Love-Scenes—In Descriptions of Natural Scenery, etc.—In Allegorical Poems and Sensational Plays.

WE will examine now the form of representation which, in contrast to pure, has been termed alloyed. This latter, as has been said, while following in the main the methods of picturing the thoughts that are used in pure representation, always introduces something into the picture in addition to what would naturally be *perceived* in connection with circumstances like those that are being detailed. At first thought, it might be supposed that these additions would not greatly impair the poetry in which we find them. But the fallacy of this supposition will appear, when we recall that poetry is an art, and that all art is representative. It follows from this that the purer the representation, the purer will be the art, and in the degree in which any thing is added to the representation,—any thing, that is, of such a nature that in like circumstances it could not presumably

GENESIS OF ALLOYED REPRESENTATION. 263

have been perceived,—in that degree will the product be likely to lose its artistic qualities.

Some who may not recognize the truth of this statement, when viewed from a theoretical standpoint, may, when viewed from a practical. Let us look at it in this way then: whatever is added to the representation must come, in the last analysis, from the artist; and from him, when not exercising his legitimate artistic functions; when, instead of giving us a picture of nature and man, as he finds them, he has begun to give us his own explanations and theories concerning them. Now all explanation and theories, as we know, are necessarily the outgrowth—if not of ignorance or superstition—at least of the intellectual or spiritual condition of the age in which one lives. For this reason, to a succeeding age they are not satisfactory, even if they do not prove to be wholly fallacious; and a work of science or philosophy that is made up of them usually dies, because men outgrow their need of it, and do not care to keep it alive. A work of artistic poetry, on the contrary, lives because its pages image the phenomena of nature, and of human life, which can really be *perceived*, and most of these remain from age to age unchanged. A writer who confines himself to these, which alone can be used legitimately in representation, is, as Jonson[1] said of Shakespear, " not of an age but for all time "; and this fact can be affirmed of men like him alone. Out of the thousands of poems written in the past, only those have come down to us, and are termed classic, which are characterized by an absence of explanations and theories, and a presence of that kind of representation which has here been termed pure. How important, then, it is for the poet of the present to under-

---

[1] To the memory of my beloved master William Shakespear.

stand just what the nature and requirements of this pure representation are, and what are the methods of rendering it alloyed that should be avoided.

We shall start at the beginning of our subject, if we notice, first, certain influences tending to divert the poet from his legitimate work, and causing him to depart from the methods of pure representation. These will be considered in the present chapter.

Taking up first in order *direct* representation, it follows, from what has been said already, that composition in the plain language of this form can be nothing except prose, the moment the writer ceases to think in pictures; the moment, therefore, that, without using figurative language, he begins to be didactic or argumentative. Notice how easy it would be to glide into prose from a passage like the following. All that saves it, as it is, are the pictures of William, of the two women, and of the old man, which, as we read it, rise up irresistibly before the imagination.

> "O Sir, when William died, he died at peace
> With all men ; for I asked him, and he said,
> He could not ever rue his marrying me.
> I had been a patient wife : but, Sir, he said
> That he was wrong to cross his father thus :
> 'God bless him !' he said, 'and may he never know
> The troubles I have gone through !' Then he turned
> His face and passed—unhappy that I am !
> But now, Sir, let me have my boy, for you
> Will make him hard, and he will learn to slight
> His father's memory ; and take Dora back,
> And let all this be as it was before."
> So Mary said, and Dora hid her face
> By Mary. There was silence in the room ;
> And all at once the old man burst in sobs :—
> "I have been to blame—to blame ! I have killed my son !"
> —*Dora : Tennyson.*

Following chapters will contain so many contrasted passages of pure and alloyed representation in the direct form, that it would be superfluous to introduce any more of them here. Besides this, whatever poetic principles their introduction would illustrate, can be brought out as well while we go on to consider what is a far more important part of our present discussion, namely, the influences tending to divert the poet from his legitimate work when composing in *figurative* language.

As all illegitimate tendencies are usually developed in some way from legitimate ones, perhaps the best method of approaching our present subject is to start by recalling what has been said before with reference to the necessity, in order to express certain phases of thought, of a poet's writing in figurative language. From this necessity it follows that he will be impelled to use figures whenever, for any reason, he feels that plain language will not serve his purpose. Two circumstances, inclusive, in a broad way, of many others, will justify him, as we can see, in having this feeling: first, where the impression to be conveyed is very great or complex in its nature. Very frequently, in these circumstances, plain *direct* representation might not only fail to do justice to the subject, but might positively misrepresent it. Milton wished to convey an impression of the size and power of Satan. It would scarcely have been possible for him to do this adequately without making his representation *illustrative;* and by taking this course he has furnished us with an example of a pure and legitimate use of this form.

> Thus Satan talking to his nearest mate,
> With head uplift above the wave, and eyes
> That sparkling blazed ; his other parts besides
> Prone on the flood, extended long and large,

> Lay floating many a rood, in bulk as huge
> As whom the fables name of monstrous size,
> Titanian, or Earth-born, that warr'd on Jove,
> Briareüs, or Typhon, whom the den
> By ancient Tarsus held, or that sea-beast
> Leviathan, which God of all his works
> Created hugest that swim th' ocean stream :
> Him haply slumb'ring on the Norway foam,
> The pilot of some small night-founder'd skiff
> Deeming some island, oft, as seamen tell,
> With fixed anchor in his scaly rind
> Moors by his side under the lea, while night
> Invests the sea, and wished for morn delays :
> So stretched out huge in length the arch-fiend lay,
> Chained on the burning lake, nor ever thence
> Had risen or heav'd his head.
> —*Paradise Lost*, 1.

The second circumstance that justifies a writer in feeling that he must not use *direct* representation is this:—not the fact that the impression to be conveyed is too great or complex to be represented truthfully in this manner, but just the opposite:—the fact that it is too small and simple to be represented adequately in this manner. When the scene to be described is one that in itself is fitted to awaken the deepest and grandest feelings and thoughts, then, as in the concluding paragraph of "Paradise Lost," given a few pages back, direct representation is all that is needed. Wherever, in fact, the ideas to be presented are sublime or pathetic in themselves, the one thing necessary is that the reader should realize them as they are ; and any indirectness in the style rather hinders than furthers this. A celebrated preacher once said that passages in his sermons that were full of thought he delivered calmly, but when he came to passages that were destitute of it, he instinctively felt that it was time for him to "holler." A similar principle is apt to control style in poetry. Indeed, the main reason for the large preponderance of direct over illustrative representation in the works of Homer and of the Greek tragedians, is undoubtedly this,—that most of the persons and actions of which they treated were heroic in their nature. They needed only to be represented as they were, in order to awaken admiration. It is the boast of our modern times, however, that we have learned to take an interest in common men and actions. The poet feels that he misses that which perhaps is noblest in his mission if he fail to help the humblest of his fellows, physically, mentally, socially, morally, and spiritually, by doing his best to lead them out of the condition of poor Peter Bell. He, as you may remember,

> Had danced his round with Highland lasses;
> And he had lain beside his asses
> On lofty Cheviot Hills:
> * * * * * *
> And all along the indented coast,
> Bespattered with the salt-sea foam;
> Where'er a knot of houses lay,
> On headland, or in hollow bay;—
> Sure never man like him did roam!
> * * * * * *
> He travelled here, he travelled there:—
> But not the value of a hair
> Was heart or head the better.
> * * * * * *
> In vain through every changeful year,
> Did Nature lead him as before;
> A primrose by a river's brim,
> A yellow primrose was to him,
> And it was nothing more.
> —*Peter Bell: Wordsworth.*

Out of this condition it is the duty of the poet to bring

mankind by revealing to them, by "the light [1] that never was on sea or land," the poetry that lies concealed in the surroundings and experiences of ordinary life.

Inasmuch, however, as this poetry lies concealed in ordinary life, the poet is compelled to do more than simply to represent ordinary life. He must make this appear to be more than it seems to be; and he must do so by making more of his poetic form than can be done in *direct* representation. We all know how ladies taking up a temporay residence for the summer in small seaside cottages, erected without paint or plaster, make up for the lack of other beautifying elements, by tacking all over the walls Japanese fans and screens of innumerable hues, intermingled with wreaths of evergreen and myrtle; or how, when they rent furnished houses in which the colors of the carpets, chairs, and wall papers do not harmonize, they spread tidies, afghans, and ornaments of all possible shades over sofas and mantles, so as to produce effects pleasing by way of combination and variety, where it is impossible to have simplicity aud unity. All this is an illustration of cheap ornamentation. Yet it is justifiable in such circumstances. The tendency producing it is exercised unjustifiably only when an architect or upholsterer, with an opportunity to rely upon more worthy methods, tries to produce similar results not as means but as ends. *Illustrative* representation in poetry is often produced by bringing together all sorts of elements, very much as the Japanese fans are brought together in seaside cottages; and it is justifiable when it is necessary to make thought attractive which otherwise would not be so. To illustrate how poetry can make this sort of thought attractive, take this description of a luncheon in Tenny-

---

[1] Elegiac stanzas suggested by a picture of Peele Castle : Woodsworth.

son's *Audley Court*. In most of the passage we have *direct* representation; but all the better for this reason, it serves to illustrate what I mean by saying that form can make the unpoetic seem poetic. What could be more unpoetic or commonplace than a meal? Yet notice how by the introduction of picturesque elements like "wrought with horse and hound," "dusky," "costly made," "Like fossils of the rock," "golden" "Imbedded," and the graphic account of the conversation,—all such as could be observed by one looking on, the poet has rendered the whole poetic. It is an admirable illustration of a legitimate way in which by richness of form a poet can make up for poverty of ideas.

> There, on a slope of orchard, Francis laid
> A damask napkin wrought with horse and hound,
> Brought out a dusky loaf that smelt of home,
> And, half-cut down, a pasty costly-made,
> Where quail and pigeon, lark and leveret lay,
> Like fossils of the rock, with golden yolks
> Imbedded and injellied; last, with these,
> A flask of cider from his father's vats,
> Prime, which I knew; and so we sat and ate,
> And talked old matters over; who was dead,
> Who married, who was like to be, and how
> The races went, and who would rent the hall;
> Then touched upon the game, how scarce it was
> This season; glancing thence, discussed the farm,
> The fourfold system and the price of grain;
> And struck upon the corn-laws, where we split,
> And came again together on the king
> With heated faces, till he laughed aloud;
> And, while the blackbird on the pippin hung
> To hear him, clapt his hand in mine and sang.
> —*Audley Court: Tennyson.*

There is much more poetry in a sunset than in a luncheon. Yet both are ordinary occurrences; and few can fail to recognize that it is the use of *illustrative* representation in the following that has enabled Wordsworth to lift this particular sunset entirely above any thing at all ordinary.

> A single step, that freed me from the skirts,
> Of the blind vapor, opened to my view
> Glory beyond all glory ever seen
> By waking sense or by the dreaming soul !
> The appearance, instantaneously disclosed,
> Was of a mighty city,—boldly say
> A wilderness of building, sinking far
> And self-withdrawn into a boundless depth,
> Far sinking into splendor,—without end !
> Fabric it seemed of diamond and of gold,
> With alabaster domes, and silver spires,
> And blazing terrace upon terrace, high
> Uplifted ; here, serene pavilions bright,
> In avenues disposed ; there, towers begirt
> With battlements that on their restless fronts
> Bore stars,—illumination of all gems !
>   *   *   *   *   *   *   *
> O 't was an unimaginable sight !
> Clouds, mists, streams, watery rocks, and emerald turf,
> Clouds of all tincture, rocks and sapphire sky,
> Confused, commingled, mutually inflamed,
> Molten together and composing thus,
> Each lost in each, that marvellous array
> Of temple, palace, citadel, and huge
> Fantastic pomp of structure without name,
> In fleecy fold voluminous enwrapped.
>   *   *   *   *   *   *   *
> This little Vale a dwelling-place of Man
> Lay low beneath my feet ; 't was visible,—
> I saw not, but I felt that it was there.
> That which I *saw* was the revealed abode
> Of Spirits in beatitude.
>   —*Excursion*, 2 : *Wordsworth.*

These quotations, though themselves containing nothing objectionable, will render it easy for us to understand how naturally this tendency to crowd outside elements into the form passes into alloyed representation. In Longfellow's *Evangeline*, and Tennyson's *Enoch Arden* we have told us stories respectively of a peasant and a sailor. There is much in the surroundings, appearances, actions, thoughts, and feelings of people of these classes which is unpoetic, uninteresting, sometimes even repelling to persons sufficiently cultivated and refined to enjoy poetry of the highest order. At the same time there are genuinely poetic elements in almost every thing that has to do with human life. By making a great deal of these elements, and very little or nothing at all of others, the poet, in a legitimate way, can cause that to seem attractive which otherwise might not seem so. Longfellow does this in the following passage from *Evangeline*.

> Cheerily neighed the steeds, with dew on their manes and their fetlocks,
> While aloft on their shoulders the wooden and ponderous saddles
> Painted with brilliant dyes, and adorned with tassels of crimson,
> Nodded in bright array, like holyhocks heavy with blossoms.
> Patiently stood the cows meanwhile, and yielded their udders
> Unto the milkmaid's hand ; whilst loud and in regular cadence
> Into the sounding pails the foaming streamlets descended.
> Lowing of cattle and peals of laughter were heard in the farm-yard,
> Echoed back by the barns. Anon, they sank into stillness ;
> Heavily closed, with a jarring sound, the valves of the barn-doors,
> Rattled the wooden bars, and all for a season was silent.

But closely connected with this rendering attractive of certain forms of life, through bringing some of its elements to the front and keeping others in the background, is an endeavor to do the same, through introducing into the description elements that could not possibly be supposed to be there. For instance, immediately following the passage from *Evangeline* just given, is one describing her father, and his thoughts as he sits by his fireside.

Indoors, warm by the wide-mouthed fireplace, idly the farmer
Sat in his elbow-chair, and watched how the flames and the smoke-wreathes
Struggled together like foes in a burning city.   Behind him
Nodding and mocking along the wall, with gestures fantastic,
Darted his own huge shadow, aud vanished away into darkness.
Faces, clumsily carved in oak, on the back of his arm-chair,
Laughed in the flickering light, and the pewter plates on the dresser
Caught and reflected the flame, as shields of armies the sunshine.
—*Evangeline : Longfellow.*

The question connected with our line of thought, suggested by this passage, is this : Would this peasant, brought up as he had been, and with his surroundings, be likely to think of " foes in a burning city," " gestures fantastic," " shields of armies," etc. ? If not, then the representation is not pure. The passage indicates only an exceedingly slight tendency in the direction of alloyed representation ; but the very slightness of the tendency will enable us to trace it in its further development. Here is a passage from Tennyson's *Enoch Arden :*

> The mountain wooded to the peak, the lawns
> And winding glades high up like ways to heaven,
> The slender coco's drooping crown of plumes,
> The lightning flash of insect and of bird,
> The lustre of the long convolvuluses
> That coil'd around the stately stems, and ran
> E'en to the limit of the land, the glows
> And glories of the broad belt of the world,—
> All these he saw ; but what he fain had seen
> He could not see, the kindly human face,
> Nor ever hear a kindly voice, but heard
> The myriad shriek of wheeling ocean-fowl,
> The league-long roller thundering on the reef,
> The moving whisper of huge trees that branched
> And blossomed in the zenith, or the sweep
> Of some precipitous rivulet to the wave,
> As down the shore he ranged, or all day long
> Sat often in the seaward gazing gorge

> A shipwrecked sailor, waiting for a sail:
> No sail from day to day, but every day
> The sunrise broken into scarlet shafts
> Among the palms and ferns and precipices.

Walter Bagehot, who quotes this passage in his "Literary Studies," as an illustration of what he terms ornate poetry, says of this sailor: "The beauties of nature would not have so much occupied him. He would have known little of the scarlet shafts of sunrise and nothing of the long convolvuluses. As in 'Robinson Crusoe,' his own petty contrivances and his small ailments would have been the principal subjects to him." Such criticism may appear to some a little hypercritical. An extremely poetical sailor is certainly conceivable. Even if one could not possibly have had the thoughts here indicated, or at least not such thoughts exclusively, or to the extent represented by Tennyson, we feel that if any thing could justify a poet in misrepresenting the facts, it would be a desire to show a common ground of sympathy between readers of poetry and such a character, even at the expense of attributing to the latter thoughts and feelings of a more refined nature than he really would have experienced. But to see what the tendency here exemplified can do, when, without any motive to justify it, it is carried slightly further, notice, in the following, how the extravagance of the language, carried to the extreme of sentimentality, ruins the representation, because it is impossible to conceive of its being true to life. The fundamental fault of the passage lies in the fact that the subject requires no such excess of illustration. A direct account of what two young people falling in love at first sight would actually do and say in the circumstances, would have been far more effective. Not recognizing this, the poet,—an inexperienced writer, who most likely would have developed great excellence had he lived,—has put into the mouths of the two language possible only to a blasé society beau and belle making love in play. According to the poem, a lady approaching discovers a slumbering poet and exclaims:

>Ha ! what is this ?   A bright and wandered youth,
>Thick in the light of his own beauty, sleeps
>Like young Apollo, in his golden curls !
>At the oak-roots I 've seen full many a flower,
>But never one so fair.   A lovely youth
>With dainty cheeks and ringlets like a girl,
>And slumber-parted lips 't were sweet to kiss !
>Ye envious lids ! . . .
>   So, here 's a well-worn book
>From which he drinks such joy as doth a pale
>And dim-eyed worker, who escapes, in Spring,
>The thousand-streeted and smoke-smothered town,
>And treads awhile the breezy hills of health.
>   [Lady opens the book, a slip of paper falls out, she reads.]
>   *   *   *   *   *   *
>Oh, 't is a sleeping poet ! and his verse
>Sings like the Siren-isles . . .
>Hist ! he awakes . . .
>
>   WALTER (awakening).
>   Fair lady, in my dream
>Methought I was a weak and lonely bird,
>In search of summer, wandered on the sea,
>Toiling through mists, drenched by the arrowy rain,
>Struck by the heartless winds ; at last, methought
>I came upon an isle in whose sweet air
>I dried my feathers, smoothed my ruffled breast,
>And skimmed delight from off the waving woods.
>Thy coming, lady, reads this dream of mine :
>I am the swallow, thou the summer land.
>
>   LADY.
>Sweet, sweet is flattery to mortal ears,
>And, if I drink thy praise too greedily,

> My fault I 'll match with grosser instances.
> Do not the royal souls that van the world
> Hunger for praises ? Does not the hero burn
> To blow his triumphs in the trumpet's mouth?
> And do not poets' brows throb feverous
> Till they are cooled with laurels ? Therefore, sir,
> If such dote more on praise than all the wealth
> Of precious-wombèd earth and pearlèd-mains,
> Blame not the cheeks of simple maidenhood.
> —*Life Drama*, 2 : *Alex. Smith.*

No wonder that this tough specimen of "simple maidenhood" should have prayed so fervently not to be blamed—putting her word into the plural also—for her *cheek* in using such language to the poet before an introduction to him, and in prefacing it too with a peep at his manuscript.

There is an intimate connection between representation rendered inappropriate by the general character of the thought, and that rendered so by the smallness of the thought. In the following the same poet tells us of a youth who heard a woman singing. He had never seen her; but

> When she ceased
> The charmèd woods and breezes silent stood,
> As if all ear to catch her voice again.
> Uprose the dreamer from his couch of flowers,
> With awful expectation in his look,
> And happy tears upon his pallid face,
> With eager steps, as if toward a heaven,
> He onward went, and, lo ! he saw her stand,
> Fairer than Dian, in the forest glade.
> His footsteps startled her, and quick she turned
> Her face,—looks met like swords. He clasped his hands,
> And fell upon his knees ; the while there broke
> A sudden splendor o'er his yearning face ;
> 'T was a pale prayer in its very self.
> * * * * * *

> Thus like a worshipper before a shrine,
> He earnest syllabled, and, rising up,
> He led that lovely stranger tenderly
> Through the green forest toward the burning west.
> —*Idem*, 3.

In our next quotation the same tendency has passed beyond the stage of sentimentality into that of obscurity. The thought in it is so small for the kind of representation given it, as to be at times altogether invisible. It is intended to describe hot weather and a shower; and is a singular exemplification of the way in which extremes meet; for while the poet evidently supposes himself to be illustrating his subject, he is really trying to explain it. His endeavor to exercise his imaginative tendency has led him to argue; and while he thinks himself influenced by a poetic motive, it is really prosaic. Thus his style is a failure in two regards: it is both too figurative and too philosophical.

> Should Solstice, stalking through the sickening bowers,
> Suck the warm dew-drops, lap the falling showers;
> Kneel with parched lip, and bending from its brink,
> From dripping palm the scanty river drink;
> Nymphs! o'er the soil ten thousand points erect,
> And high in air the electric flame collect.
> Soon shall dark mists with self-attraction shroud
> The blazing day, and sail in wilds of cloud;
> Each silvery flower the streams aërial quaff,
> Bow her sweet head, and infant harvests laugh.
> —*The Botanic Garden, Part First* : E. *Darwin.*

By comparing any of the clean-cut, clear descriptions of Homer with this passage, in which, on account of the far-fetched illustrative nature of the form, it needs often a second thought to detect what the poet is talking about, one will have a sufficiently forcible exemplification of the difference between poetic form that is representative, and that which, on account of the addition to it of elements having to do merely with the illustrative methods of presenting the thought, is not representative.

The fault now under consideration characterizes, as will be noticed, all poems in which the subject does not justify the treatment,—from those like Spenser's *Faerie Queene*, (in which the allegory meant to illustrate the thought, and therefore an element merely of the form, is made to appear the principal thing, because developed to such an extent that one forgets all about what the subject of the poem is,) down to sensational plays, and romances of the lowest order, in which the characters, for serious, not comic purposes, are placed in situations and made to utter sentiments inconceivable in their circumstances. There is no necessity for quoting from such works here.

CHAPTER XXIV.

EXPLANATORY ALLOY IN DIRECT REPRESENTATION.

Alloy, if carrying to Extreme the Tendency in Plain Language, becomes Didactic ; if the Tendency in Figurative Language, it becomes Ornate —Didactic Alloy explains, and appeals to the Elaborative Faculty, not the Imagination—Rhetoric instead of Poetry—Examples of Didactic Alloy where Representation purports to be Direct—In Cases where the Thought is Philosophical—How Thought of the same Kind can be Expressed Poetically—In Cases where the Thought is Picturesque, as in Descriptions of Natural Scenery—How similar Scenes can be described Poetically—Didactic Descriptions of Persons—Similar Representative Descriptions—How Illustrative Representation helps the Appeal to the Imagination—In Descriptions of Natural Scenery—Of Persons—The Sensuous and the Sensual.

THE reader who has followed our line of thought to this point, probably understands by this time the general nature of the difference between pure and alloyed representation. But he cannot understand the extent of the inartistic influence which the latter introduces into poetry as a representative art, until he has traced its developments a little further. That will be done for him in this and following chapters.

It has been said that whatever is added to representation of such a nature as to change it from pure to alloyed, must come from the poet. This is true, and yet he may not always be himself the primary source of these additions. He may get them either from his own mind or from nature,—a term used here to apply to every thing external to himself. If he get them from his own mind, he will carry into excessive development the tendency which has been termed the instinctive, underlying ejaculatory sounds and all plain language; and his product will manifest a preponderance of the features making up the *thought* that he desires to express. If he get his additions from nature, he will carry into excessive development the tendency, which has been termed the reflective, underlying imitative sounds and all figurative language; and his product will manifest a preponderance of the features employed in the form for the purpose of *amplifying* and *illustrating* his thought. The first tendency, carried to an extreme, will deprive the form of representation, and make it *explanatory* or *didactic;* the second will overload it with representation, and make it *florid* or *ornate*.

Taking up these tendencies in their order, we will examine now the former of them, and first, as exemplified in poetry modelled upon *direct* representation. In this form, as we have seen, the poet uses no similies nor metaphors. He states precisely what he wishes to say— only what he says, if put in the form of poetry, must *represent* his thought. If it merely *present* this, he gives us a product not of the ideal art of poetry, but of the practical art of rhetoric. This latter appeals to the mind through what Sir William Hamilton termed the elaborative faculty, and is characterized by a particularizing of details in explanatory words and clauses, termed amplification,—all of which details together enable the hearer to weigh the evidence that is offered, and to draw from it trustworthy conclusions. Poetry, on the contrary, appeals to the representative faculty, and is characterized by an absence of any more details or explanatory elements than are needed in order to form a picture, and this for the reason that nothing appeals so strongly to the imagination as a hint. At the same time, as poetry and rhetoric both communicate ideas, there is a constant tendency for the one to pass into the other, for the poet to forget that the poetical depends not upon ideas alone, but also upon the forms given to the ideas,—in fact, to forget that, while great poetry must necessarily embody great thoughts, very genuine poetry, at times, may do no more than give to the merest "airy nothings a local habitation and a name."

To exemplify what has been said, let us begin with some quotations from Wordsworth. They are specimens of rhetoric, pure and simple, presenting, but not in any sense representing, the thought. By consequence, they are almost wholly lacking in the suggestive and inspiring effects with which true poetry appeals to the imagination:

>   O for the coming of that glorious time
>   When, prizing knowledge as her noblest wealth
>   And best protection, this imperial Realm,
>   While she exacts allegiance, shall admit
>   An obligation, on her part, to *teach*
>   Them who are born to serve her and obey ;
>   Binding herself by statute to secure
>   For all the children whom her soil maintains
>   The rudiments of letters, and inform
>   The mind with moral and religious truth,
>   Both understood and practised,—so that none,
>   However destitute, be left to droop,
>   By timely culture unsustained.
>   *   *   *   *   *   *   *
>   The discipline of slavery is unknown
>   Among us,—hence the more do we require
>   The discipline of virtue ; order else
>   Cannot subsist, nor confidence, nor peace.
>   Thus, duties rising out of good possessed,
>   And prudent caution needful to avert
>   Impending evil, equally require

> That the whole people should be taught and trained.
> So shall licentiousness and black resolve
> Be rooted out, and virtuous habits take
> Their place ; and genuine piety descend
> Like an inheritance from age to age.
>
>   *   *   *   *   *   *
>
> Vast the circumference of hope,—and ye
> Are at its centre, British Lawgivers ;
> . . . Your country must complete
> Her glorious destiny. Begin even now,
>
>   *   *   *   *   *   *
>
> Now when destruction is a prime pursuit
> Show to the wretched nations for what end
> The powers of civil polity were given.
>
>   —*Excursion*, 9.

Some may suppose that the thought presented in these passages is not fitted for representation, and be inclined to justify the poet's treatment of it on this ground. The truth is, however, that there is very little thought that cannot be expressed in a representative way. As a proof of this, look at the following passages from Tennyson's *Princess*. They contain thoughts of essentially the same character as those from the *Excursion ;* yet their forms, if not always those of *direct* representation, are, at least, those of representation of some sort, which is the important matter, just now, for us to consider.

>   O lift your natures up,
> Embrace our aims ; work out your freedom ! . . .
> Knowledge is now no more a fountain sealed :
> Drink deep, until the habits of the slave,
> The sins of emptiness, gossip, and spite,
> And slander die. Better not be at all
> Than not be noble.
>
>   *   *   *   *   *   *
>
> Let there be light, and there was light : 't is so :
> For was, and is, and will be, are but is ;
> And all creation is one act at once,
> The birth of light ; but we that are not all,

As parts, can see but parts, now this, now that,
And live, perforce, from thought to thought, and make
One act a phantom of succession : thus
Our weakness somewhat shapes the shadow, Time ;
But in the shadow will we work.

* * * * * * *

But trim our sails and let old by-gones be,
While down the stream that floats us each and all
To the issue, goes, like glittering bergs of ice,
Throne after throne, and molten on the waste
Becomes a cloud ; for all things serve their time
Toward that great year of equal mights and rights.

* * * * * * *

And knowledge in our own land make her free,
And ever following those two crownèd twins,
Commerce and conquest, shower the fiery grain
Of Freedom broadcast over all that orbs
Between the Northern and the Southern morn.
—*Princess : Tennyson.*

In the following, also, a very similar line of thought is not merely presented or stated, but represented or pictured :

For I dipped into the future, far as human eye could see,
Saw the Vision of the world, and all the wonder that would be ;

Saw the heavens fill with commerce, argosies of magic sails,
Pilots of the purple twilight, dropping down with costly bales ;

Heard the heavens fill with shouting, and there rained a ghastly dew
From the nations' airy navies grappling in the central blue ;

Far along the world-wide whisper of the South wind rushing warm
With the standards of the peoples plunging through the thunder-storm ;

Till the war-drum throbbed no longer, and the battle-flags were furled
In the Parliament of man, the Federation of the world ;

There the common-sense of most shall hold a fretful realm in awe,
And the kindly earth shall slumber, lapt in universal law.
—*Locksley Hall : Tennyson.*

THE DIDACTIC IN DIRECT REPRESENTATION. 283

The following, too, though it contains representation that is both illustrative and alloyed, will serve to show how the kind of thought expressed in the passage from the *Excursion* may be treated representatively.

> We sleep and wake and sleep, but all things move;
> The Sun flies forward to his brother Sun;
> The dark Earth follows, wheeled in her ellipse;
> And human things returning on themselves,
> Move onward, leading up the golden year.
>
> Ah! though the times when some new thought can bud
> Are but as poets' seasons when they flower,
> Yet seas that daily gain upon the shore
> Have ebb and flow, conditioning their march,
> And slow and sure comes up the golden year.
>
> When wealth no more shall rest in moulded heaps,
> But smit with freer light shall slowly melt
> In many streams to fatten lower lands,
> And light shall spread, and man be liker man
> Through all the seasons of the golden year.
>   *   *   *   *   *   *   *
> Fly happy, happy sails, and bear the Press;
> Fly happy with the mission of the Cross;
> Knit land to land, and blowing havenward,
> With silks, and fruits, and spices, clear of toll,
> Enrich the markets of the golden year.
>
> But we grow old. Ah! when shall all men's good
> Be each man's rule, and universal Peace
> Lie like a shaft of light across the land,
> And like a lane of beams athwart the sea,
> Through all the circle of the golden year?
>   —*The Golden Year: Tennyson.*

As the principle under consideration is important, the reader will excuse one further quotation exemplifying better perhaps than any of those already considered the way in which ideas of this kind may be expressed very clearly and forcibly, and yet representatively. In the following, the poet has to say that he is tired of the buzz and bustle of the world, and wishes to live in retirement. This is the prose of his statement. Notice now how he represents this thought, and in doing so turns it into poetry. Most of the representation here, too, is *direct* and *pure*.

> Let us swear an oath, and keep it with an equal mind,
> In the hollow Lotus-land to live, and lie reclined
> On the hills like Gods together, careless of mankind.
> For they lie beside their nectar, and the bolts are hurled
> Far below them in the valleys, and the clouds are lightly curled
> Round their golden houses, girdled with a gleaming world ;
> Where they smile in secret, looking over wasted lands,
> Blight and famine, plague and earthquake, roaring deeps and fiery sands,
> Clanging fights, and flaming towns, and sinking ships, and praying hands.
> —*The Lotus Eaters: Tennyson.*

Could there be a more significant picture of the trouble of this life, or a more fitting climax for it than the helplessness of these "praying hands"? Poetry does not reveal truth to us in logic, but in light.

It is not only, however, in the expression of thought in itself unpicturesque, that the poet is in danger of giving us rhetoric instead of poetry. Even in descriptions of objects and persons in which, at first, it might be supposed that it would be impossible to do any thing except represent, the same tendency is manifest. In the following from Southey's *Madoc in Wales*, the descriptions scarcely include one feature that might not be true of any one of a score of rivers or mountains. Therefore the lines are almost wholly lacking in the specificness noticed in Chapter XXII. as characterizing the descriptions of Homer. This fact alone might be enough to condemn them. But their lack of this trait is not the chief reason why they are mentioned here ; but because, owing

THE DIDACTIC IN DIRECT REPRESENTATION. 285

to the lack of it, they read like something written in a man's study, not out of doors where he had a view of the objects delineated. In other words, they read like something taken out of his own brain. For this reason they furnish good examples of direct representation in which too much attention relatively is given to the thoughts that come from the author as contrasted with that which comes from nature.

> The land bent westward soon,
> And, thus confirmed, we voyaged on to seek
> The river inlet, following at the will
> Of our new friend ; and we learnt after him,
> Well pleased and proud to teach what this was called,
> What that, with no unprofitable pains.
> * * * * * * *
> At length we came
> Where the great river, amid shoals, and banks,
> And islands, growth of its own gathering spoils,
> Through many a branching channel, wide and full,
> Rushed to the main.
> —*Madoc in Wales*, 5 : *Southey.*

> We travelled in the mountains ; then a plain
> Opened below, and rose upon the sight,
> Like boundless ocean from a hill-top seen.
> A beautiful and populous plain it was ;
> Fair woods were there, and fertilizing streams,
> And pastures spreading wide, and villages
> In fruitful groves embowered, and stately towns,
> And many a single dwelling specking it.
> As though for many years the land had been
> The land of peace.
> —*Idem*, 6.

As contrasted with this, notice the following. In reading it, we feel that it definitely represents some real scene which we ourselves at once imagine that we see. Therefore it is better poetry than that in the quotation from Southey.

> On either side
> Is level fen, a prospect wild and wide,
> With dikes on either hand, by ocean's self supplied.
> Far on the right, the distant sea is seen,
> And salt the springs that feed the marsh between ;
> Beneath an ancient bridge the straightened flood
> Rolls through its sloping banks of slimy mud ;
> Near it a sunken boat resists the tide,
> That frets and hurries to the opposing side ;
> The rushes sharp that on the borders grow,
> Bend their brown flowerets to the stream below,
> Impure in all its course, in all its progress slow.
> —*Lover's Journey : Crabbe.*

There is poetry, however, higher in its quality than this, —poetry in which we not only feel that the things described actually exist or existed, but that the man describing them saw at the supposed time of the description just what he says that he saw. Crabbe's description reads a little as if the narrator had gone out some morning and taken notes, as one would for a county map, and then had come back and copied off what he gives us. But in reading the following, from Tennyson's *Gardener's Daughter*, we derive no such impression. In fact, a man taking notes would not confine himself to the things here mentioned. It is only natural to suppose, therefore, that they were seen by the narrator just as they are represented in the picture. In another place may be explained what is meant by saying that this description for this reason gives expression to a poetic motive. At present, it is sufficient to direct attention to the fact that we have arrived now, through a different course, at the same conclusion as that reached while examining the poetry of Homer in Chapter XXII. The representation below seems real and life-like, because only a few things are mentioned, and these just the ones that would impress the mind of an observer amid such surroundings. The description is not indefinite and characterless, like that of Southey, but specific and typical; it is not complete and circumstantial, like the photographic picture of Crabbe, but fragmentary and suggestive—a rapid sketch of salient outlines, which the imagination is left to fill in for itself. There is some *illustrative* representation in it, but this need not injure it for our present purpose.

> Not wholly in the busy world, nor quite
> Beyond it, blooms the garden that I love.
> News from the humming city comes to it
> In sound of funeral or of marriage bells ;
> And, sitting muffled in dark leaves, you hear
> The windy clanging of the minster clock ;
> Although between it and the garden lies
> A league of grass, washed by a slow, broad stream,
> That, stirred with languid pulses of the oar,
> Waves all its lazy lilies, and creeps on,
> Barge-laden, to three arches of a bridge
> Crowned with the minster-towers.
> —*Gardener's Daughter : Tennyson.*

It will be well to close this phase of our subject with an example of representation that is not only *pure*, but, from beginning to end, *direct*.

> So saying, by the hand he took me, raised,
> And over fields and waters, as in air
> Smooth sliding without step, last led me up
> A woody mountain ; whose high top was plain,
> A circuit wide, enclosed, with goodliest trees
> Planted, with walks and bowers, that what I saw
> Of earth before scarce pleasant seem'd. Each tree
> Loaden with fairest fruit, that hung to the eye
> Tempting, stirr'd in me sudden appetite
> To pluck and eat ; whereat I wak'd, and found
> Before mine eyes all real, as the dream
> Had lively shadow'd ; here had new begun
> My wandering, had not he, who was my guide

> Up hither, from among the trees appear'd,
> Presence Divine. Rejoicing, but with awe,
> In adoration at his feet I fell,
> Submiss: He rear'd me, and, Whom thou sought'st I am,
> Said mildly, Author of all this thou seest
> Above, or round about thee, or beneath.
> —*Paradise Lost*, 8: *Milton.*

Now let us go back and take up examples in which, in descriptions of *persons*, too much attention, relatively, is paid to the thought as contrasted with the form. The following is a passage of this kind. Through a series of explanations, it appeals directly to the understanding, scarcely at all to the imagination.

> I admire
> Him and his fortunes, who hath wrought thy safety;
> Yea as my mind predicts, with thine his own.
> Obscure and friendless he the army sought;
> Bent upon peril in the range of death.
> Resolved to hunt for fame and with his sword
> To gain distinction which his birth denied.
> In this attempt unknown he might have perished,
> And gained with all his valor but oblivion.
> Now graced by thee his virtue serves no more
> Beneath despair. The soldier now of hope,
> He stands conspicuous: fame and great renown
> Are brought within the compass of his sword.
> —*Douglas*, 2: *Home.*

Here is another passage of the same sort:

> Turn up thine eyes to Cato!
> There mayest thou see to what a godlike height
> The Roman virtues lift up mortal man.
> While good and just and anxious for his friends
> He's still severely bent against himself;
> Renouncing sleep, and rest, and food, and ease,
> He strives with thirst and hunger, toil and heat;
> And, when his fortune sets before him all
> The pomp and pleasures that his soul can wish,
> His rigid virtues will accept of none.
> —*Cato*, 1, 4: *Addison.*

Contrast with this the following description of Ogier the Dane in William Morris' *Earthly Paradise*. The representation here is just as *direct* as in the foregoing, but, in a sense not true of it, each sentence presents a picture.

> Great things he suffered, great delights he had,
> Unto great kings he gave good deeds for bad;
> He ruled o'er kingdoms, where his name no more
> Is had in memory, and on many a shore
> He left his sweat and blood, to win a name
> Passing the bounds of earthly creature's fame.
> A love he won and lost, a well-loved son
> Whose little day of promise soon was done.
> A tender wife he had, that he must leave
> Before his heart her love could well receive.
> —*Ogier the Dane.*

Of course some will think that these lines are not far removed from the level of prose. But they could not well be made more poetic without using *illustrative* representation, the introduction of which into passages of this kind is much the best way of making them appeal to the imagination. To recognize this fact one has only to compare the following descriptions of natural scenery with those given a few moments ago. The first deviates only slightly from the methods of *direct* representation.

> In front
> The sea lay laughing at a distance; near,
> The solid mountains shone, bright as the clouds,
> Grain-tinctured, drenched in empyrean light;
> And in the meadows and the lower grounds
> Was all the sweetness of a common dawn,—
> Dews, vapors, and the melody of birds,
> And laborers going forth to till the fields.
> —*The Prelude,* 4: *Wordsworth.*

In the second the figures stand out more clearly:

> At my feet
> Rested a silent sea of hoary mist.
> A hundred hills their dusky backs upheaved
> All over this still ocean ; and beyond,
> Far, far beyond, the solid vapors stretched,
> In headlands, tongues, and promontory shapes,
> Into the main Atlantic, that appeared
> To dwindle, and give up his majesty,
> Usurped upon far as the sight could reach.
> —*Prelude*, 14 : *Wordsworth.*

Now look at the effects of *illustrative* representation upon descriptions of *persons*, as in this:

> O what a noble mind is here o'erthrown !
> The courtier's, scholar's, soldier's eye, tongue, sword :
> The expectancy and rose of the fair State,
> The glass of fashion, and the mould of form,
> The observed of all observers.
> —*Hamlet*, iii., 1 : *Shakespear.*

And in this:

> He was not born to shame :
> Upon his brow shame is ashamed to sit ;
> For 't is a throne where honor may be crowned
> Sole monarch of the universal earth.
> —*Romeo and Juliet*, iii., 2 : *Idem.*

And in these series of pictures presented to the imagination in Sir Richard Vernon's description of Prince Harry and his troops:

> All furnished, all in arms ;
> All plumed like estridges that wing the wind ;
> Bated like eagles having lately bathed ;
> Glittering in golden coats, like images ;
> As full of spirit as the month of May,
> And gorgeous as the sun at midsummer ;
> Wanton as youthful goats, wild as young bulls.
> I saw young Harry,—with his beaver on,
> His cuisses on his thighs, gallantly armed,—
> Rise from the ground like feathered Mercury,
> And vaulted with such ease into his seat,

> As if an angel dropped down from the clouds,
> To turn and wind a fiery Pegasus,
> And witch the world with noble horsemanship.
> —1 *Henry IV.*, iv., 1 : *Shakespear.*

Notice, too, to what an extent the element of beauty is introduced into the following, through the use of *illustrative* representation :

> For up the porch there grew an Eastern rose
> That, flowering high, the last night's gale had caught,
> And blown across the walk. One arm aloft—
> Gowned in pure white, that fitted to the shape—
> Holding the bush, to fix it back, she stood.
> A single stream of all her soft brown hair
> Poured on one side : the shadow of the flowers
> Stole all the golden gloss, and, wavering
> Lovingly lower, trembled on her waist—
> Ah, happy shade !—and still went wavering down,
> But ere it touched a foot that might have danced
> The green sward into greener circles, dipt
> And mixed with shadows of the common ground !
> But the full day dwelt on her brows, and sunned
> Her violet eyes, and all her Hebe-bloom,
> And doubled his own warmth against her lips,
> And on the bounteous wave of such a breast
> As never pencil drew. Half light, half shade,
> She stood, a sight to make an old man young.
> —*The Gardener's Daughter : Tennyson.*

Milton says that poetry must be simple, sensuous, and passionate. The above certainly meets all these requirements. Read this too from Shakespear's *Antony and Cleopatra :*

> I will tell you.
> The barge she sat in, like a burnished throne,
> Burned on the water : the poop was beaten gold ;
> Purple the sails, and so perfumed, that
> The winds were love-sick with them ; the oars were silver;
> Which to the tune of flutes kept stroke, and made
> The water, which they beat, to follow faster,

> As amorous of their strokes. For her own person,
> It beggared all description : she did lie
> In her pavilion (cloth of gold, of tissue)
> O'er-picturing that Venus where we see
> The fancy out-work nature : on each side her
> Stood pretty dimpled boys, like smiling Cupids,
> With divers colored fans, whose wind did seem
> To glow the delicate cheeks which they did cool,
> And what they did, undid. . . .
> Her gentlewomen, like the Nereids,
> So many mermaids, tended her i' th' eyes,
> And made their bends adoring : at the helm
> A seeming mermaid steers ; the silken tackle
> Swell with the touches of those flower-soft hands
> That yarely frame the office. From the barge
> A strange invisible perfume hits the sense
> Of the adjacent wharfs. The city cast
> Her people out upon her ; and Antony,
> Enthron'd i' th' market-place, did sit alone,
> Whistling to th' air ; which, but for vacancy,
> Had gone to gaze on Cleopatra too,
> And made a gap in nature.
>
> —*Antony and Cleopatra*, ii., 2 : *Shakespear.*

Perhaps no poetical passage could exemplify better than this that which distinguishes the sensuous from the sensual. Describing conditions which some of our modern poets would think would justify them in throwing every shred of drapery overboard, it reveals nothing that the most delicate taste cannot enjoy. The picture appeals solely to the imagination, and to nothing lower, which proves that Shakespear, although a poet, had enough practical sense to know that verse which does not appeal to the highest æsthetic nature cannot be in the highest sense artistic.

CHAPTER XXV.

EXPLANATORY ALLOY IN ILLUSTRATIVE REPRESENTATION.

Illustrations that are not always necessarily representative—Their Development gradually traced in Descriptions of Natural Scenery—Practical Bearing of this on the Composition of Orations—Why Common People hear some gladly and others not at all—Obscure Styles not Brilliant—Examples of Obscure Historical and Mythological References in Poetry—Alloyed Representation Short-lived—How References to possibly unknown Things are made in Poetry that lives—Mixture of Main and Illustrating Thought so as to destroy Representation—Examples of how this Result may be prevented.

IT must not be supposed that a poet, even though he uses illustrative representation, can overcome—merely by doing this—the tendency in his verse to pay too much attention relatively to thought as contrasted with form, and thus to make his representation not pure but alloyed. Alloyed illustrative representation is a fault on a larger scale, similar to that of the "blending" of metaphors in which plain and figurative language are both used with reference to the same object in the same clause or sentence (see Chapter XVIII.). To understand the nature of this fault we must go back to *pure* representation for a moment. The sixth line of the following is a departure from *pure* representation. It expresses what could not have been *perceived*: it explains.

> So saying, from the pavement he half rose,
> Slowly, with pain, reclining on his arm,
> And looking wistfully with wide blue eyes

> As in a picture. Him Sir Bedivere
> Remorsefully regarded through his tears,
> And would have spoken, but he found not words.
> —*Mort D'Arthur : Tennyson.*

Even in Homer, notwithstanding assertions made to the contrary, we find exceptional passages identical in character with this :

> Back he sprang,
> Hiding amid the crowd, that so the Greeks
> Might not behold the wounded limb, and scoff.
> —*Iliad*, 12 : *Bryant's Trs.*

This last line is not characteristic of Homer. But there are numberless ones like it in the works of modern writers, for the reason that all of us modern people are more accustomed than the ancient to look beneath the surface of things ; and therefore we are more prone in our descriptions to assign real or imaginary motives to the actions of those whom we are watching. The moment, however, that this analyzing of motives becomes characteristic of description, the style is evidently in danger of becoming less representative. To show the effect produced upon it, notice this quotation from Crabbe's *Parish Register*. It is certainly poetry ; series of pictures are called up as we read it ; the general is embodied in the concrete ; the versification adds to the interest that we take in the ideas expressed in it ; and yet nothing could be more unlike the poetry of Homer ; and this because it is not *pure* representation, but representation *alloyed* with much that is merely a direct presentation of the writer's own thoughts.

> Phoebe Dawson gayly crossed the green ;
> In haste to see and happy to be seen ;
> Her air, her manners, all who saw, admired,
> Courteous though coy, and gentle though retired ;

THE EXPLANATORY IN ILLUSTRATIONS. 295

> The joy of youth and health her eyes displayed,
> And ease of heart her every look conveyed ;
> A native skill her simple robes expressed,
> As with untutored elegance she dressed ;
> The lads around admired so fair a sight,
> And Phoebe felt, and felt she gave, delight.
>
> *   *   *   *   *   *
>
> Lo ! now with red rent cloak and bonnet black,
> And torn green gown loose hanging at her back,
> One who an infant in her arms sustains,
> And seems in patience striving with her pains,
> Pinched are her looks, as one who pines for bread,
> Whose cares are growing, and whose hopes are fled ;
> Pale her parched lips, her heavy eyes sunk low,
> And tears unnoticed from their channels flow ;
> Serene her manner, till some sudden pain
> Frets the meek soul, and then she 's calm again.

To understand how this explanatory poetry, in which thought that is not at all representative is constantly being thrust into the form, can be produced even when figurative language is used, let us trace the gradual development of the tendency from its beginning. In the following description of evening, analogies are drawn between certain effects usually seen in connection with evening, and certain others usually seen in connection with human beings. In each case, however, only such effects are mentioned as are externally perceptible, like those represented in the words *twilight, silence, Hesperus,* and *moon* on the one hand, and in the words *still, gray, livery, clad, accompanied, pleased, led, rode, rising, majesty,* and *apparent queen,* on the other. For this reason, as we read the description, the picture of what is done by a human being, as well as of the evening effect to which this is likened, comes at once before the imagination.

> Now came still evening on, and twilight gray
> Had in her sober livery all things clad ;

> Silence accompanied ; for beast and bird,
> They to their grassy couch, these to their nests,
> Were slunk, all but the wakeful nightingale ;
> She all night long her amorous discant sung ;
> Silence was pleased ; now glowed the firmament
> With living sapphires ; Hesperus that led
> The starry host, rode brightest, till the moon,
> Rising in clouded majesty, at length
> Apparent queen, unveiled her peerless light,
> And o'er the dark her silver mantle threw.
> —*Paradise Lost*, 4 : *Milton*.

A similar analogy is given us in the following; but in certain places, somewhat subtle to detect, as in the words *needing*, *suffices*, and *ostentatious*, the appearances of the natural objects mentioned are likened not to what is perceptible in human beings, but to imperceptible motives which can only be surmised by an observer. The harm done to the representation by such words happens, in this passage, to be very evident. For, in the end, the last of them, *ostentatious*, runs the poet, as it seems, entirely off his track. That it is less ostentatious to wear a moon or jewel *in a zone* than *on high*, is inferred, not perceived by him, and, in order to give us his view of the Evening's modesty, he apparently forgets all about his picture of her *in the west;* for he says that the low moon, which decorates her, is of an ampler *round*. But the evening moon never is this except when *in the east*. He may mean, indeed, the dim old moon encircling as it does at times the crescent; but few would derive this impression from his words. Or he may mean to have the *round* refer to the zone of the Evening herself, and so make her corpulent enough to fit the girdle of the whole horizon! But whatever he may mean, the moment we try to frame a picture from this or any of his later phrases, we find that the alloy at first introduced very slightly has finally injured his picture very greatly.

> Come, Evening, once again, season of peace ;
> Return, sweet Evening, and continue long !
> Methinks I see thee in the streaky west,
> With matron step slow-moving, while the Night
> Treads on thy sweeping train ; one hand employed
> In letting fall the curtain of repose
> On bird and beast, the other charged for man
> With sweet oblivion of the cares of day :
> Not sumptuously adorned, nor needing aid,
> Like homely feathered Night, of clustering gems ;
> A star or two, just twinkling on thy brow,
> Suffices thee ; save that the moon is thine
> No less than hers, not worn indeed on high
> With ostentatious pageantry, but set
> With modest grandeur in thy purple zone,
> Resplendent less, but of an ampler round.
> —*The Task ; Winter Evening : Cowper.*

A little further development of the tendency under consideration leads to a style in which there appears to be in the figures still less distinctness of representation. As we read the following, the imagination does not perceive clearly whether the *orb, ocean, Vesper, night, clouds, breezes, moon*, etc., are meant to be likened to human or to some other beings ; nor is there any thing to tell us why these beings act as is indicated. That is to say, we fail to see pictures here, because the representation is alloyed by the introduction of too many of the thoughts of the writer. Instead of referring us to what can be seen in a sentient being, to which a material object is compared, he refers us to what may or may not be an explanation of what might be seen in such a being. Men sometimes *forget*—not often, however,—because they are *hushed*. So, he says, it is with the *ocean ;* and the same principle is exemplified in many other of his words.

> The sun's bright orb, declining all serene,
> Now glanced obliquely o'er the woodland scene ;

Creation smiles around ; on every spray
The warbling birds exalt their evening lay ;
* * * * * *
The crystal streams that velvet meadows lave,
To the green ocean roll with chiding wave.
The glassy ocean hushed forgets to roar,
But trembling murmurs on the sandy shore.
* * * * * *
While glowing Vesper leads the starry train,
And night slow draws her veil o'er land and main,
Emerging clouds the azure east invade,
And wrap the lucid spheres in gradual shade ;
* * * * * *
Deep midnight now involves the livid skies,
When eastern breezes, yet enervate, rise ;
The waning moon behind a watery shroud,
Pale glimmer'd o'er the long-protracted cloud ;
A mighty halo round her silver throne
With parting meteors crossed, portentous shone ;
This in the troubled sky full oft prevails,
Oft deemed a signal of tempestuous gales.
—*Shipwreck*, 1 : *Falconer.*

The same indistinctness of representation, though with less in it of the explanatory element, characterizes the poetry of Thomson. Here is what he has to say of an evening :

The western sun withdraws the shorten'd day ;
And humid Evening, gliding o'er the sky,
In her chill progress, to the ground condensed
The vapors throws. Where creeping waters ooze,
Where marshes stagnate, and where rivers wind,
Cluster the rolling fogs, and swim along
The dusky mantled lawn. Meanwhile the Moon,
Full-orbed, and breaking through the scattered clouds,
Shows her broad Visage in the crimson'd east.
Turn'd to the sun direct, her spotted Disk,
Where mountains rise, umbrageous dales descend,

> And caverns deep, as optic tube descries,
> A smaller earth, gives us his blaze again,
> Void of its flame, and sheds a softer day.
> Now through the passing Cloud she seems to stoop,
> Now up the pale Cerulean rides sublime.
> Wide the pale Deluge floats, and, streaming mild
> O'er the sky'd mountain to the shadowy vale,
> While rocks and floods reflect the quivering gleam,
> The whole air whitens with a boundless tide
> Of silver radiance, trembling round the world.
> —*Seasons ; Autumn.*

There is a practical bearing of the tendency under consideration upon rhetoric and oratory. Certain public speakers like F. W. Robertson, Beecher, and Spurgeon are able to hold the attention of both the cultivated and the uncultivated; others equally great in their way, like Everett, Storrs, and James Martineau, appeal only to the cultivated. Why is this? Of course their thought, aside from their style, has something to do with it, but is there not something in their style also that accounts for it? If we examine the rhetoric of orators of the former class, we find that the *presentation* of the thought in one clause or sentence is seldom mixed with its *representation* in another; in short, that whatever representation is attempted is *pure*. Robertson, for instance, says in one of his sermons:

"As the free air is to one out of health the cause of cold and diseased lungs, so to the healthy man it is a source of great vigor. The rotten fruit is sweet to the worm, but nauseous to the palate of man. It is the same air and the same fruit, acting differently upon different beings. To different men a different world: to one all pollution; to another all purity."

And Beecher says, as reported in the "Life Thoughts":
"But when once faith has taught the soul that it has

wings, then it begins to fly, and, flying, finds that all God's domain is its liberty. And as the swallow that comes back to roost in its hard hole at night is quite content, so that the morning gives it again all the bright heavens for its soaring ground, so may men close quartered and cramped in bodily accommodations be quite patient of their narrow bounds, for their thoughts may fly out every day gloriously. And as in autumn these children of the chimney gather in flocks and fly away to heavens without a winter, so men shall find a day when they too shall migrate; and rising into a higher sphere without storm or winter, shall remember the troubles of this mortal life, as birds in Florida may be supposed to remember the Northern chills which drove them forth to a fairer clime."

This last is representation as *pure* as any thing in Homer. Beecher's pictures are equally *pure*, too, in his metaphors. "A lowly home has reared many high natures." "The heart of friends is the mirror of good men," etc.

In the rhetoric of the other class of orators, however, the representation is alloyed with presentation to such an extent that minds unacquainted with the methods of literary workmanship do not always recognize either the illustrating picture and enjoy it, or the illustrated thought, which seems to them to be merely lumbered by material in which others see pictures. Nothing could be finer of its kind than the following from Dr. Storr's address on "The Early American Spirit"; yet notice how both pictures and thoughts are affected by the way in which they are welded together:

"All of them came out of communities which had had to face portentous problems, and which were at the time profoundly stirred by vast moral and political forces.

They bore them imbedded in their consciousness, entering whether articulated or not, with a dominant force into their thought, into their life. They transported to these coasts, by the simple act of transferring their life hither, a power and a promise from the greatest age of European advancement. They could not have helped it if they would. They could more easily have left behind the speech which they had learned in childhood than they could have dropped on their stormy way across the ocean the self-reliance, the indomitable courage, the constructive energy, and the great aspiration, of which the lands they left were full.

* * * * * * *

"It is easy to exaggerate their religious enthusiasm till all the other traits of their characters are dimmed by its excessive brightness. Our filial pride inclines us to this; for, if we could, we should love to feel, all of us, that we are sprung from untitled nobles, from saints who need no canonization, from men of such heroic mould, and women of such tender devoutness that the world elsewhere was not worthy of them; that they brought to these coasts a wholly unique celestial life, through the scanty cabins which were to it as a manger and the quaint apparel which furnished its swaddling clothes; that airs Elysian played around them, while they took the wilderness as was said of the Lady Arabella Johnson, 'on their way to heaven.'"

There is nothing obscure in this style to a cultivated man, but there is to an uncultivated one, because, while composed in a representative style, it is not in the highest sense representative. It degenerates very easily, too, into a style in which, even among the cultivated, the figures hinder rather than help the presentation of the thought. In the following we have an example of this effect, a passage in many respects admirably composed, but ordinary people will be obliged to think twice before understanding what it means. "Vice has this additional condemnation,—that the present is dogged and hunted down by the evil companionship of the past, that its words have the taint and its suggestions the stain of a worn-out debauch; that it cannot shake itself loose from the foul memories which hang about it, nor rebuke the malignant and sneering devils now evoked even by the purest objects."

This is a method of writing not uncommon in our day, and it is called brilliant. But no style is really brilliant the figures and ideas of which do not stand out in bright light and clear relief; and no writer of the first class, notwithstanding the example of Carlyle, and, to some extent, of Emerson, obscures his thought by an endeavor to render it poetically representative. We have found how true this is as applied to the poetry of the best writers; it is equally true as applied to their prose. The fact is that a man who knows best what poetry is, knows best what poetry is not; and when he tries to write prose he gives men the benefit of his knowledge. Nothing, indeed, can be more simple and direct than the prose of Shakespear, Coleridge, Goethe, Wordsworth, and Byron. A man judging from it might suppose that these writers, as compared with men like Professor Wilson, Hartley Coleridge, and Carlyle, had but little representative ability.

At present, however, we are dealing with poetry. The bearing upon it of what has been said is this,—that modern poetry, like modern prose, tends to alloyed representation. The similarity of the following poetry and the last of our prose quotations will be recognized at once; also that the same tendency underlies both, viz., the crowding together of thought and illustration in the form, in such a way that neither of the two stands forth in clear relief. Here the tendency is only slightly suggested:

> O Mother State, how quenched thy Sinai fires!
>   Is there none left of thy staunch Mayflower breed?
> No spark among the ashes of thy sires,
>   Of Virtue's altar-flame the kindling seed?
> Are these thy great men, these that cringe and creep,
>   And writhe through slimy ways to place and power?—
> How long, O Lord, before thy wrath shall reap
>   Our frail-stemmed summer prosperings in their flower?
> O for one hour of that undaunted stock
> That went with Vane and Sidney to the block!
>
> O for a whiff of Naseby, that would sweep,
>   With its stern Puritan besom, all this chaff
>   From the Lord's threshing-floor! Yet more than half
> The victory is attained, when one or two,
>   Through the fool's laughter and the traitor's scorn,
>   Beside thy sepulchre can abide the morn,
> Crucified Truth, when thou shalt rise anew.
>   —*To John G. Palfrey: Lowell.*

Here there is a much further development of the tendency:

> Meantime, just meditate my madrigal
> O' the mugwort that conceals a dewdrop safe!
> What, dullard? we and you in smothery chafe,
> Babes, baldheads, stumbled thus far into Zin
> The Horrid, getting neither out nor in,
> A hungry sun above us, sands that bung
> Our throats,—each dromedary lolls a tongue,
> Each camel churns a sick and frothy chap,
> And you 'twixt tales of Potiphar's mishap,
> And sonnets on the earliest ass that spoke,
> Remark, you wonder any one needs choke
> With founts about! Potsherd him, Gibeonites!
> While awkwardly enough your Moses smites
> The rock, though he forego his Promised Land,

> Thereby, have Satan claim his carcass, and
> Figure as Metaphysic Poet . . . ah!
> Mark ye the dim first oozings? Meribah!
> Then, quaffing at the fount, my courage gained,
> Recall—not that I prompt ye—who explained . . .
> "Presumptuous!" interrupts one.
> —*Sordello*, 3 : *R. Browning.*

In addition to what has been said already, it will be noticed that in the first of these quotations, phrases like *Sinai fires, Mayflower breed, whiff of Naseby, Puritan besom,* etc., and in the second, words like *Zin the Horrid, Potiphar's, ass, Gibeonites, Moses, Meribah,* etc., call up no definite pictures, though at first they seem to do so. They merely call up ideas, which, in turn, call up pictures to the poet's mind, on account of the facts which he has come to associate with these words. They call up the same ideas in the minds of others, only so far as these happen to have the same associations with the terms that the poet has. But suppose the people of India or China, or of any clime or age having no such associations, were to read the poetry; for them there would be no pictures represented—scarcely any ideas presented by this kind of language. In saying this, it is not meant that all allusions to such things as are mentioned here for the sake of illustration should be banished from poetry; it is meant merely that this sort of material should not be crowded into the form in such a way as to interfere with clearness of representation. Some of the allusions, with very slight alterations, might be made intelligible and forcible to readers the most ignorant of the facts mentioned, and the most devoid of sympathy with the principles exemplified by them. All of the allusions would injure the poetry less, if they stood in passages by themselves, instead of being crowded, as they are, into every part of it. In that case there might be, aside from them, enough of *pure* representation in the poetry to render it of permanent and universal interest. Some of us, perhaps, have seen old paintings, the costumes in which, representing the fashions of the day, made the figures seem almost ridiculous; but, notwithstanding this, the faces of the forms thus clothed, because *pure* representations of nature, were beautiful or attractive. We have seen, also, pictures of North American Indians, in which not only the forms were so robed, but the faces so painted, that what may be termed the *alloyed* representation of their day, left in its portraiture no *pure* representation of nature whatsoever for us really to admire. The kind of poetry of which we have just been treating, is in danger at some time of producing similar effects. Often not even in small, scattered parts of it, is there any *pure* representation. When, therefore, the fashion of the time to which it is addressed goes by, nothing will be left to render it of permanent interest. We come back here, therefore, to the place where we started. Art is representative, and that which is not representative in the highest sense does not meet the requirements of art, and therefore cannot live as true art does. Allusions in poetry that lives are separated from the main thought, as in the following, which, though not wholly to be commended, can be read with intelligence even by one who does not recall the particulars of the myths to which reference is made.

> Thus saying, from her husband's hand, her hand
> Soft she withdrew; and like a wood-nymph light,
> Oread or Dryad, or of Delia's train,
> Betook her to the groves, but Delia's self
> In gait surpassed, and goddess-like deport,
> Though not as she with bow and quiver armed,

> But with such gard'ning tools as art, yet rude,
> Guiltless of fire had form'd, or angels brought.
> —*Paradise Lost,* 9: *Milton.*

> Not less but more heroic than the wrath
> Of stern Achilles on his foe pursued
> Thrice fugitive about Troy walls : or rage
> Of Turnus for Lavinia disespous'd,
> Or Neptune's ire or Juno's, that so long
> Perplex'd the Greek and Cytherea's son.
> —*Idem,* 9.

Sometimes, too, such allusions in the best poetry, are explained or rendered picturesque, as in the following:

> Do you believe me yet, or shall I call
> Antiquity from the old schools of Greece
> To testify the arms of chastity?
> Hence had the huntress Dian her dread bow,
> Fair silver-shafted queen, for ever chaste,
> Wherewith she tamed the brinded lioness
> And spotted mountain pard, but set at nought
> The frivolous bolt of Cupid ; gods and men
> Fear'd her stern frown, and she was queen o' th' woods.
> What was that snaky-headed Gorgon shield,
> That wise Minerva wore, unconquer'd virgin,
> Wherewith she freezed her foes to congeal'd stone,
> But rigid looks of chaste austerity,
> And noble grace that dash'd brute violence
> With sudden adoration and blank awe ?
> —*Comus: Milton.*

It is not merely in historical or mythological allusions, however, that the main thought of a passage can be so mixed with the illustrating figures as to destroy their representative character. The same tendency will be recognized in the following:

> Yes, the pine is the mother of legends ; what food
> For their grim roots is left when the thousand-yeared wood—
> The dim-aisled cathedral, whose tall arches spring
> Light, sinewy, graceful, firm-set as the wing

> From Michael's white shoulder—is hewn and defaced
> By iconoclast axes in desperate waste,
> And its wrecks seek the ocean it prophesied long,
> Cassandra-like, crooning its mystical song?
> Then the legends go with them—even yet on the sea
> A wild virtue is left in the touch of the tree,
> And the sailor's night watches are thrilled to the core
> With the lineal offspring of Odin and Thor.
> — *The Growth of the Legend: Lowell.*

In contrast with this, notice how clearly both thoughts and figures, and the thoughts by means of the figures, stand out in poetry that is truly representative:

> Truth forever on the scaffold, Wrong forever on the throne,—
> Yet that scaffold sways the Future, and, behind the dim unknown,
> Standeth God within the shadow, keeping watch above his own.
> — *The Present Crisis: Lowell.*

> Virtue? a fig! 't is in ourselves that we are thus or thus. Our bodies are gardens to the which our wills are gardeners; so that if we will plant nettles, or sew lettuce; set hyssop, and weed up thyme; supply it with one gender of herbs, or distract it with many; either to have it sterile with idleness, or manured with industry; why the power and corrigible authority of this lies in our wills.
> —*Othello*, i., 3: *Shakespear.*

> You have seen
> Sunshine and rain at once; her smiles and tears
> Were like a better May; those happy smilets,
> That played on her ripe lips seemed not to know
> What guests were in her eyes.
> —*Lear*, iv., 3: *Idem.*

> Through tatter'd clothes small vices do appear;
> Robes and furr'd gowns hide all. Plate sin with gold,
> And the strong lance of justice hurtless breaks;
> Arm it in rags, a pigmy's straw does pierce it . . .
> . . . Get thee glass eyes;
> And like a scurvy politician seem
> To see the things thou dost not.
> —*Idem*, iv., 6.

CHAPTER XXVI.

ORNAMENTAL ALLOY IN REPRESENTATION.

Poetic Development of the far-fetched Simile in the Illustrating of Illustrations—Examples of this from several Modern Writers—Whose Representation or Illustration fails to represent or illustrate—Poetic Development of the Mixed Metaphor—Examples from Modern Poets—In what will this result—More Examples—How the Tendency leads the Poet from his Main Thought to pursue Suggestions made even by Sounds—Representing thus a Lack of Sanity or of Discipline, neither of which is what Art should represent.

OUR examination of the effects upon poetry of the didactic tendency, in which considerations of thought overbalance those of form, have led us to trace certain phases of failure to a lack of representation. We have now to examine the effects of the ornate tendency, in which considerations of form overbalance those of thought, and in which therefore there is failure because of an excess of representation.

It is simply natural for one who has obtained facility in illustrating his ideas to overdo the matter, at times, and to carry his art so far as to re-illustrate that which has been sufficiently illustrated or is itself illustrative. The first form that we need to notice, in which this tendency shows itself, is a poetic development and extension of what rhetoricians term the "far-fetched" simile, a simile in which minor points of resemblance are sought out and dwelt upon in minute detail and at unnecessary length. Attention has been directed in another place to the way in which the exclusively allegorical treatment in Spenser's *Faerie Queene* causes us to lose sight of the main subject of the poem. An allegory, as has been said, is mainly an extended simile. The poetic fault of which I am to speak is sometimes found in similes, sometimes in allegories, and sometimes in episodes filled with metaphorical language, partaking partly of the distinctive nature of both. These passages seem to be suggested as illustrations of the main subject, but they are so extended and elaborated that they really obscure it. As the reader goes on to peruse them, he either forgets altogether what the subject to be illustrated is, or he finds himself unable to separate that which belongs only to it, from that which belongs only to the illustration.

It is largely owing to passages manifesting this characteristic that Robert Browning's writings seem obscure to so many. Most persons would be obliged to read the following, for example, two or three times before understanding it, and this because of the difficulty they experience in separating the particulars of the passage that go with the main thought from those that go with the illustrating thought; in other words, the excess of representation in the form interferes with its clearness.

> The man is witless of the size, the sum,
> The value, in proportion of all things,
> *   *   *   *   *
> Should his child sicken unto death,—why, look
> For scarce abatement of his cheerfulness,
> Or pretermission of his daily craft—
> While a word, gesture, glance, from that same child
> At play, or in school, or laid asleep,
> Will start him to an agony of fear,
> Exasperation, just as like! demand
> The reason why—"'t is but a word," object—
> "A gesture"—he regards thee as our lord

> Who lived there in the pyramid alone,
> Looked at us, dost thou mind, when being young
> We both would unadvisedly recite
> Some charm's beginning, from that book of his,
> Able to bid the sun throb wide and burst
> All into stars, as suns grown old are wont.
> Thou and the child have each a veil alike
> Thrown o'er your heads from under which ye both
> Stretch your blind hands and trifle with a match
> Over a mine of Greek fire, did ye know!
> He holds on firmly to some thread of life—
> (It is the life to lead perforcedly)
> Which runs across some vast distracting orb
> Of glory on either side that meagre thread,
> Which, conscious of, he must not enter yet—
> The spiritual life around the earthly life!
> The law of that is known to him as this—
> His heart and brain move there, his feet stay here.
> So is the man perplexed with impulses
> Sudden to start off crosswise, not straight on,
> Proclaiming what is Right and Wrong across—
> And not along,—this black thread through the blaze—
> "It should be" balked by "here it cannot be."
>
> —*An Epistle.*

It must be confessed, however, that these episodes of Browning are often very charming to those who have come to understand them, *e. g.*:

> And hereupon they bade me daub away.
> Thank you! my head being crammed, their walls a blank,
> Never was such prompt disemburdening.
> First, every sort of monk, the black and white,
> I drew them, fat and lean: then, folks at church,
> From good old gossips waiting to confess
> Their cribs of barrel-droppings, candle-ends,—
> To the breathless fellow at the altar-foot
> Fresh from his murder, safe and sitting there
> With the little children round him in a row
> Of admiration, half for his beard and half
> For that white anger of his victim's son

ORNAMENT IN POETRY.

> Shaking a fist at him with one fierce arm,
> Signing himself with the other because of Christ
> (Whose sad face on the cross sees only this
> After the passion of a thousand years)
> Till some poor girl, her apron o'er her head,
> Which the intense eyes looked through, came at eve
> On tiptoe, said a word, dropped in a loaf,
> Her pair of ear-rings and a bunch of flowers
> The brute took growling, prayed, and then was gone.
> I painted all, then cried, " 't is ask and have,—
> Choose, for more 's ready ! "—laid the ladder flat,
> And showed my covered bit of cloister wall.
> —*Fra Lippo Lippi.*

This way of turning from the main thought of a passage, in order to amplify and illustrate the illustration, characterizes still more the poetry of a later school. Notice how, in the following from Gerald Massey, the "Oak" is used to illustrate the condition of England, and then the picture of Victory further on is used to illustrate the condition of the oak.

> And England slumbered in the lap of Peace,
> Beneath her grand old Oak which, hale and strong,
> Rode down the storm, and wrestled with the winds,
> To rise in pomp of bloom, and pæan of song,
> Green with the sap of many hundred springs ;
> And tossed its giant arms in wanton life,
> Like Victory smiling in the sun of Glory.
> —*Glimpses of the War: Massey.*

But it is Swinburne who has developed most fully, and apparently with design, this method of catching at the illustrating thought as if it were the main thought, and going on to illustrate it, and then catching at this second illustration once more, and treating it in the same way, and so on *ad infinitum.* Notice this from his *Evening on the Broads :*

> All over the gray soft shallow
> Hover the colors and clouds of **twilight, void of** a star.
> As a bird unfledged in the broad winged night, whose winglets are callow
> Yet, but soon with their plumes will she cover her brood from afar,
> Cover the brood of her worlds that cumber the skies with their blossom
> Thick as the darkness of leaf-shadowed spring is encumbered with flowers.
> World upon world is enwound in the bountiful girth of her bosom,
> Warm and lustrous with life lovely to look on as ours.
> Still is the sunset adrift as a spirit in doubt that dissembles
> Still with itself, being sick of division and dimmed by dismay—
> Nay, not so ; but with love and delight beyond passion it trembles,
> Fearful and fain of the night, lovely with love of the day :
> Fain and fearful of rest that is like unto death, and begotten
> Out of the womb of the tomb, born of the seed of the grave :
> Lovely with shadows of loves that are only not wholly forgotten,
> Only not wholly suppressed by the dark as a wreck by the wave.

The fault in this mode of illustrating, or representing, lies in the fact that it does not illustrate nor represent. The poet, in writing it, has made the form an end and not a means. His thoughts, and methods of developing them, are suggested by the representation, and not by that which it is supposed to represent, and which his readers naturally expect it to represent. Accordingly, his readers cannot distinguish the main thought from the illustrating thought, nor this again from the re-illustrating thought, and the whole passage is necessarily more or less obscure. The poet has not made his subject stand forth in clear, concrete outlines, as art should do ; but has so veneered and besmeared it with excess of ornamentation that no one can tell very decidedly just what his subject is. Besides this, there is another fundamental error in this style ; but as it underlies also the next fault that is to be mentioned, reference will be made to it after we have considered that.

The second form that we need to notice, of the tendency now under consideration, is allied to the "mixed metaphor" in the same way as we found that the first was to the "far-fetched simile." Using "mixed metaphors" is a fault from which, as most of us know, our very best poets are not altogether exempt. Shakespear makes Hamlet ask

> Whether 't is nobler in the mind to suffer
> The slings and arrows of outrageous fortune ;
> Or to take *arms* against a *sea* of troubles,
> And by opposing end them ?
> —*Hamlet*, iii., 1.

And Milton says :

> How sweetly did they float upon the wings
> Of silence, through the empty-vaulted night,
> At every fall smoothing the raven *down*
> Of *darkness* till it *smiled!*
> —*Comus*.

Poets, like other people, are careless at times. Very likely this fact will account for these passages. Possibly, however, the mixed metaphors were used with a design,—in the first case, to represent confusion of thought, and in the second antithesis. But what are we to say of the following from Tennyson?

> For I *dipt* into the future far as human eye could *see*.
> —*Locksley Hall*.

> With that she kissed
> His forehead, then, a moment after, clung
> About him and betwixt them *blossomed* up
> From out a common *vein* of memory
> Sweet household talk, and phrases of the hearth.
> —*Princess*.

> A classic lecture, rich in sentiment
> With *scraps* of *thunderous* Epic *lilted* out
> By violet-hooded doctors, elegies
> And quoted odes, and jewels five words long,
> That on the stretched forefinger of all time
> Sparkle forever.
> —*Princess*.

> " Be it so," the other, "that we still may *lead*
> The *new light up* and *culminate* in *peace*."
>
> —*Idem.*

There are several questions which passages like these suggest,—passages so numerous as to be almost characteristic of the style of Tennyson. Are they consciously designed to crowd the form with that which shall ornament it? Do they add to the attractiveness of the form? Do they do this without interfering with the pureness of its representation? Have they any thing to do with the fact that those who have never read poetry of the school of Tennyson need to learn how to understand it? If people of our own day need to learn this, will not people of future days need to do the same? If so, after this kind of poetry ceases to be the fashion, will anybody ever take the trouble to learn to understand it?—in other words, is there not danger that this poetry, simply because its representation is not pure, will not become classic? Possibly it may. Even the quotations just given are no more mixed in their way than some of the music of Wagner; and that is supposed to be the music of the future. Music, certainly, develops a taste for itself, and changes its methods in every age. At least such has always been its history in the past. Is it the same with poetry? There are sufficient excellencies in that of Tennyson to cause it to deserve to live. He has been the favorite poet of most of us, and has exerted incomparably more poetic influence upon his age than any of his contemporaries. But if he is to live, will it be in spite of, or on account of, faults such as we are now considering? If on account of them, and if future poets are to imitate and develop his peculiarities, what is to become of poetry? Notice what some of his followers are doing already. This is from Gerald Massey's *New Year's Eve in Exile*. There is much in this poet's writings that is fine, and his spirit is earnest, but these are the very reasons why he should avoid a mixture such as this:

> But God 's in heaven, and yet the Day shall dawn—
> Break from the dark upon her golden wings,
> Her quick, ripe splendors rend and burn the gloom,
> Her living tides of glory burst, and foam,
> And hurry along the darken'd streets of night.
> Cloud after cloud shall light a rainbow-roof,
> And build a Triumph-Arch for conquering Day
> To flash her beauty—trail her grandeurs through,
> And take the World in her white arms of light.
> And Earth shall fling aside her mask of gloom,
> And lift her tearful face. O there will be
> Blood on it thick as dews! The children's blood
> Splasht in the Mother's face! And there must be
> A red sunrise of retribution yet!
> —*New Year's Eve in Exile: Massey.*

Here we have a thing that comes on *golden wings* and *bursts her living tides*, that is at once *quick* and *ripe*, and that *rends* and *burns*, and this thing is a day which usually dawns slowly; we have also clouds that *light* a *rainbow*, and also build what appears to be a similar rainbow *Arch*, which they, and not the sun, would have to do, if it were to be seen in the east, where alone the day could *trail her grandeurs through* it at sunrise. Finally, what connection there is between the sentence beginning, "The children's blood," and the context one fails to recognize, unless in the poet's mind the subject, which is the *Day*, has become mixed with something else. It has. The word *world*, used in illustration, has made him think of *earth;* but only for a little. Soon the word *blood* makes him think of *red sunrise;* not one of glory now, but—*of retribution.*

In this matter of mixing metaphors, however, of all

poets able to do better work, Swinburne caps the climax. In the following single sentence, at least so we must judge where we have nothing but the punctuation marks to indicate the sense, we are told of fire *kissing* and *killing*, which is like light *riotous* and *red* flaming round *bent*—a word suggested by the *round*, perhaps—*brows;* and at the same time the fire, or the brows, or Semiramis, or the dead body—nobody can tell which—is *kindling* like *dawn steely* snows where treading *feet feel* snaky lines of blood *hiss*, in which, as is evident (?), they resemble *creeping things* that *writhe* but do not have, as one might suppose, *stings* to *scare adulterers* from an *imperial bed, bowed* —possibly *boughed* misspelt—with a load of *lust*. After this, the same *blood*, or something else, goes on to *chill*, as if that could put it out, a *gust* that *made her body a fire*, which now seems to have passed over the whole body from the brow to the heel, and is about to *change* a *high bright spirit* from *taint of fraud*. One supposing that no practical end is to be attained by trying to have poets avoid alloyed illustrative representation, will be in a fair way to have his doubts removed after he has made one honest attempt to put into plain prose these remarkable adventures of the amorous fire as related in this choice specimen of florid poetic art:

> As fire that kisses, killing with a kiss,
>   He saw the light of death, riotous and red,
> Flame round the bent brows of Semiramis
>   Re-risen and mightier, from the Assyrian dead,
> Kindling, as dawn a frost-bound precipice,
>   The steely snows of Russia, for the tread
> Of feet that felt before them crawl and hiss
>   The snaky lines of blood violently shed
>   Like living creeping things
>   That writhe but have no stings

> To scare adulterers from the imperial bed
>   Bowed with its load of lust,
>   Or chill the ravenous gust
> That made her body a fire from heel to head ;
> Or change her high bright spirit and clear,
> For all its mortal stains, from taint of fraud or fear.
>   —*Song for the Centenary of W. S. Landor.*

The artistic mistake here, just as in the case of that allied to the "far-fetched simile," is that the figure, the design of which, when rightly used, is to represent, does not represent. It does the opposite. Instead of making the thought more concrete, and thus giving it more definiteness of form, it gives it indefiniteness.

But there is another mistake made in these methods, which is psychological as well as artistic. As has been seen, in all of these cases in which the clearness of representation is obscured by the excess of it, the course of the thought turns from the main subject, as if the writer had forgotten it, while going on to develop that which is suggested by the illustration. In the quotation above from Massey, for example, it is easy enough to see that, in the fifth line from the last, the phrase *mask of gloom* suggested *tearful face*, and this again *dews*, and this *blood*, and this the *splashing* of it, and all these things together, the *red* sunrise of retribution. In the quotation from Swinburne, beginning

> All over the gray soft shallow,

quoted on page 312, we hear first of a *bird;* this suggests a *brood;* this suggests *world's coursing skies*, this suggests *blossoms*, this *flowers*, this *putting flowers in a bosom*, etc., while, in the last passage quoted from him, *fire* suggests *light, kindling light* suggests *dawn,* dawn suggests its effects on *snow,* snow the effects of *feet treading it,* treading suggests *crawling,* and crawling suggests *creeping.* Worse than this, certain words seem suggested merely by their sounds which alliterate with words near them. Now, suppose a man in conversation were to let his thoughts run on in this way, deviating from the line of his argument or description, whenever he happened to strike a word the sense or sound of which suggested something different from that of which he started out to speak. What should we think of him? One of two things,—either that he was insane, or had a very poorly disciplined mind. Precisely this is what is represented, so far as any thing is represented, by this kind of poetry. Yet, as we all know, the finest and highest art must represent the finest and highest efforts of the finest and highest powers of the mind. If this be so, then poetry modelled upon a form which is the legitimate and natural expression of an insane or a poorly disciplined mind, is not poetry of the finest and highest order.

CHAPTER XXVII.

REPRESENTATION IN POEMS CONSIDERED AS WHOLES.

Form in Words and Sentences—How Visible Appearances give an Impression of Form—How Movable Appearances do the Same—Consistency and Continuity in a Sentence Necessary to give it an Effect of Form—A Poem a Series of Representations and of Sentences—Must have Manifest Consistency and Continuity giving it Manifest Unity and Progress, also Definiteness and Completeness—Form modelled on Direct Representation—How Figures can be carried out with Manifest Consistency and Continuity—Complete and Broken Figures—Examples of Poems with Forms modelled on the Methods of Illustrative Representation—How Excellence of Form in all Poems of whatever Length should be determined—Certain Poems not representing Unity and Progress—Great Poets see Pictures when conceiving their Poems; Inferior Poets think of Arguments—Same Principles applied to Smaller Poems—The Moral in Poetry should be represented not presented—Poetic Excellence determined not by the Thought but by the Form of the Thought, which must be a Form of Representation.

WE have been considering the representative nature of poetry. It remains for us to consider the representative nature of a poem. All the products of art, it was said at the opening of this work, are acknowledged to have what is termed a form. In what sense can a poem be said to have form, and what is necessary to cause the form to be what it should be? In order to determine this, let us go back for moment to the method in which thought attains form in ordinary language of which poetry is a development. When we have noticed the principles that operate there, we shall have something to aid us in solving our question here.

These principles are very simple. Sounds, or letters symbolizing them in a material sphere, represent a thought in the immaterial mind, and thus give it a form embodied in a word. Two or more words put together give form to compound words, phrases, or sentences. Let us examine the last of these for a moment. It is the most complex of the three, yet very simple as compared with the collection of words in a whole poem. At the same time, too, it is the most complete form of expression of the three—in fact, in its way an absolutely complete form of expression. A whole poem is more complete only in the sense that it is composed of a large number of these sentences. As mere vehicles of expression, therefore, every principle that applies to them applies to the poem as a whole, and if we can find out in what sense they can be said to have form, we can have something to guide us in determining in what sense a poem can be said to have form.

What do we mean, then, by saying that a sentence has form? If it were a visible object we should say it had form in the degree in which it appeared to be *one* object, by which we should mean in the degree in which, owing to the effects of outlines, colors, or some other features, every part of the object seemed to be connected with every other part of it throughout the entire extent of space which it occupied. A sentence is not visible in space, but is apprehended in time,—in words that follow one another. Its substance is movement, and if we apply to it the same criterions as those usually applied to visible objects, changing only the terms that are necessary to refer to it as an object whose substance is movement, we must say that it appears to have form in the degree in which it appears to be *one movement* by which we mean in the degree in which every part of its movement seems to be connected with every other part of it, and this throughout the whole extent of time which it occupies. The first of these conditions, when every part of the movement seems to be connected with every other part of it, gives to the whole the effect of *consistency*. The second of the conditions, when this connected movement seems to extend throughout the whole time occupied by it, gives to the whole the effect of *continuity*. In a perfect sentence, consistency is manifest, because every word or clause is related in some way to every other; and continuity, because every word or clause is related in some way to a subject which represents the beginning of a movement; to a predicate, which represents the continuation and sometimes the end of the movement; and also, when needed, to an object, which represents the end of the movement. It is for these reasons that a perfect sentence seems to us to have form: it has consistency and continuity.

If this be true of a sentence, which is a series of words representing thought, why should it not be true of a poem, which is also a series of words representing thought? A poem is made up of series of sentences, or, as we have found, of series of representations, some of them continuing through many sentences. If the poem, as a whole, is to have form, and one that can be readily recognized, it follows, from what has been said, that its different sentences or representations of movements or actions must all manifest their relationships to one another, thus producing the effect of *consistency;* and also their relationships to the general forward movement, thus producing the effect of *continuity*.

From its very nature a whole poem is always more or less complex; and the human mind is so constituted that one can never understand that which is complex until it has been analyzed sufficiently to make possible some kind of a classification of its parts. For this classification there is needed a basis, and this is always found primarily in some one feature which all the parts possess in common, as when the whole family of birds are classed together because they all have feathers. The mind cannot understand, therefore, that *consistency* exists in any complex series of sentences or thoughts represented by them, unless perceiving one kind of movement or action which all manifest; nor *continuity* unless perceiving one direction which all the movements or actions take. Hence it is that the action represented in art, if the art-product is to appear to have an artistic form, must be characterized by what are termed *unity* and *progress*, unity being the result of effects produced by apparent consistency, and progress, of the effects of apparent continuity.

Once more, unity as influenced by progress in an art-product renders its æsthetic effects clearly distinguishable from all other effects produced side by side with it. In other words, progress in unity gives *definiteness* to form. On the other hand, progress as influenced by unity in an art-product renders its æsthetic effects clearly distinguishable from all other effects produced before or after it, because these are separated from it, both at its beginning and at its end. In other words, unity in progress gives *completeness* to form.

A poem is a development of language, and language is a representation of thought, and thought is always in motion. Every poem, therefore, must represent *thought in motion*. But more than this, it must manifest unity.

Therefore it must represent *one thought* to which all other thoughts that it contains must be related and subordinated. More than this, too, it must manifest progress. Therefore it must represent this one thought as *moving in one direction*, as *having one end* toward the attainment of which all the movements of all the related and subordinated thoughts of the entire poem tend.

A production in which these requirements are fulfilled, and, for reasons given on the last page, such a production only, will have a form that will appear to be *definite* and *complete*.

Now let us examine some poems, and find out, if we can, how far they fulfil these requirements. Notice, first, the following representation of a very common thought that comes to all of us when gazing on something that we are not to see again. The unity of the poem is embodied in the idea expressed in the word *forever*, and its progress in the amplification of this idea, by extending it successively to the river as it flows near the speaker (first stanza), away from him (second stanza), and with other surroundings in space (third stanza), and in time (fourth stanza).

> Flow down, cold rivulet, to the sea,
>   Thy tribute wave deliver :
> No more by thee my steps shall be,
>   Forever and forever.
>
> Flow, softly flow, by lawn and lea,
>   A rivulet then a river :
> Nowhere by thee my steps shall be.
>   Forever and forever.
>
> But here will sigh thine alder tree,
>   And here thine aspen shiver ;
> And here by thee will hum the bee
>   Forever and forever.

> A thousand suns will stream on thee,
> A thousand moons will quiver;
> But not by thee my steps shall be,
> Forever and forever.
>
> —*A Farewell: Tennyson.*

Better examples of the *direct* representation of complete phases of action are the following, because in all of them the unity and progress are more apparent. All bring out distinctly a single idea, and this is unfolded progressively without a word at the beginning or end or in the middle not necessary to complete the picture.

> Home they brought her warrior dead;
> She nor swoon'd, nor utter'd cry:
> All her maidens, watching, said,
> "She must weep or she will die."
>
> Then they praised him, soft and low,
> Call'd him worthy to be loved,
> Truest friend and noblest foe;
> Yet she neither spoke nor moved.
>
> Stole a maiden from her place,
> Lightly to the warrior stept,
> Took the face-cloth from the face:
> Yet she neither moved nor wept.
>
> Rose a nurse of ninety years,
> Set his child upon her knee—
> Like summer tempest came her tears—
> "Sweet my child, I live for thee."
>
> —*The Princess: Tennyson.*

> As through the land at eve we went,
> And plucked the ripened ears,
> We fell out, my wife and I,
> O, we fell out, I know not why,
> And kiss'd again with tears.
>
> For when we came where lies the child
> We lost in other years,

> There above the little grave,
> O, there above the little grave,
> We kiss'd again with tears.
> 		—*The Princess : Tennyson.*

> As beautiful Kitty one morning was tripping,
> With a pitcher of milk from the fair of Coleraine,
> When she saw me, she stumbled, the pitcher it tumbled,
> And all the sweet buttermilk watered the plain.
>
> "O what shall I do now? 't was looking at you now!
> Sure, sure, such a pitcher I 'll n'er meet again!
> 'T was the pride of my dairy; O' Barney M'Cleary!
> You 're sent as a plague to the girls of Coleraine!"
>
> I sat down beside her,—and gently did chide her,
> That such a misfortune should give her such pain,
> A kiss then I gave her,—before I did leave her,
> She vowed for such pleasure she 'd break it again.
>
> 'T was hay-making season—I can't tell the reason—
> Misfortunes will never come singly—'t is plain;
> For, very soon after poor Kitty's disaster,
> The devil a pitcher was whole in Coleraine.
> 		—*Kitty of Coleraine : C. D. Shanly.*

The two following lyrics are still more effective, for the reason that they reveal still more clearly the characteristics which we are now considering. Think what either of them would be aside from the *form* in which the facts in them are represented. And what in the form makes it so effective? What but its concreteness, revealed through the consistency and continuity, the unity and progress that characterize the representation?

> "O Mary, go and call the cattle home,
> And call the cattle home,
> And call the cattle home,
> Across the sands o' Dee!"
> The western wind was wild and dank wi' foam,
> And all alone went she.

> The creeping tide came up along the sand,
>   And o'er and o'er the sand,
>   And round and round the sand,
> As far as eye could see ;
> The blinding mist came down and hid the land :
>   And never home came she.
>
> " O is it weed, or fish, or floating hair—
>   A tress o' golden hair,
>   A drownèd maiden's hair—
> Above the nets at sea ?
> Was never salmon yet that shone so fair,
>   Among the stakes on Dee."
>
> They rowed her in across the rolling foam—
>   The cruel, crawling foam,
>   The cruel, hungry foam—
> To her grave beside the sea ;
> But still the boatmen hear her call the cattle home
>   Across the sands o' Dee.
>   —*O Mary, Go and Call the Cattle Home : Kingsley.*

Three fishers went sailing out into the West,—
  Out into the West as the sun went down ;
Each thought of the woman who loved him the best,
  And the children stood watching them out of the town ;
For men must work and women must weep ;
And there 's little to earn, and many to keep,
  Though the harbor bar be moaning.

Three wives sat up in the lighthouse tower,
  And trimmed their lamps as the sun went down ;
And they looked at the squall and they looked at the shower,
And the night rack came rolling up, rugged and brown ;
But men must work, and women must weep,
Though storms be sudden, and waters deep,
  And the harbor bar be moaning.

Three corpses lay out on the shining sands
  In the morning gleam as the tide went down,
And the women are watching and wringing their hands
  For those who will never come back to the town ;

> For men must work and women must weep—
> And the sooner it's over the sooner to sleep—
> And good-by to the bar and its moaning.
> —*The Fishermen : Idem.*

These poems, in which, as must have been noticed, the representation in each case is also *definite* and *complete*, have unity, because they unfold only one prominent idea; and progress, because the particulars leading up to the clearest expression of this idea are unfolded successively and logically—unfolded in most of them, in fact, according to the method of the climax.

Now notice how the same principles apply to poems in which *illustrative* representation is used. This, as we have found, either pictures the movements of the mind through the operations of external nature, or pictures the latter through other operations of external nature analogous to them. *Direct* representation is developed from the methods according to which plain language is formed; *illustrative* representation from those according to which distinctively figurative language is formed. In the latter some one process or order of events is represented in words that image another. This image is thoroughly intelligible and enjoyable in the degree in which its outlines are *definite* and *complete*, causing the form to appear single and unbroken, in which, therefore, the analogy between the two things, compared,—of course, in the brief, suggestive way that appeals best to the imagination—is carried out with *consistency* and *continuity* from beginning to end. In fact, the fundamental reason why similes and metaphors, when far-fetched or mixed, are not artistic, is because, on account of too much or too little of the illustrative element in them, their analogies are not carried out successfully. For a good illustration of how they can be carried out successfully, observe the following from Mrs. Spafford's (Harriet E. Prescott) *Sir Rohan's Ghost:*

> Sir Rohan had a ghost; not by any means a common ghost that appeared at midnight on the striking of a bell, and trailed its winding sheet through the upper halls nearest the roof, but a ghost that, sleeping or waking, never left him—

Now notice how the same description of the ghost, as an outward apparition, is continued in order to represent its influence over the inward states and whole experience of Sir Rohan:

> a ghost whose long hair coiled round and stifled the fair creations of his dreams, and whose white garments swept leprously into his sunlight.

A sentence or series of sentences in which there is throughout this consistency and continuity of meaning is artistic. That effort of Sir Boyle Roche in the House of Parliament, in which he exclaimed: "I smell a rat. I see him floating in the air. I will nip him in the bud,"—was not artistic. His image had been broken even before he had nipped it.

It follows from what has been said, that an artistic poem, constructed according to the methods of illustrative representation, must be characterized throughout by consistency and continuity. So far as possible, the two things compared must be alike in their beginnings, middles, and ends; they must start, move, and stop when sustaining analogous relations.

To see how this is feasible, notice the following poem translated from the German. The one feature of excellence in it is the fact that it brings out distinctly and completely the likeness between the two things compared—*i. e.*, between the fate of a woman at different periods of her life and that of a rose-bush at different seasons of the year; in the one case by words like *child*, *maiden*, *mother*, and *mound*, and in the other by words like *buds, blossoms, leaves*, and *withered*, as well as *May* and *autumn*. Because these different stages in human life and natural life are so distinctly and completely imaged, the one in the other, none of us can fail to feel the representative and, in connection with this, the artistic and æsthetic effects of the poem.

> A child sleeps under a rose-bush fair.
> The buds swell out in the soft May air.
> Sweetly it rests and on dream-wings flies
> To play with the angels in paradise :
>   And the years glide by.
>
> A maiden stands by the rose-bush fair.
> The dewy blossoms perfume the air.
> She presses her hand to her throbbing breast,
> With love's first wonderful rapture blest :
>   And the years glide by.
>
> A mother kneels by the rose-bush fair,
> Soft sigh the leaves in the evening air.
> Sorrowing thoughts of the past arise,
> And tears of anguish bedim her eyes :
>   And the years glide by.
>
> Naked and lone stands the rose-bush fair,
> Whirled are the leaves in the autumn air,
> Withered and dead they fall to the ground,
> And silently cover a new-made mound :
>   And the years glide by.
>   —*The Rose-bush : Trs. by W. Caldwell.*

Some may be inclined to criticise this poem on the ground that the words quoted a moment ago indicating the analogies between nature and life by which its form is suggested are too numerous, leaving too little to the imagination, and giving something of a mechanical effect to the whole. This criticism, however, need not be directed against the method in general, only against this particular application of it. Here is another poem constructed upon similar principles. Probably the same criticism would not be made upon it. The comparison in it, is between the spring-time of nature and of human life, in which, as is intimated, love is at its strongest. The unity of thought in the poem and its progress, not so much in time as in space, *i. e.*, from the generic to the specific, from universal material nature to the maiden, and then to her particular feelings toward her lover, with just enough of a suggestion of the disappointment of the writer to let us surmise it,—is all very effective.

> The sun had scattered each opal cloud,
>   And the flowers had waked from their winter's rest,
> The song of the skylark rang free and loud,
>   And ah! there were eggs in the swallow's nest!
> And for joy of the spring that so sweet appears,
> I sang with the singing of twenty years.
>
> Out from the meadows there passed a maid,—
>   How can I tell you why she was fair?
> To see was to love as she bent her head
>   Over the brooklet that murmured there.
> As I gazed, in an April of hopes and fears,
> I dreamed with the dreaming of twenty years.
>
> Next,—for I saw her just once again,—
>   Just once in that rare spring-tide,—
> I felt a heart-throb of vague sweet pain,
>   For I noticed that some one was by her side!
> And I turned, with a passion of sudden tears,
> For they loved with the loving of twenty years.
>   —*Twenty Years: Trs. from the French of E. Barateau.*

In the following, in which also the progress is in space, and from the generic to the specific, the *art*, or the *effort* to give *form* to the thought, is less apparent than in the foregoing. For this reason it is more artistic. In fact it would scarcely be possible to conceive of any thing more easy and graceful.

> Nature, thy fair and smiling face
>   Has now a double power to bless,
> For 't is the glass in which I trace
>   My absent Fanny's loveliness.
>
> Her heavenly eyes above me shine,
>   The rose reflects her modest blush,
> She breathes in every eglantine,
>   She sings in every warbling thrush.
>
> That *her* dear form alone I see
>   Need not excite surprise in any,
> For Fanny 's all the world to me,
>   And all the world to me is Fanny.
>   — *To Fanny: Horace Smith.*

It will be noticed that whatever merit the following poem has is owing entirely to the consistency with which the comparison of the human body to a house is carried out from beginning to end.

I.

> Life and Thought have gone away
>   Side by side,
>   Leaving door and windows wide;
> Careless tenants they!

II.

> All within is dark as night:
> In the windows is no light;
> And no murmur at the door,
> So frequent on its hinge before.

III.

> Close the door, the shutters close,
>   Or through the windows we shall see

> The nakedness and vacancy
> Of the dark deserted house.
>
> IV.
>
> Come away ; no more of mirth
> Is here or merry-making sound.
> The house was builded of the earth,
> And shall fall again to ground.
>
> V.
>
> Come away ; for Life and Thought
> Here no longer dwell ;
> But in a city glorious—
> A great and distant city—have bought
> A mansion incorruptible.
> Would they could have stayed with us !
> —*The Deserted House : Tennyson.*

The charm of each of the following, too, is owing to the completeness of the parallelism indicated between the main thought and the illustrating thought, both of which are unfolded with unity and progress. The poems would be still more successful artistically, were it not for the alloyed representation attendant upon the use of a word like *lover*, in the third stanza of the first poem, and of some of the adjectives in the selection from Bryant ; but both, as they are, illustrate well the principal feature which we are now considering.

> Up to her chamber window
> A slight wire trellis goes,
> And up this Romeo's ladder
> Clambers a bold white rose.
>
> I lounge in the ilex shadows,
> I see the lady lean,
> Unclasping her silken girdle,
> The curtain's folds between.

She smiles on her rose-white lover,
She reaches out her hand
And helps him in at the window—
I see it where I stand!

To her scarlet lip she holds him,
And kisses him many a time—
Ah me! it was he that won her
Because he dared to climb!
—*Nocturne: T. B. Aldrich.*

A brook came stealing from the ground;
  You scarcely saw its silvery gleam
Among the herbs that hung around
  The borders of that winding stream,
The pretty stream, the placid stream,
The softly gliding, bashful stream.

A breeze came wandering from the sky,
  Light as the whispers of a dream;
He put the o'erhanging grasses by,
  And softly stooped to kiss the stream,
The pretty stream, the flattered stream,
The shy yet unreluctant stream.

The water, as the wind passed o'er,
  Shot upward many a glancing beam,
Dimpled and quivered more and more,
  And tripped along a livelier stream;
The flattered stream, the simpering stream,
The fond, delighted, silly stream.

Away the airy wanderer flew
  To where the fields with blossoms teem,
To sparkling springs and rivers blue,
  And left alone that little stream,
The flattered stream, the cheated stream,
The sad, forsaken, lonely stream.

The careless wind came never back;
  He wanders yet the fields, I deem;
But, on its melancholy track,
  Complaining went that little stream,

> The cheated stream, the hopeless stream,
> The ever-murmuring, mourning stream,
> —*The Wind and the Stream*: W. C. Bryant.

Still finer,—because it represents a grander thought, appealing to us literally with the voice of nature and of the God behind nature, as well as because the comparison in it to human life is indicated in the subtlest, as, also, for the imagination, the most powerful way,—is the following:

> The moon is at her full, and, riding high,
>   Floods the calm fields with light.
> The airs that hover in the summer sky
>   Are all asleep to-night.
>
> There comes no voice from the great woodlands round
>   That murmured all the day;
> Beneath the shadow of their boughs, the ground
>   Is not more still than they.
>
> But ever heaves and moans the restless Deep;
>   His rising tide I hear,
> Afar I see the glimmering billows leap;
>   I see them breaking near.
>
> Each wave springs upward, climbing toward the fair
>   Pure light that sits on high—
> Springs eagerly, and faintly sinks, to where
>   The mother waters lie.
>
> Upward again it swells; the moonbeams show
>   Again its glimmering crest;
> Again it feels the fatal weight below,
>   And sinks, but not to rest.
>
> Again, and yet again, until the Deep
>   Recalls his brood of waves;
> And with a sullen moan, abashed, they creep
>   Back to his inner caves.
>
> Brief respite! they shall rush from that recess
>   With noise and tumult soon,
> And fling themselves, with unavailing stress,
>   Up toward the placid moon.

> O restless Sea, that, in thy prison here,
>   Dost struggle and complain ;
> Through the slow centuries yearning to be near
>   To that fair orb in vain :
>
> The glorious source of light and heat must warm
>   Thy billows from on high,
> And change them to the cloudy trains that form
>   The curtain of the sky.
>
> Then only may they leave the waste of brine
>   In which they welter here,
> And rise above the hills of earth, and shine
>   In a serener sphere.
>   —*The Tides : W. C. Bryant.*

The chief criticisms that can be made on Bryant's poetry, of which these two quotations furnish fair specimens, are the tendencies in it to alloyed representation already mentioned, and to slowness of movement. The following, however, manifests neither of these characteristics; and, although it does not present either a very great or an original thought, being evidently suggested by Goethe's *Erl-King*, it presents what thought it has artistically, and in strict accordance with the methods which we have been considering.

> " O father, let us hence—for hark,
>   A fearful murmur shakes the air ;
> The clouds are coming swift and dark ;—
>   What horrid shapes they wear !
> A wingèd giant sails the sky ;
> O father, father, let us fly ! "
>
> " Hush, child ; it is a grateful sound,
>   That beating of the summer shower ;
> Here, where the boughs hang close around,
>   We 'll pass a pleasant hour,
> Till the fresh wind, that brings the rain,
> Has swept the broad heaven clear again."

> " Nay, father, let us haste,—for see
>   That horrid thing with hornèd brow,—
> His wings o'erhang this very tree,
>   He scowls upon us now ;
> His huge black arm is lifted high ;
>   O father, father, let us fly ! "
>
> " Hush, child " ; but, as the father spoke,
>   Downward the livid firebolt came,
> Close to his ear the thunder broke,
>   And, blasted by the flame,
> The child lay dead ; while dark and still,
> Swept the grim cloud along the hill.
>   —*A Presentiment : Bryant.*

The principles thus illustrated measure artistic excellence in all poems of whatever length. Just as in a short poem, so in a long one, the development of the main idea, whether by representing what is said, as in the dramatic form, or what is done, as in the narrative or epic, must be consistent and continuous throughout. Every poem, as a whole, even if as long as *Othello, Faust, Paradise Lost*, or *The Æneid*, must furnish, with *unity* and *progress*, what may be termed *a complete moving image* of the action which it is designed to represent. *Othello*, for instance, gives us a complete view of the successive stages of jealousy, as developed both in a frank, magnanimous character like Othello, and in a deceitful, malicious character like Iago. So *Paradise Lost* gives us a complete view of the author's theory of the causes, character, and results of the loss of paradise. It would be a misappropriation of time in this place to present a thorough analysis of any of these poems in order to prove this statement. Besides, there is no necessity for doing it. Such analyses have often been made, and the truth of the statement will be acknowledged by all acquainted with them. The difference, therefore, between the ability to produce a long poem and a short one is the same that exists between a greater and smaller degree of capacity in other departments,—a difference in the ability to hold the thought persistently to a single subject, both complicated and comprehensive, until every thing in it has been classified and arranged and aimed, in accordance with one formative conception.

The moment that we try to do so, we shall be able to recall numbers of poems, great and small, that fail to manifest this unity and progress. All such works as Thomson's *Seasons*, Cowper's *Task*, Campbell's *Pleasures of Hope*, and Wordsworth's *Excursion* must be classed with these. What unity and progress they reveal,—and some might claim these qualities for them,—is of the logical, not representative, kind. There is in them no consistency nor continuity of action. As wholes they are not made up of related parts of single onward movements. In fact, they scarcely represent movements at all. The *Excursion*, even according to its author, was planned to have the effect of a cathedral with one central nave and many side chapels. The plan was only too faithfully carried out. For, although composed in words that ought to move, it is an embodiment of slowness, having all the solidity and stolidity of a structure of stone, and for this reason few read it through.

None of these poems deserve to be placed in the highest rank, because they lack the qualities which, as we have found, must characterize the products of an art, whose form is apprehensible in time. They lack the qualities because they lack the *form* that necessarily would show these; and they lack the form—*i. e.*, the *representative form*,—because their authors did not start to compose them with *representative conceptions*. When Dante, Shakespear, and Milton first conceived their greatest works, it must have been a *picture* that appeared to loom before their imaginations. It is doubtful whether Wordsworth, Cowper, and Campbell thought of anything except an *argument*.

In smaller poems similar defects are not so noticeable; but it would be well for poetic culture if they were. Longfellow outgrew the period of his *Excelsior;* but the world that welcomed it admiringly when it first appeared might welcome it with equal rapture now; yet the lack of representative truth in its conception makes it so unreal and absurd that nothing but repeated experiences at school exhibitions should convince one that it can be read or heard with a sober countenance. Look at its beginning:

> The shades of night were falling fast
> As through an Alpine village passed
> A youth, who bore, 'mid snow and ice,
> A banner with the strange device
> Excelsior!

At its middle:

> "O stay," the maiden said, "and rest
> Thy weary head upon this breast!"
> A tear stood in his bright blue eye,
> But still he answered with a sigh,
> Excelsior!

And at its end:

> There in the twilight cold and gray,
> Lifeless, but beautiful, he lay,
> And from the sky, serene and far,
> A voice fell like a falling star,
> Excelsior!

It is impossible to believe that the series of events described here could ever have been *perceived*, except, perhaps, in a dream; which this tale does not purport to represent. Of course there is in the poem an underlying moral; but this could have been brought out just as well, and better, in connection with a form representative of what really takes place on the earth. The following is a specimen of Longfellow's more artistic method:

> The day is cold, and dark, and dreary;
> It rains, and the wind is never weary;
> The vine still clings to the mouldering wall,
> But at every gust the dead leaves fall,
> And the day is dark and dreary.
>
> My life is cold, and dark, and dreary;
> It rains, and the wind is never weary;
> My thoughts still cling to the mouldering Past,
> But the hopes of youth fall thick in the blast,
> And the days are dark and dreary.
>
> Be still, sad heart! and cease repining;
> Behind the clouds is the sun still shining;
> Thy fate is the common fate of all,
> Into each life some rain must fall,
> Some days must be dark and dreary.
> —*The Rainy Day : Longfellow.*

Even in the last stanza of this, however, some would say that there is too much of a tendency to moralize. This tendency which Longfellow manifests, in common with Whittier and most of our American poets, is something that of course, in its way, is inartistic; not that a poem should have no moral, but, as has been said before, that this should be represented rather than stated. But the power to represent, as all art should represent,—as well as the artistic sense to appreciate such a representation when it has been produced,—seems, as yet, not to have been fully developed among us. Most of us appear to think that thought alone constitutes poetry, or, if not this, at least thought in connection with a strong and metrical expression of it, without regard to other features necessary to render its character in all respects representative.

The truth is, however,—and this is the truth which the whole line of our argument has been intended to emphasize,—that poetry is more than thought; it is more even than a strong and metrical expression of thought. The mere fact that a girl was drowned on the sands of Dee, or that three fishermen were lost at sea, is not enough to account for the interest that we take in Charles Kingsley's *O Mary, Go and Call the Cattle Home*, and *The Fishermen*. It is his poetry that interests us; and by his poetry we mean the representative way in which he has told these tales. So with reference to any statements of facts or opinions. If Wordsworth had said that Milton had a bright intellect and lived a comparatively solitary life, few would have found his words particularly interesting, or noteworthy; but when, in his sonnet on that poet, he said:

> Thy soul was like a star and dwelt apart,

the representative nature of his statement, giving it form and beauty—which latter exists, if at all, as a characteristic of form,—made his expression at once attractive and fitted it to be remembered. So, again, it is not Pope's authority, nor the thought in the following lines, which gives them such a value that they are inserted in every book of quotations; it is the representative form in which the thoughts are expressed, without which form, mere statements to the effect that order must characterize heaven, or that wise and good men are cautious, would not be deemed deserving of remembrance.

> Order is heaven's first law.
> —*Essay on Man*, 4.

> For fools rush in where angels fear to tread.
> —*Essay on Criticism*, 3.
>
> Damn with faint praise.
> —*Epis. to Dr. Arbuthnot.*
>
> Praise undeserved is scandal in disguise.
> —*Epis. of Horace*, ii., 1 ; *Trs.*
>
> Honor and shame from no condition rise ;
> Act well your part, there all the honor lies.
> —*Essay on Man*, 4.

In one word, then, the important thing that needs to be borne in mind in judging of poetry, is that it is an art, and partakes of the nature of the fine arts ; and that, as such, its one essential is a representative form appealing to a man through that which causes him to admire the beautiful. Tennyson has expressed this truth well in what he calls *The Moral* of his *Day-Dream.*

> So, Lady Flora, take my lay,
>   And if you find no moral there,
> Go, look in any glass and say,
>   What moral is in being fair.
> O to what uses shall we put
>   The wildweed-flower that simply blows ?
> And is there any moral shut
>   Within the bosom of the rose ?

But he has suggested in his next stanza another truth that needs to be considered in connection with the last, before all the facts concerning the functions of poetry in the world can be understood.

> But any man that walks the mead
>   In bud, or blade, or bloom, may find,
> According as his humors lead,
>   A meaning suited to his mind.
> And liberal applications lie
>   In Art like Nature, dearest friend,
> So 't were to cramp its use, if I
>   Should hook it to some useful end.

CHAPTER XXVIII.

THE USEFUL ENDS OF POETIC REPRESENTATION.

These are all developed from Possibilities and Methods of Expression underlying equally the Formation of Poetic and of all Language—Poetry forced to recognize that Nature symbolizes Processes of Thought—Influence of this Recognition upon Conceptions of Truth, Human and Divine, Scientific and Theologic—And its Effects upon Feeling and Action—Conclusion.

PERHAPS this discussion of poetry as a representative art can be brought to a close in no better way than by dwelling for a moment upon the thought suggested by the stanza at the end of the last chapter. Poetry is not, in a technical sense, a useful art, yet its forms have their uses, and many uses—as many, in fact, as have the forms of nature itself, which poetry, when it fulfils its mission, employs in its representations. To give a complete list of these uses here would be irrelevant. It is sufficient to suggest, that in the last analysis all of them are developed from possibilities and methods of expression, underlying the formation of all language but especially of poetic language.

Language involves, as we have found, a representation of mental facts and processes through the use of analogous external facts and processes, which alone are apprehensible to others, and which alone, therefore, can make others apprehend our thoughts. But facts and processes fitted to furnish such representations may be perceived on every side of us in the objects and operations of what we term nature. It is the poet, however, who is most conscious of these analogies, for he, instead of accepting those noticed by others and embodied in conventional words, is constantly seeking for new ones and using these. To the poet, and the reader of poetry, therefore, all nature appears to be, in a peculiar sense, a representation, a repetition, a projection into the realm of matter, of the immaterial processes of thought within the mind. This, as I interpret it, is what Wordsworth meant when he said:

> I have learned
> To look on nature not as in the hour
> Of thoughtless youth, but—

because finding in nature the representations of human thought—

> hearing oftentimes
> The still, sad music of humanity.
> —*Lines Composed a few Miles above Tintern Abbey.*

There is, accordingly, a literal as well as a figurative sense, in which the poet

> Finds tongues in trees, books in the running brooks,
> Sermons in stones, and good in every thing.
> —*As You Like It*, ii., 1 : *Shakespear.*

Whatever others may say or think,

> To him who in the love of Nature holds
> Communion with her visible forms, she speaks
> A various language.
> —*Thanatopsis : Bryant.*

In a true sense of the term she has a voice; and she has more than this: she has a voice which says something, which imparts definite intelligence. We have found how in every process in one department of nature, the mind of poetry finds the image of a process in another department of nature. "Flower," says Tennyson,—

> Flower in the crannied wall,
> I pluck you out of the crannies ;—
> Hold you here, root and all, in my hand,
> Little flower—but if I could understand
> What you are, root and all, and all in all,
> I should know what God and man is.
>
> —*Flower in the Crannied Wall.*

To extend this thought, here is a rose-bush. When it begins to grow, it is small and weak and simple. As it develops, it becomes large and strong and complex. So does every other plant in nature ; so does a man ; so does a nation ; so does all humanity ; so, as far as we can know, does the entire substance that develops for the formation of our globe. One mode of operation, one process, we find everywhere. If this be so, then to the ear skilled to listen to the voice in nature, what is all the universe but a mighty auditorium—in which every tale is re-echoed endlessly beneath, about, and above, through every nook of its grand crypts and aisles and arches? But, again, if all created things bear harmonious reports with reference to the laws controlling them, what inference must follow from this ? In view of it, what else can a man do but attribute all these processes, one in mode, to a single source ?—and, more than this, what can he do but accept the import of these processes, the methods indicated in them, the principles exemplified by them, as applicable to all things,—in other words, as revelations of the universal truth ? So the poet finds not only thought in nature, but also truth.

Once more, subtly connected with these facts are others. If nature can represent the thought, frame the language of the human mind,—why, according to the same analogy, can it not represent the thought, frame the language of a greater Creative Mind? And if all nature represent the same kind of thought, *i. e.*, analogous thought, or truth that is harmonious, why is not this Creative Mind one mind? We all know how it is with man when he represents in language any thing true with reference to his inner self. Take that experience, in some of the manifestations of which religious people believe that he most resembles the Unseen One. Think how love, which is begotten often in a single glance, and is matured in a single thrill, gives vent to its invisible intensity. How infinite in range and in variety are those material forms of earth and air and fire and water which are used by man as figures through which to represent the emotion within him! What extended though sweet tales, what endless repetitions of comparisons from hills and valleys, streams and oceans, flowers and clouds, are made to revolve about that soul which, through their visible agency, endeavors to picture in poetry spiritual conditions and relations which would remain unrevealed but for the possibility of thus indirectly symbolizing them. Now if this be so with human love, why should not the Great Heart whose calm beating works the pulses of the universe, express divine love through similar processes evolving infinitely and eternally into forms not ideal and poetic, but real and tangible,—in fact, into forms which we term those of nature. This is the question with which, wittingly or unwittingly, poetry and poetic faith always have confronted and always must confront merely natural science and scientific skepticism. Therefore, Bailey wrote the truth, when he said

> Poetry is itself a thing of God—
> He made his prophets poets, and the more

> We feel of poesy, do we become
> Like God in love and power.
> —*Festus.*

This interpretation of the meaning of nature, natural and human, by those who have learned to interpret it, while striving to have it convey their own meanings, lies at the basis of all the practical uses of poetry. Therefore it is that its products bring with them an atmosphere consoling and inspiring, both enlightening and expanding the conceptions and experiences of the reader. Just as each specific application of Christianity,—all its warnings, consolations, and encouragements, which develop purity within and righteousness without, in the individual, in society, or in the state, spring from the one general conception of universal and divine love manifested in the form of Christ, so do all the specific applications of poetry spring from the one general conception of universal and divine truth manifested through the forms of material and human nature. When each of us can say with Wordsworth—

> I have learned
> To look on nature, not as in the hour
> Of thoughtless youth, but hearing oftentimes
> The still, sad music of humanity,

Then too we may be able to add with him—

> And I have felt
> A presence that disturbs me with the joy
> Of elevated thoughts ; a sense sublime
> Of something far more deeply interfused,
> Whose dwelling is the light of setting suns,
> And the round ocean, and the living air,
> And the blue sky, and in the mind of man :—
> A motion and a spirit, that impels
> All thinking things, all objects of all thought,
> And rolls through all things.
>   —*Lines Composed a few Miles above Tintern Abbey.*

INDEX.

Abou Ben Adhem, 216.
Abruptness, eloc. and poetic, 82–88.
Accent, how marks for, read in Greek poetry, 107; relation of, to regularity of effect, 82–88; to loudness and softness, 50–56; what different kinds represent in elocution, 32; in poetic measures which they determine, 57–81; source of English rhythm and tunes of verse, 27, 104–114.
Adams, S. F., 74.
Addison, 154, 203, 259, 288.
Admiration. See Delight.
Affirmation, how represented, 92. See Assurance, Dictation, Positiveness, etc.
Afternoon at a Parsonage, 159.
Agreement as a factor in forming language, 11, 174.
Alcaic verse, 21.
Aldrich, T. B., 230, 333.
Alexander's feast, 101.
Alexander, J. W., 79.
Allegorical poetry, 277, 309.
Allegory, figure, 200.
Allen, Grant, 20, 189.
Alliteration, what it represents, 116.
Alloy, 212.
Alloyed representation, 212, 262–318; direct, 264; genesis of, 262–277; illustrative, 265; is short-lived, 305.
All 's well that ends well, 94.
Alteration of words, 157.
Amazement, 128–149.
American flag, the 141.
Amphibrach metre, 60, 70.
Ancient Mariner, 77, 237.
Annabel Lee, 70.

Anticipation, how represented, 92, 109–114.
Antithesis, 196.
Antony and Cleopatra, 292.
Aphæresis, 158.
Apocope, 158.
Apophasis, 196.
Apostrophe, 196.
Arbitrary symbols and words, 174.
Aristotle, 25, 31.
Arnold, Matthew, 48, 222, 229.
Arts, all representative, 3, 4; developed according to principle of comparison, 27.
Aspiration, metre representing, 65, 67.
Association, its influence in determining meanings of phrases, 164, 180–185; in forming words from sounds, 5–7; in forming new words from old words, 174, 175; in making words unpoetic and poetic, 187–193; and language plain, 195.
Assonance, what it represents, 116.
Assurance, how represented, 62–64, 71, 112–114.
Audley Court, 269.
Aurora Leigh, 237.
Autumn, 299.
Aux Italiens, 86, 244.
Awe, how represented, 128, 131, 136–149.
Aytoun, 51.

Bacon, 137.
Bagehot, 273.
Bailey, 2, 345.
Bains Carew, 78.
Barateau, 330.

347

Barbara Frietchie, 84, 133.
Barton, 67.
Battle of Ivry, 49, 77.
Bayley, 119.
Beecher, H. W., 299, 300.
Bells, The, 143, 169.
Bells of Shandon, 85, 112.
Beppo, 85.
Bernard, 79.
Bertha in the Lane, 167.
Bigelow Papers, 79, 160.
Bird Let Loose, The, 234.
Birthday Ode, 101.
Bishop of Rum-ti-Foo, 94.
Black, W., 191.
Black Regiment, 110.
Boadicea, 9.
Boker, 110.
Botanic Garden, 276.
Break, break, break, 221.
Breathing, and length of line, 25.
Breton, N., 106.
Bridge of Sighs, 72, 114.
Broadswords of Scotland, 75.
Bristowe tragedy, 157.
Brooke, 259.
Brown, M. T., 15, 17.
Browning, Mrs. E. B., 40, 111, 159, 167, 237.
Browning, R., 9, 46, 53, 73, 110, 114, 131, 132, 139, 148, 163, 164, 165, 170, 201, 304, 309–311.
Bryant, W. C., see Iliad, 230, 334, 335, 336, 343.
Burns, 144, 158, 159, 224.
Byron, 80, 85, 91, 130, 139, 147, 204, 207, 302.
By the North Sea, 170.

Cæsura, 26, 39.
Caldwell, W., 329.
Callanan, J. J., 69.
Campbell, 87, 101, 105, 110, 111, 116, 133, 337, 338.
Captivity, The, 101.
Caractacus, 67.
Carillon, 63, 79, 86, 111.
Carlyle, 302.
Cataract of Lodore, 88.
Cato, 259, 288.
Chapman, 138.
Charge, Light Brigade, 71, 84, 110.

Chatterton, 157.
Chaucer, 194.
Chesterfield, 14.
Childe Harold, 80, 139, 204.
Children of Lord's Supper, 47.
Christabel, 45, 81.
Choree, 63.
Churchill, J. W., 15.
Classic, metres, 29, 30; historical development of Greek poetry, 22; representation pure, 240–261, 263.
Climax, 196, 284.
Cloud, The, 76, 80, 104, 105.
Coleridge, H., 302.
Coleridge, S. T., 45, 77, 81, 191, 237, 302.
Coles, A., 64.
Columbus, Voyage of, 133.
Come Rest in this Bosom, 113.
Complaint, metre representing, 65, 66.
Comus, 306, 313.
Comparison, principle of, at the basis of all art, 27; in forming words, 8, 174, 175, 187; in determining meaning of phrases, 180–185; words formed from, not necessarily poetic, 186, 208; but are figurative, 195; how comparisons are used appropriately in poetry, 190, 206, 225–239, 260, 265–270, 281–284, 287–295, 299–307; how inappropriately, 190, 200–203, 271, 272, 296–318.
Completeness in form, 322–327.
Comus, 306, 313.
Conclusive effects. See Assurance, Positiveness, etc.
Concord Monument, Hymn at completion of, 236.
Confidence. See Assurance, Positiveness, etc.
Consistency in form, 321–327.
Contempt, how represented, 128, **148, 149.**
Continuity in form, 321–327.
Coriolanus, 129, 138, 162, 166.
Courage. See Determination.
Course of Time, 163.
Cowley, 159.
Cowper, 70, 297, 337, 338.

Crabbe, 286, 287, 294.
Cranch, 227.
Cupid and Psyche, 219.
Cymbeline, 54, 166.

Dactyl, 60, 72.
Dance and poetry, 22, 95.
Dante, 155, 194.
Darkness, 147.
Darwin, C., 144.
Darwin, E., 156, 276.
Davis, T., 113.
Day Dream, The, 132, 341.
Definiteness in form, 322–327.
Delaumosne, 17.
Delight, how represented, 72, 82, 86, 127, 128, 132–149.
Delsarte, 17.
Decisiveness, how represented, 62–67, 92, 113.
Deserted Village, 27.
Deserted House, 332.
Descriptive poetry, 203–207, 209–277, 284–307 ; referring to nat. scenery, 284–289, 293–299 — to persons, 288, 291.
Despondency, 229.
Determination, metre representing, 65–67, 71, 72, 109–113, 128, 133–149.
Dictation, metre representing, 62–64, 70–72, 113.
Didactic poetry, 278–292.
Dies Iræ, 64.
Diiambic metre, 61, 77.
Diinitial metre, 61, 77.
Dimond, 69.
Dionysius, 64.
Discoursive elocution, 33.
Diterminal measure, 61, 77.
Ditrochaic measure, 61, 77.
Divided, 159.
Dobell, 84.
Donders, 98.
Dora, 264.
Douglas, 288.
Drake, 141.
Drama of Exile, 167.
Dramatic elocution, 33.
Dream of Eugene Aram, 131.
Dryden, 101, 155, 156, 157, 259.
Duration, elocutionary, and what it represents, 33–38 ; poetic, and what it represents, 38–49.
Dyer, 87.
Dying Christian to his Soul, 121

Earl o'Quarter-Deck, 153.
Earthly Paradise, 219, 233, 249, 289.
Eden, Language of, 11.
Ejaculations, influence in formation of language, 5, 11, 174.
Ejaculatory tendency in elocution, 33.
Elegant extracts, 216, 239.
Elegy, Gray's, 42, 137.
Ellen McJones Aberdeen, 52.
Ellipsis, 161.
Elocution, influence in language, 18—in poetry, 21 ; its elements classified, 32–36 ; discoursive 33 ; dramatic, 33.
Eloquence of thought, metre representing, 68, 74, 86 ; quality, 127.
Emerson, 83, 236, 302.
Emotive tendency in forming language, 13 ; in character, 14 ; in elocution, 35 ; in duration, 44 ; in force, 50, 58, 82–87 ; in pitch, 90–95, 115 ; in quality, 126–149, 203–207, 265–267.
Emphasis, as influenced by rhymes, 120. See Accent, Force, Stress.
Enallage, 165.
End-cut words, 158.
End-stopped lines, 41.
English, Metrical possibilities of, 30.
Enthusiasm, how represented, 72, 128.
Enoch Arden, 272.
Epigram, Pope, 239.
Epilogue, Browning, 132 ; Swinburne, 87, 146.
Epistle, An, 310 ; to Arbuthnot, 341.
Epistles of Horace, 341.
Essay on Criticism, 44, 55, 341 ; on Man, 120, 340, 341 ; on Satire, 156.
Evangeline, 76, 114, 271, 272.
Evelyn Hope, 73.
Evening on the Broads, 311, 317.
Everett, E., 299.

Eve of St. Agnes, 152, 153, 163, 167.
Eve of St. John, 122.
Excelsior, 338.
Excursion, 26, 270, 281, **337**.
Exile of Erin, 110.
Explanatory alloy, 279–307.

Faerie Queen, 40, 138, 142, 143.
Fairies' song, 78.
Falconer, 298.
Fanny, To, 331.
Farewell, A., 324.
Farrer, 6.
Feeling, how represented, 12–18, 35; how different kinds represented, 127–149. See Emotive.
Feet, Eng. and classic, how produced, 28; classification of English, 60. See Measures.
Felise, 144.
Ferdinando and Elvira, 41, 52, 114.
Festus, 2, 346.
Figurative language, 195–207, 228; when to be used, 206, 265; when poetic and representative, and when not so, 208–212, 293–318. See Indirect and Illustrative Representation.
Figures of rhetoric, not always representative, 195–197, 265; when representative, 197–200.
First Kiss, 105.
Fishermen, The, 327.
Fisher's Cottage, 221.
Flower in Crannied Wall, 344.
Force, elocutionary, 33, 50; what it represents, 34, 35; its kinds, 50; degrees of, in elocution and poetry, 51–56; gradations of, 57–81; regularity of, 82–88; significance of metres determined by it, 57–81.
Form in words and sentences, 320; in poems, 322–341; when modelled on direct representation, 323; on illustrative representation, 327.
Fra Lippo Lippi, 311.
French language, 24, 191, 192.
Fright, how represented, 127–149.
Front-cut in words, 158.
Frothingham, 48.

Gardener's Daughter, 43, 287, 291.
Garden of Cymodoce, 116.
Gathering Song, 71.
Gentle Alice Brown, 99.
Gerhardt, 79.
Gilbert, 30, 41, 52, 78, 94, 114, 160, 223.
Glimpses of the War, 311.
Glorious things of thee are spoken, 65.
Goethe, 48, 124, 194, 248, 302, 335.
Golden Legend, 63.
Golden Year, 283.
Goldsmith, 27, 101, 121, 184.
Good Old Plow, 76.
Goose, Mother, 29.
Gougaune Barra, 69.
Go where glory waits thee, 62.
Greek, development of its poetic forms, 22; direct representation in tragedies, 267; how accents pronounced in reading verse, 107; metres, 29, 30, 60–81. See Classic and Homer.
Grief, metre representing, 73. See Pathos.
Growth of the legend, 307.
Guest, 45, 137.
Guttural, meaning of, elocutionary and poetic, 127–149.
Gradation, 116. See Force and Stress.
Gray, 42, 137, 144.
Grant, 86.

Halcro's verses, 85.
Hamilton, Sir W., 279.
Hamlet, 207, 219, 290, 313.
Hammond, 117.
Harrington, 216.
Hawtrey, 49.
Heine, 220.
Hegel, 17.
Helmholtz, 98.
Henry VIII., 27, 41; 1 Henry IV., 83, 143, 207, 291; 2 Henry IV., 138; Henry V., 166, 167; 2 Henry VI., 142, 236; 3 Henry VI., 234.
Heretic's Tragedy, 131.
Herder, 7.

INDEX.   351

Hermann and Dorothea, 48, 248.
Herrick, 111.
Hesitation, in sense of doubt, 92, 113, 123.
Heyse, 10.
Heywood, 167.
Hexameter, Classic and English, 47, 76.
Hiawatha, 63, 166.
High tide, 167.
History English Rhythms, 45, 137.
Hogg, 100.
Holmes, O. W., 3.
Holy Cross Day, 9, 148.
Home, 259, 288.
Homer, 46, 47, 155, 193, 205, 207, 216, 217, 232, 235, 236, 240-261, 284, 294; his representative methods, 240-261.
Homeric verse, 21.
Horror. See Awe.
Hood, 72, 76, 114, 131.
Hope. See Anticipation.
How they brought the good news, 9, 46, 110.
Hugo, 236.
Humboldt, W. von, 248.
Hunt, L., 78, 215.
Hunting song, 51.
Hymn on the Nativity, 159, 168.
Hyperbaton, 154.
Hyperbole, 200.
Hyperion 155.

Iambic, or Iambus, 60, 67.
Idyls of King, 87, 236.
Iliad, Bryant's translation, 205, 207, 217, 232, 236, 242, 246, 247, 251-256, 259, 260, 294; Hawtrey's 49; Pope's 42, 54.
Illustrations, why used, 206, 226, 265, 290; when not representative, 293-318. See Figurative Language, and Representation, Illustrative and Indirect.
I love my Jean, 222.
Il Penseroso, 55, 144.
Imagery, 196.
Imitative principle, in forming language, 7-11; in elocution, 34; in elocutionary duration, 37-49; force, 51-56; accent and metre,

80-88; tunes of verse, 94-102, 115-120; in letter sounds, 128-149.
Important ideas, how represented in elocution and poetry, 38, 39, 41-49, 52-56, 79-81, 90-92, 115-121, 133, 139-142.
In a Year, 53.
Indignation. See Contempt.
Inflections, elocutionary, 90-94; poetic, 103-125.
Ingelow, J., 156, 159, 163, 166, 167.
Ingoldsby Legends, 100.
In Memoriam, 111, 123.
Insertion of useless words, 152.
Instinctive tendency, in character, 14; in elocution, 35; in ejaculatory expression, 14-17; in forming through association words from sounds, 5; new words from old words, 175; in making representation direct, 230; representing what in duration, 37, in force, 50, 58-68, 82; in pitch, 90-93; in quality, 127.
Interjection, 196.
Interrogation, 196.
Intonations, representative character of, 19, 88-125; physical reason for, 20.
Inversion of words, 154.
Irony, 196.
Is there for honest poverty, 158.

Jebb, 67.
John, King, 124, 125.
Jonson, 263.
Julius Cæsar, 134, 155, 218.

Keats, 152, 153, 155, 163, 167.
Key, musical, high or low elocutionary and poetic, 89-102.
Key, P. B., 75.
Kingsley, 224, 235, 326, 327, 340.
Kirkham, 51.
Kiss, The, 111; The First, 111.
Kitty, 86; of Colraine, 325.

Lady of the Lake, 100, 145, 162, 163, 167, 258.
L'Allegro, 99, 137, 144.
Lament, 159.

Landor, Song for Centenary of, 317.
Lanier, 93.
Language, plain and figurative, 195–207; poetry an artistic development of, 4; how it represents thought in single words, 4–11; and processes of thought in successive words, 12, 180–185, 320–333.
Latin. See Classic.
Lear, King, 139, 141, 146, 307.
Le Byron de nos Jours, 163.
Leland, 221.
Lessing, 251.
Letter from Italy, 203; Letters, 83.
Lewis, 100.
Life Drama, 199, 230, 274, 275.
Line, length of exhalation, 25–27; end of, representing what when accented and unaccented, 104–125; when masculine or feminine, 104–114, 118–125; end-stopped and run-on lines, 41; inartistic endings, 40; rhyme and blank verse, 118–125.
Little Mattie, 40.
Lochinvar, 39, 46, 110.
Lockhart, 75.
Locksley Hall, 40, 85, 112, 203, 282, 313.
Longfellow, 31, 47, 63, 76, 79, 86, 111, 114, 152, 157, 166, 229, 231, 271, 338, 339.
Lord of Burleigh, 154.
Lord of the Isles, 153.
Lost Love, The, 121.
Lotus Eaters, 55, 284.
Loudness, how represented in poetry, 51–55.
Louse on Lady's Bonnet, 224.
Love divine all loves excelling, 119.
Lover's Journey, 286.
Lovers of Gudrun, 232, 248.
Love's Labor Lost, 117, 191.
Love's Philosophy, 85.
Lowell, 79, 160, 303, 307.
Lute Song, 116.
Lytton 86, 244.

Macaulay, 49, 77.
Macbeth, J. W. V., 198; The play, 129, 130, 131, 140; 142, 158, 227, 238.

MacDonald, 153.
Macgregor's Gathering, 76.
Machiavelli, 14.
Mad Dog, Elegy on, 121.
Madoc in Wales, 285.
Mahogany tree, 83.
Mahony, F., 85, 112.
Maniac, 100.
Manly Heart, 159.
Man who never laughed again, The 154, 159.
Marino Faliero, 130.
Marmion, 110, 145.
Martineau, J., 299.
Massey, G., 53, 159, 163, 311, 315, 317.
Master Hugues, 114.
Maud, 39, 54, 66, 129, 130, 238.
McMaster, 141.
Meanings of elocutionary and poetic forms, 32–149; duration, 37–50; force, 50–88; inflections, melody, pitch, tunes of verse, 89–125; the different poetic metres, 41–49, 60–68; of words as developed by association and comparison, in sounds, 4–9, 126–149, 150–172; in phrases, 164, 180–185; in spiritual as contrasted with material applications, 176, 228.
Measures, blending of different, to prevent monotony, 75; to represent movements, 38–49, 79–88; classification of English, and their classic analogues, what each represents, 58–81; compound, 61, 71; di-initial, 61, 77; di-terminal, 61, 77; double, 60, 62–67; initial, 60, 62, 70; median, 60, 68; pathetic, 72, 73; quadruple, 49, 61, 77; terminal, 60, 65, 74; triple, 46–49, 60, 68–81.
Melody, elocutionary, musical, and poetic, 90–125.
Mercenary Marriage, A, 207.
Merkel, 98.
Merman, The, 132.
Metaphor, 199, 235–239; ancient and modern, 235; faults in, 200, 293–318; metaphorical representation, 228.
Metonomy, 197.

Metres. See Measures, Feet.
Metrical essay, 3.
Mid-cut in words, 158.
Mid-Summer Night's Dream, 75, 109.
Milton, 27, 40, 43, 53, 55, 56, 80, 83, 87, 99, 114, 129, 132, 134, 136, 137, 138, 140, 141, 142, 143, 144, 145, 146, 147, 155, 159, 168, 171, 201, 218, 226, 233, 265, 288, 291, 296, 306, 313, 338.
Milton, Sonnet on, 340.
Misuse of words, 165.
Mitford, 135.
Monotony in melody, 75, 115–120.
Moore, 62, 113, 234.
Moral, in poetry, how can be represented, 339–346.
Morris, W., 154, 159, 170, 219, 234, 248, 249, 289.
Mort d'Arthur, 146, 206, 215, 294.
Movement, how represented in elocutionary and poetic duration, 37–49; force, 50–88; pitch, 89–125; quality, 126–149; in grammatical arrangements of words, 180–184; in intonations, 12; in progress of form, 322; in poetry of Homer, 251–261.
Müller, M., 9, 10, 176, 182.
Mulock, 53, 207.
Music, 22–24, 95–125. See Melody.
My faith looks up to thee, 112.
My Psalm, 53, 230.

Nearer my God to Thee, 74.
Napoleon, 14, 109.
Negative effects, how represented, 92, 145.
New Testament, 15.
Newton, 65.
New Year's Eve in Exile, 315.
Nocturne, 333.
Nymph's Reply, 66.

Obscurity, 156, 164, 276, 296, 309–318; not brilliancy, 302, 303; in allusions, 304.
Odyssey, 55, 138, 202.
Ogier the Dane, 289.
Old Continentals, 141.
Old Oaken Bucket, 69.

O Mary go and call, etc., 326.
Omission of words, 161; figure of rhetoric, 196.
Only a Woman, 53.
Onomatopœia, 9, 197.
On the Detraction, 40.
On the Cliffs, 101, 118.
Orations, style of, 299–302.
Ornamental alloy, 279, 307–318.
Ornate, 279, 307–318.
Orotund quality, elocutionary and poetic, 127–149.
Orris, S. S., 15.
O Sacred Head, etc., 79.
Osgood, F. S., 75.
Othello, 129, 137, 237 307

Palestine, Sketches of, 117
Palfrey, To J. G., 303.
Palmer, 112.
Paradise Lost, 27, 40, 43, 55, 56, 80, 83, 87, 114, 129, 132, 134, 136, 137, 138, 140, 141, 142, 143, 146, 147, 155, 201, 218, 226, 233, 266, 288, 296, 306,
Paradise Regained, 137, 145.
Paralipsis, 196.
Parallelism, 25.
Parish Register, 294.
Pathos, how represented, 69, 72, 73, 114.
Patten, G. W., 79.
Patti, A., 126.
Pause, source of verse, 25, 39, 40; inartistic, 40; what represents in elocution, 32, 38; in poetry, 39, 40.
Pectoral quality in elocution and poetry, 127-149.
Percy, 223.
Persistency, metre representing, 65–67, 71.
Peter Bell, 267.
Phillis the Fair, 106.
Philosophical, The, how made poetic, 204–207, 209–212, 225–230, 281–284,
Phrases, source of verse, 25; ideas derived from them, as well as from words, 164; how meanings of, determined by association and comparison, 180–185.

354 POETRY AS A REPRESENTATIVE ART.

Pictures, in plain language, 210.
Pinafore, 30, 160, 222.
Pitch, elocutionary, 33 ; what represents, 34, 35, 85–125 ; rising and falling, 103–114.
Plain Language distingushed from figurative, 195–207; when should be used, 203 ; when plain is poetic and representative, 208–224.
Plato, 15.
Pleasures of Hope, 101, 116, 133.
Pleonasm, 152.
Poe, 9, 55, 70, 143, 168, 169.
Pollock, 163.
Poor Man's Wife, A, 163.
Pope, 42, 44, 54, 55, 120, 121, 156, 157, 202, 239, 340, 341.
Portrait, A, 111.
Portrait, The, 167.
Positiveness, metre representing, 62–64, 71, 92.
Precision, metre representing, 62.
Precocious Baby, The, 52, 94.
Prelude, 289, 290.
Presentation, distinguished from Representation, 208–212, 339, 340. See Alloyed Representation.
Present Crisis, 307.
Presentiment, A, 336.
Princess, 9, 55, 144, 145, 149, 226, 282, 313, 324.
Progress in poetic form, 322. See Movement.
Progress of Poesy, 144.
Prometheus Unbound, 190.
Prose, how differing from poetry, 186, 208–212, 279–290, 339, 340.
Psalms, The, 26.
Psalm of Life, 31, 152, 229.
Pure quality, elocutionary and poetic, 128–149.
Pure representation, 208–261 ; all classic representation, pure, 263 ; in Homer, 241–261.
Push, metre representing, 58, 65–67.

Quality, el. 33–35 ; and poetic, what each kind represents, 126–149.
Quantity of syllables, as basis of metre, English and classic, 29, 38–49 ; elocutionary and poetic representation by means of, 38, 49, 98–102, 126–149.

Railroad Rhyme, 42, 122.
Rainy Day, The, 339.
Raleigh, 66.
Rapidity, how represented in elocution and poetry, 39, 41–49, 52, 68 ; in rhyme, 118–125.
Rapture, metre representing, 74. See Delight.
Raven, 9, 55, 168.
Read, T. B., 9, 46.
Recitative, 21.
Reflective tendency, in character, 14 ; in elocution, 34 ; in imitative expression, 14–17 ; in forming words from sounds, 8 ; new words from old words by comparison, 173 ; in making representation indirect or illustrative, 231 ; representing what in duration, 37 ; in force, 50, 58, 68, 82 ; in pitch, 90–93 ; in quality, 127.
Regularity of movement, produced by force, 82–88 ; by rhyme, 118–125.
Representation in conception of great poems, 337 ; in distinction from presentation, 208–212 ; in expressing thought and feeling, limits of, 213 (see Philosophy) ; in expressing the moral, 339 ; in mixture of main and illustrative thought, 296–307 ; in poems as wholes, 319–341 ; in sense, 173–346 ; in sound, 1–172 ; in thought as well as style, 211 ; useful ends of, 342–346. See Alloyed, Composite, Direct, Illustrative, Indirect, Pure.
Rhapsody of Life's Progress, 159.
Rhetoric, figures of, not all representative, 196, 197 ; how different from poetry, 279.
Rhyme, Effects of, 118–125.
Rhythm, 19, 27, 28, 35–87.
Richard II., 201 ; III., 133.
Rienzi's Address, 135.
Ring and the Book, 164, 165.
Robertson, Rev. T. W., 299.
Roche, 328.

Rogers, 133.
Rokeby, 58, 201.
Roman. See Classic.
Romeo and Juliet, 129, 290.
Rosebush, The, 329.
Rowe, 259.
Ruins of Rome, 87.

Sailor Boy's Dream, 69.
Samson Agonistes, 53.
Sapphic verse, 21.
Satisfaction, how represented, 82, 127.
Saturday Review, 193.
Saxe, 42, 122.
Schmidt, J. H. H., 22, 23, 29, 63, 67, 72, 108.
Scholar and Carpenter, 156.
Scott, 39, 46, 51, 54, 71, 76, 85, 100, 109, 110, 122, 145, 153, 162, 163, 167, 201, 223, 258.
Seasons, The, 299.
Seige of Corinth, 207.
Selkirk, 70.
Seminole's Defiance, 79.
Sensuous and sensual, 292.
Serenade at the Villa, 139.
Shakespeare, 27, 41, 53, 54, 63, 75, 83, 91, 93, 107, 109, 117, 124, 125, 129, 130, 131, 133, 134, 137, 138, 139, 140, 141, 142, 143, 146, 155, 158, 162, 166, 167, 171, 191, 193, 201, 205, 207, 218, 227, 233, 236, 237, 238, 290, 291, 292, 307, 313, 338, 343; prose of, 302; sonnet on, 159.
Shanly, C. D., 325.
Shelley, 66, 76, 80, 85, 104, 105, 190.
Shelling, 17.
Sheridan's Ride, 9, 46.
She was a Phantom of Delight, 190, 202.
Shipwreck, 298.
Sidney, Sir P., 2.
Simile, 199, 232; faults in, 200–203, 308–312.
Sing Heigh-Ho, 235.
Sky Lark, The, 100.
Slowness in elocution, 39; in poetry, 41–49; 52.
Smith, Alex., 199, 230, 274, 275; H., 331.

Smooth force, elocutionary and poetic, 82–88.
Softness, how represented in poetry, 53–55, 86.
Soldier's Dream, 87.
Song and Poetry, 22.
Song of the Shirt, 76.
Sordello, 201, 304.
Soul in expression, same as emotion, 13, 15–17.
Sounds, how representing thought in duration, 37–49; force, 50–88; intonations, 18–36; pitch, 89–125; quality of word-forms, 4–18, 126–149; how not representing thought, 150–172; when poetic sounds are inartistic, 171.
Southey, 88, 124, 249, 250, 257, 258, 260, 284, 285.
Spafford, H. E. P., 328.
Spencer, H., 15, 17, 20, 22, 23, 191, 233.
Spenser, E., 31, 40, 138, 140, 143, 171, 277, 309.
Spenserian verse, 21.
Spinning-Wheel Song, 69.
Spurgeon, 299.
Star-Spangled Banner, 75.
St. Cecilia's Day, 155.
Still we wait for thine appearing, 119.
Storrs, R. H., 299, 300.
Strength, how represented in poetry, 52-55.
Stress, elocutionary and poetic, 57, 58; analogy between it and poetic measures, 58–60.
St. Simeon Stylites, 82.
Suckling, 115, 116.
Summing up in Italy, 40.
Superfluity, 152.
Surprise, how represented, 128–149.
Swinburne, 87, 101, 102, 116, 118, 144, 146, 169, 170, 311, 312, 316, 317.
Symbols, words not arbitrary, 174. See Meanings, Sounds, Words.
Syncope, 158.
Synecdoche, 198.

Taming of the Shrew, 143.
Task, The, 297.

356   POETRY AS A REPRESENTATIVE ART.

Tears of the Muses, 140.
Tempest, The, 63, 139.
Tennyson, 9, 39, 40, 43, 51, 52, 54, 55, 66, 71, 82, 84, 85, 87, 101, 110, 111, 112, 113, 116, 122, 129, 130, 132, 134, 144, 145, 146, 149, 154, 157, 194, 203, 206, 215, 221, 224, 226, 230, 236, 238, 264, 269, 271, 272, 281, 282, 283, 284, 287, 291, 294, 313, 324, 332, 341, 344.
Thackeray, 83.
Thalaba 124, 250, 257.
Thalassius, 102, 118,
Thanatopsis, 343.
The Spacious Firmament on High, 154.
The Sun is Warm, 66.
Thompson, 298, 337.
Thought, 227.
Tides, The, 335.
Time. See Duration.
Timon of Athens, 53.
Tintern Abbey, 2, 178, 343, 346.
Toccata of Galuppi's, 132.
To-day and To-morrow, 53.
To Labor is to Pray, 75.
To Mr. Hobbes, 159.
Tommy's dead, 84.
Too Late, 222.
Transposition of words, 154.
Tree of Liberty, 158.
Trench, 176, 178.
Triumph, metre representing, 74.
Trochee, 60, 63, 67.
Troilus and Cressida, 140, 236.
Trope, 198.
Tunes of Verse, 21, 27, 89–125.
Twa Dogs, 144.
Twelfth Night, 107.
Twenty Years, 330.
Two April Mornings, 205.
Two Voices, 51, 66, 101, 113.

Unbeloved, The, 159.
Under my Window, 75.
Unimportant ideas. See Important.
Unity, effects of, as produced by rhyme, 118–125 ; by form in arrangement of thought, 322.

Variety in poetic melody, 115–125.
Vehemence, metre representing, 74, 82.
Veron, 172.
Virgil, 46, 47, 155.
Vision, 196.

Wagner, 314.
Waller, J. F., 69.
Washington, 14.
Waterloo, Charge at, 54.
Weakness, how represented in poetry, 53–56.
Wedding, Ballad upon, 115.
Wedgeworth, 145.
Weight, how represented in poetry, 52, 53, 55.
Welcome, The, 113.
Wellington, Ode on, 52, 84, 116, 134.
Westminster Bridge, 40.
Westwood, T., 75.
When gathering Clouds, 86.
Whitney, 8, 10.
Whittier, 53, 84, 86, 133, 230, 339.
Will, 14.
Wilfulness, 14.
Wilmot, 119.
Wilson, 302.
Wind and Stream, The, 334.
Winstanley, 159, 166, 167.
Winter Evening, 297.
Winter's Tale, 166.
Wither, 159.
Woodworth, S., 69.
Words, why Anglo-Saxon preferred by poets, 191–194 ; conventional and imaginative, 187 ; poetic and unpoetic, 186–194 ; primary, formed from association and comparison, 5–8 ; secondary, ditto, 174–179 ; sounds of, representing sense, 9, 127–149, 178.
Wordsworth, 1, 26, 40, 121, 151, 156, 178, 190, 202, 205, 267, 270, 280, 289, 290, 338, 340, 343, 346, prose of, 302 ; plan of Excursion, 337.
Wreck of Grace of Sunderland, 163.

POEMS BY PROF. GEO. L. RAYMOND

A Life in Song. 16°, cloth extra, gilt top $1.25

"Mr. Raymond is a poet, with all that the name implies. He has the true fire—there is no disputing that. There is thought of an elevated character, the diction is pure, the versification is true, the meter correct, and . . . affords innumerable quotations to fortify and instruct one for the struggles of life."—*Hartford Post.*

"Marked by a fertility and strength of imagination worthy of our first poets. . . . The versification throughout is graceful and thoroughly artistic, the imagery varied and spontaneous, . . . the multitude of contemporary bardlings may find in its sincerity of purpose and loftiness of aim a salutary inspiration."—*The Literary World* (Boston).

"Original and noble thoughts, gracefully put into verse. . . . Mr. Raymond thoroughly understands the true poet's science, man."—*The Literary World* (London).

"Here, for instance, are lines which, if printed in letters of gold on the front of every pulpit, and practised by every one behind one, would transform the face of the theological world. . . . In short, if you are in search of ideas that are unconventional and up-to-date, get 'A Life in Song,' and read it."—*Unity.*

"The poet has 'a burden' as conscious and urgent as the prophet of old. His is a 'story with a purpose,' and very deftly and effectively is it sung into the ear of the cultivated listener. . . . Wonderful versatility and mastery of the poetic art are shown in the manipulation of speech to the service of thought. . . . Professor Raymond has revealed a metrical genius of the highest order."—*The Watchman.*

"A remarkably fine study of the hopes, aspirations, and disappointments of . . . an American modern life. . . . Is not only dramatic in tendency, but is singularly realistic and acute. . . . The volume will appeal to a large class of readers by reason of its clear, musical, flexible verse, its fine thought, and its intense human interest."—*Boston Transcript.*

Ballads, and Other Poems. 16°, cloth extra, gilt top . . $1.25

"Notable examples of what may be wrought of native material by one who has a tasteful ear and practised hand. . . . There is true enjoyment in all that he has written."—*Boston Globe.*

"A very unusual success, a success to which genuine poetic power has not more contributed than wide reading and extensive preparation. The ballads overflow, not only with the general, but with the very particular truths of history."—*Cincinnati Times.*

"A work of true genius, brimful of imagination and sweet humanity."—*The Fireside* (London).

"Fine and strong, its thought original and suggestive, while its expression is the very perfection of narrative style."—*The N. Y. Critic.*

"Proves beyond doubt that Mr. Raymond is the possessor of a poetic faculty which is worthy of the most careful and conscientious cultivation."—*N. Y. Evening Post.*

"A very thoughtful study of character . . . great knowledge of aims and motives. . . . Such as read this poem will derive from it a benefit more lasting than the mere pleasure of the moment."—*The Spectator* (London).

"Mr. Raymond is a poet emphatically, and not a scribbler in rhyme."—*Literary Churchman* (London).

The Aztec God and Other Dramas. 16°, cloth extra, gilt top . $1.25

"The three dramas included in this volume represent a felicitous, intense, and melodious expression of art both from the artistic and poetic point of view. . . . Mr. Raymond's power is above all that of psychologist, and added thereto are the richest products of the imagination both in form and spirit. The book clearly discloses the work of a man possessed of an extremely refined critical poise, of a culture pure and classical, and a sensitive conception of what is sweetest and most ravishing in tone-quality. The most delicately perceptive ear could not detect a flaw in the mellow and rich music of the blank verse."—*Public Opinion.*

". . . The plot is exceedingly interesting and well executed. . . . It is careful work, strong and thoughtful in its conception."—*Worcester Spy.*

"As fine lines as are to be found anywhere in English. . . . Sublime thought fairly leaps in sublime expression. . . . As remarkable for its force of epigram as for its loftiness of conception."—*Cleveland World.*

"There are countless quotable passages in Professor Raymond's fine verse. . . . The work is one of unusual power and brilliancy, and the thinker or the student of literature will find the book deserving of careful study."—*Toledo Blade.*

". . . 'Columbus' one finds a work which it is difficult to avoid injuring with fulsome praise. The character of the great discoverer is portrayed grandly and greatly. . . . It is difficult to conceive how anyone who cares for that which is best in literature . . . could fail to be strengthened and uplifted."—*N. Y. Press.*

Dante and Collected Verse. Just issued. 16°, cloth extra, gilt top. $1.25

G. P. PUTNAM'S SONS, New York and London.

OTHER WORKS BY PROF. GEO. L. RAYMOND

The Essentials of Æsthetics. 8vo. Illustrated . . Net, **$2.50**

This work, which is mainly a compendium of the author's system of Comparative Æsthetics, previously published in seven volumes, was prepared, by request, for a text-book, and for readers whose time is too limited to study the minutiæ of the subject.

"We consider Professor Raymond to possess something like an ideal equipment. . . . His own poetry is genuine and delicately constructed, his appreciations are true to high ideals, and his power of scientific analysis is unquestionable." . . . He "was known, when a student at Williams, as a musician and a poet—the latter because of taking, in his freshman year, a prize in verse over the whole college. After graduating in this country, he went through a course of æsthetics with Professor Vischer of the University of Tübingen, and also with Professor Curtius at the time when that historian of Greece was spending several hours a week with his pupils among the marbles of the Berlin Museum. Subsequently, believing that all the arts are, primarily, developments of different forms of expression through the tones and movements of the body, Professor Raymond made a thorough study, chiefly in Paris, of methods of cultivating and using the voice in both singing and speaking, and of representing thought and emotion through postures and gestures. It is a result of these studies that he afterwards developed, first, into his methods of teaching elocution and literature" (as embodied in his 'Orator's Manual' and 'The Writer') "and later into his æsthetic system. . . . A Princeton man has said of him that he has as keen a sense for a false poetic element as a bank expert for a counterfeit note; and a New York model who posed for him, when preparing illustrations for one of his books, said that he was the only man that he had ever met who could invariably, without experiment, tell him at once what posture to assume in order to represent any required sentiment."—*New York Times.*

"So lucid in expression and rich in illustration that every page contains matter of deep interest even to the general reader."—*Boston Herald.*

"Its superior in an effective all-round discussion of its subject is not in sight."
The Outlook (N. Y.)

"Dr. Raymond's book will be invaluable. He shows a knowledge both extensive and exact of the various fine arts and accompanies his ingenious and suggestive theories by copious illustrations."—*The Scotsman* (Edinburgh).

Published by G. P. PUTNAM'S SONS, 27 West 23d St., New York.

The Psychology of Inspiration. 8vo . . . . . Net, **$1.40**

An attempt to distinguish Religious from Scientific Truth and to Harmonize Christianity with Modern Thought.

Dr. J. Mark Baldwin, Professor of Psychology in John Hopkins University, says that its psychological position is "new and valuable"; Dr. W. T. Harris, late United States Commissioner of Education, says that it is sure "to prove helpful to many who find themselves on the border line between the Christian and the non-Christian beliefs"; and Dr. Edward Everett Hale says "no one has approached the subject from this point of view."

"A book that everybody should read. . . . medicinal for profest Christians, and full of guidance and encouragement for those finding themselves somewhere between the desert and the town. The sane, fair, kindly attitude taken gives of itself a profitable lesson. The author proves conclusively that his mind—and if his, why not another?—can be at one and the same time sound, sanitary, scientific, and essentially religious."—*The Examiner*, Chicago.

"It is, we think, difficult to overestimate the value of this volume at the present critical pass in the history of Christianity."—*The Arena*, Boston.

"The author has taken up a task calling for heroic effort; and has given us a volume worthy of careful study. . . . The conclusion is certainly very reasonable."
Christian Intelligencer, New York.

"The author writes with logic and a 'sweet reasonableness' that will doubtless convince many halting minds. It is an inspiring book."—*Philadelphia Inquirer.*

"Interesting, suggestive, helpful."—*Boston Congregationalist.*

"Thoughtful, reverent, suggestive."—*Lutheran Observer*, Philadelphia.

Published by **FUNK & WAGNALLS COMPANY**, 44 East 23d St., New York.

The Orators' Manual, a Text-Book of Vocal Culture and Gesture . . . in constant demand for years. , . Net, **$1.12**
The Speaker, a Collaborated Text-Book of Oratory. . . Net, **$1.00**
The Writer, a Collaborated Text-Book of Rhetoric. . . Net, **90 cts.**

Published by SILVER, BURDETT & COMPANY, 231 West 39th St., New York.